ALSO WRITTEN BY HOWARD JOHNS

Palm Springs Confidential: Playground of the Stars

Hollywood Celebrity Playground

Greed and glamour in the Mexican jungle

A STOLEN Paradi$e

by Howard Johns

Book Cover Design by Lori McKinney

Publishing by www.globaleapps.com

First Printing, 2017

ISBN- 9781976986529

AUTHOR'S NOTE

The names, characters and events in this story are factual. The Aztec customs and historical passages are authentic. Nothing has been fictionalized.

CONTENTS

ACKNOWLEDGMENTS

The evolution of this book about the making of John Huston's film *The Night of the Iguana* began in 2001, when I first visited Puerto Vallarta. It was the rainy season. By chance, I went horse riding in the hills above Mismaloya, where Arnold Schwarzenegger battled an alien monster in the science-fiction movie *Predator*. After my ride I visited the beach and explored the rocky peninsula. There was a heavy thunderstorm and I sought shelter under a broken canopy at the top of some unused stairs.

The place I chose to rest was the ramparts of a derelict building, whose remains were sticking out of the jungle. Red rock crabs eyed me cautiously from the damp walls of fetid rooms with broken ceilings. I worried if there were any snakes or scorpions waiting in the dark recesses, although they did not show themselves to me. Graffiti was scrawled on the bricks, and broken bottles and other trash littered the floors. Who had lived there, I wondered, and for how long?

Walking between the pink *amapas* and rust-colored gumbo limbo trees with their peeling bark, I located several crumbling buildings, where people once slept, showered, and ate meals on small terraces. Most of the structures were missing their roofs, the doors were gone, and the windows were nothing more than empty spaces. It was then that I realized this was once a hotel – and a very famous one, as I soon learned. The people who stayed there weren't anonymous guests, they were world-famous movie stars.

By chance I had stumbled on the hotel set and accommodations from *The Night of the Iguana*, which first brought Richard Burton and Elizabeth Taylor, along with Ava Gardner and Deborah Kerr, to Mexico.

I imagined finding various relics from its production buried like hidden treasure in the jungle. Alas, there was nothing. What happened prior to my arrival, when the hotel was constructed half a century ago, was the real and intriguing story. As I delved into the past to learn about the previous existence of this abandoned building, I unearthed curious details about a flashpoint in Puerto Vallarta's history, which dramatically changed its future.

The discovery of this knowledge both fascinated and puzzled me. My mind was overwhelmed with intriguing questions. I returned to California from my vacation and began long hours of research in various libraries, while contacting the film's surviving participants, hoping they could provide me with some answers. I had no idea when I started that it would take almost one decade to solve the perplexing mystery that revealed itself to me like a ghostly apparition on that rainy afternoon. Many times, when discouraged, I wanted to give up my investigation, but I kept coming back to Puerto Vallarta in search of clues.

Thirteen summers have since come and gone. I am indebted to many generous individuals, some now deceased, and who shared their reminiscences with me. In Puerto Vallarta, I interviewed Robert Acord, Cynthia Alpenia, Nelly Barquet, Janice Chatterton, Ricardo Farkas, Lowe Figour, Michael Figour, Don Gallery, Sylvia Garcés Reed, Celeste Huston, Janice Lavender, Lindsey Leyva, Sabrina Leyva, Javier López Núñez, Jenny McGill, Wayne McLeod, John Nation, Cachi Pérez, Robert Price, Ernesto Ramirez, Sofia Ramirez, William Reed, Raúl Romero, Rosalba Romero, John Russell, Sam Skidmore, Gary Thompson, Sergio Toledano, Narcisa Vizcarra, Cathy Von Rohr, Cheryl Woodcock, Luis Wulff, and John Youden.

The director of Biblioteca Los Mangos, Ricardo Murrieta, city historian Juan Manuel Gómez Encarnación, and the staff at Museo Historico Naval and Museo del Cuale graciously offered their assistance.

Alejandro Ramirez Acalco took evidentiary photographs and videos of the various film locations; he conducted interviews in Spanish and provided English translations of published texts and other documents. Chano Rano Contreras furnished high quality DVD and audio transfers.

In Mexico City, Guillermo Cerón of the Hemeroteca Nacional at the Centro Cultural Universitario in Coyoacán supplied archival copies of news articles from *Novedades*, *Excélsior*, *Cine Universal*, and *Cine Mundial*, which verified many important events. Seeking to obtain information about two of the film's key figures, Gabriel Figueroa and Emilio Fernández, I contacted their descendants, Gabriel Figueroa Flores and Adela Fernández, who gave me helpful advice about their ancestors.

In Los Angeles, Jenny Romero, Department of Special Collections at the Margaret Herrick Library in the Fairbanks Center for Motion Picture Study of the Academy of Motion Picture Arts and Sciences, Beverly Hills, granted me access to Ray Stark's written correspondence from *The Night of the Iguana*. Although screenwriter Gavin Lambert's contributions to the film have frequently been overlooked, he bore no one any malice and encouraged me to tell this unique story. My request to interview Elizabeth Taylor about her life in Puerto Vallarta with Richard Burton was met with a polite refusal, though she wished me good luck with the project.

Biographies and obituaries of public figures that are mentioned in this book were obtained from reference librarians Jeff Clayton, Patti Henley, Sastri Madugula and Shelly Thacker of Palm Springs City Library in California. Other individuals helped to corroborate various aspects of the making of the film.

David Bartlett of Palm Desert recounted his stepfather Sy Bartlett's involvement in Club Mismaloya. Georgianne Beebe of Winchester furnished genealogical information about her grandfather-in-law Cyril Delevanti.

Another ally in this long quest was Jon Schwartz of Larry Edmunds Bookshop in Hollywood. He provided me with *The Night of the Iguana* campaign press book and publicity stills, which were originally sent to film exhibitors and journalists. The videotape of John Huston, titled *Nuestro Amigo Americano* by Gerardo Lara, was given to me courtesy of Lucila Moctezuma, Director of Media Arts Fellowships at Renew Media, National Video Resources, in New York.

Researching and writing this elaborate chronicle of events took much longer than expected. One year of dedication grew to three years of compulsion and, eventually, six years of obsession. There was moments of joy, anger, frustration, disappointment and, finally, exhilaration as I uncovered the hidden truth. Now, thankfully, that difficult task has been completed.

Several times during my exploration I felt a strange uneasiness surrounding *The Night of the Iguana*. Call it an omen. Almost everybody connected with the movie is now dead, with the exception of Sue Lyon. I contacted her ex-husband Richard Rudman and asked him to convey my request for an interview because Lyon is distrustful of the press. But despite his intervention, she refused to talk about herself or the film. Sue, if you read this book, I hope you will be satisfied with my retelling of events as seen through the looking glass of history.

PROLOGUE

THIS EVENTFUL JOURNEY BEGINS in a lush tropical rainforest on the west coast of Mexico. The year is 1963, the place Puerto Vallarta, on the edge of the Pacific Ocean. From a far distance, the dappled green canopy of the Sierra Madre Occidental mountain range resembles jumbo-sized broccoli plants in a vast prehistoric garden. Huge birds glide through the air like pterodactyls. If a tyrannosaurus showed itself, we would not be surprised.

Sprouting between the crooked trunks of mahogany, rosewood and cedar trees are thousands of coconut, oil and fan palms, many of them reaching up one hundred feet. At this low elevation, heat and humidity saps the energy of all living things. The only audible sound is the chattering of unseen parrots in the jungle awning.

Resting in the lower treetops, illuminated by diffused shafts of sunlight, are enormous lizards, some of them the size of large dogs. At first it is difficult to spot these solitary creatures because their striped emerald-, lime-, and olive-colored markings provide excellent camouflage.

The sluggish reptiles can grow up to five feet in length and weigh as much as fifteen pounds. Each of them has knobby hornlike growths on their triangular heads and long spiked crests extending along the entire length of their backs. Their sleek bodies are covered in thickened layers of skin folded into interlocking scales that are hinged together like a medieval suit of armor. They have four powerful legs with five fearsome claws on each foot. Every animal has a long-serrated tail, as thick as a bullwhip, and almost twice the length of their bodies. Some of these lethal appendages are so long they dangle limply from the trees.

Suddenly, there is a rustling movement in the center branches. One dormant lizard snaps open its hooded eyes to reveal two shiny golden orbs. The creature's head turns in the direction of a loud thrashing sound. A long bamboo pole, swaying back and forth, is pushed upwards through the twisted foliage by a brawny Mexican boy, who clings perilously to the side of the tree like a chimpanzee.

Thirty feet below, next to a meandering stream, stand a cluster of bare-chested teenagers, holding nets and machetes, their heads turned upwards. The youths are probably no more than sixteen years of age, some of them smooth-faced, several with soft mustaches. "Iguana, iguana!" yells one of the boys. Alert to the presence of danger, the awakened lizard slowly moves away. The kid on the tree with the pole whacks the iguana and it sprints through the leaves. Pausing at the edge of the furthest branch the reptile is dragged down by its body weight and slides off the tree into a freefall.

On the ground, the youths form a circle next to the stream and quickly unfurl their nets. Iguanas are good swimmers, but boys are better ones. One nimble lad in calico shorts jumps into the stream ahead of the reptile, which plummets, legs outstretched, into the water. The boy catches the lizard in his hands, taking care not to be scratched by its sharp claws. But the youngster underestimates the tenacity of his opponent. In a flash, the lizard whips its razor-sharp tail against his attacker, leaving a painful red gash across the boy's chest and torso. Another youth leaps into the water to help his injured friend.

The two boys lose their balance and the lizard hits the ground running and escapes into the jungle. The teenagers give chase, hurling the net ahead of the fleeing reptile. One youngster springs into the air with the agility of a frog and lands on the splayed net, pinning the lizard beneath him. In the tree above, the kid with the bamboo pole continues slashing wildly at the branches, causing the other iguanas to flee for their lives. We see them dropping like ripened fruit onto the ground.

The same rainforest, it is one hour later. There are four crudely made wooden cages containing the captured iguanas, two or three to a cage, on the banks of the gurgling stream. The teenagers are squatting in front of the cages, grinning with pride at their accomplishment. One youth inhales a marijuana cigarette, he passes it to another boy, who takes a few puffs, and then hands it to his friend. A few feet away, a skewered iguana is being roasted over the burning coals of a small fire that is being tendered by one of the group. Another lizard, which has already been cooked and cut into strips, is hungrily devoured by eager young mouths.

The Puerto Vallarta coastline at sunset. The shrill blast of mariachi music wafts out of the Hotel Oceano, where customers sit on the patio opposite the main beach drinking bottles of beer and glasses of tequila. The teenagers from the jungle leave the bar in a joyful mood. The boys are clutching fistfuls of crisp American ten-dollar bills. They glance back at the hotel where two Hollywood executives wave goodbye to them. The men are wearing Hawaiian shirts, linen trousers and expensive wristwatches. Stacked in a nearby corner of the bar are the forlorn iguanas in their primitive cages. Some of the captured reptiles have little ropes tied around their scaly necks.

A waiter sets down a tray of cocktails on the men's table. Resting on a corner of the tabletop is a mimeographed screenplay in a stiffened maroon cover with two brass paper fasteners. When one of the men reaches for the ashtray, the other man picks up the script, and the cover, which is embossed in big gold letters, comes into full view:

"THE NIGHT OF THE IGUANA"
Screenplay
by
Anthony Veiller and John Huston
Based on the Broadway play
by Tennessee Williams

Gradually the center of the image turns bright white as if seared by a burning flame. The insistent mariachi beat of the cantina fades away and a majestic entr'acte swells up. We are shown a striking montage of the chief participants in this eloquent drama: the avaricious movie producer Ray Stark surrounded by comely starlets, his impulsive director John Huston foxhunting in Ireland, and the ever-luscious Elizabeth Taylor and her scowling lover Richard Burton caught *in flagrante delicto* by the Italian paparazzi.

These images are followed by a black-and-white newsreel of Ava Gardner dallying with a Spanish bullfighter, and color snapshots of Deborah Kerr skiing with her husband Peter Viertel in Switzerland. We see Sue Lyon displaying her adolescent charms for photographers at a London press junket, and Tennessee Williams posing with a group of suntanned beach boys in Key West, Florida.

Through the marvel of pinpoint geography, we have arrived at our current setting, the pastel-colored skyline of Miami Beach in 1960. A young man performs an impressive somersault from the high diving board of the Hotel Fontainebleau's swimming pool.

On the sprawling lanai of the nearby Eden Roc, thirty vacationing New Yorkers are dancing the cha-cha. The couples wiggle their hips and shuffle their feet to the percussive beat of the tune *Patricia*, a standard in the musical repertoire, played by a small orchestra.

With the clever use of time-lapse photography, day turns rapidly into night, and the brilliant shades of yellow, orange and blue that dominate the crowded beachfront at noon are replaced by luminous blacks, warm reds and soft golds of the city's pulsating nightlife. Our gaze is drawn to a large theater playbill with the words NOW PLAYING printed in a red diagonal stripe pasted to a South Beach wall illuminated by an adjoining streetlight:

ARMAND DEUTSCH
Presents
BETTE DAVIS
in
"THE WORLD OF CARL SANDBURG"
Miami Beach Auditorium
Nightly 8:00 p.m.

The advertisement features a life-size photograph of Miss Davis. Her imperious face peers out from the poster, defying us to look away. As we stare back, she smiles and batters her famous eyes...

PART ONE:

THE SEVENTH ART

"All good art is an indiscretion."

– Tennessee Williams

BETTE DAVIS HAD NEVER SEEN a real iguana. The legendary movie star, who relished playing venomous roles, had only glanced at illustrations of these peculiar looking reptiles and heard about their ferocious reputation. “I thought iguanas were poisonous,” she reacted with astonishment.

“No, no, no!” laughed the eminent playwright Tennessee Williams, who was visiting Davis backstage at the Miami Beach Auditorium on the night of January 25, 1960. Their unpublicized meeting took place in the private dressing room of the art deco theatre with its coral pink and sea foam green façade.

“Those are Komodo dragons, and they don’t eat people,” quipped Williams from behind thick, black-rimmed eyeglasses, “unless you’re already dead!”

Davis had been nominated ten times for the Academy Award and won the gold-plated statuette twice for her bravura acting in the films *Dangerous* and *Jezebel*. The evening of Williams’ visit, Davis was sitting at a makeup table framed with electric light bulbs.

Resembling a plumper version of Queen Elizabeth, the short-tempered English monarch she had portrayed two different times on the screen, Davis sipped Johnnie Walker Red Label from a whisky glass. At age fifty-one, her regal features had coarsened from years of heavy smoking, though she still possessed the soft chestnut hair and piercing light blue eyes.

The celebrated actress was performing a national tour of *The World of Carl Sandburg*, an evening of homespun poetry readings adapted by the esteemed scriptwriter Norman Corwin and interspersed with American folk songs by the virtuoso soloist Clark Allen. The traveling road show, which commenced in Davis's hometown of Portland, Maine, was slowly winding its way through a total of 108 North American cities until it reached California.

On many nights, there was more drama going on in the theater wings with Davis and her fourth husband, actor Gary Merrill, than there was on the stage. The married performers regularly fought each other, sometimes coming to angry blows. The catalyst was their addiction to alcohol. The brawling continued and so Merrill left the play before the end of his contract.

Even so, for many observers, the idea of Davis reciting Sandburg's philosophical prose and verse, while attired in a formal evening gown, hardly fit her image as a Yankee spitfire. But that was part of Davis' longstanding appeal; she liked to surprise her fans, which is the reason she agreed to do these historic readings.

It was an entirely different kind of theatrical experience – joyful, sentimental, and heartwarming – compared to Williams' tense emotional dramas with their verbal cruelty. Still, there was no denying his exalted reputation. So, she listened to him talking about lizards until he revealed the true reason for his visit. Davis glared at the reflection of Williams, who stood behind her like a fawning manservant.

A short, bashful man with wavy dark hair, deep blue eyes and a neatly-trimmed mustache, Williams had traveled 150 miles from his home in Key West, to personally offer Davis the starring role in his forthcoming play *The Night of the Iguana*, which was scheduled to open on Broadway in the winter of 1961. With his black suit and necktie, however, he looked more like an undertaker selling funeral caskets than a famed writer of plays.

“Actually, in many parts of Latin America,” Williams continued, “people eat iguanas. I’m told they taste like chicken.” Davis stared at him bug-eyed, her penciled eyebrows arched like two brown caterpillars. “I don’t believe it!” she snorted, a faint smile crossing her scarlet lips. Although Davis doubted the veracity of his claims, she was amused by Williams’ soft-spoken Southern charm.

The actress reached for a packet of Chesterfields, thrust one of the unfiltered cigarettes into her puckered mouth and lit the white cylindrical tip with a solid gold lighter. Then she exhaled, blowing smoke into the air. “Surely, you’re joking,” she responded in her emphatic, clipped tones. “No,” he drawled sweetly, “I assure you I’m not.”

It would take one hour before the chill thawed between the overbearing star and the high-strung dramatist. Davis broke the ice by offering the forty-eight-year-old writer a glass of Scotch, which he gladly accepted. Williams proceeded to tell her the story of an Episcopalian minister who is accused of sexual misconduct.

The angry priest denounces God from the pulpit of his West Virginia church and runs away to Mexico. While working as a bus tour guide, he meets three beautiful women, representing innocence, guilt and betrayal. But the man must resist the strong impulse to sleep with each of them if he is to make peace with himself and find salvation.

Williams was convinced that Davis would be perfect for the lead female character in the play: a widowed hotel proprietor, who falls in love with the expelled reverend.

The part, as he described, was ideally suited for Davis: “She is a stout swarthy woman in her middle forties – affable and rapaciously lusty... Maxine always laughs with a harsh, loud bark, opening her mouth like a seal expecting a fish to be thrown to it.”

Listening to Williams speak, Davis warmed to the play's dramatic possibilities. Her long film career, which spanned four decades, had begun to slow down. Always restless, she was actively pursuing work on television and in the theatre.

A new play by Tennessee Williams afforded Davis the opportunity of staging a major acting comeback. "So these iguanas," she inquired, hinting at the play's symbolism, "are they predators?"

Williams grinned at her. "Well, actually they are metaphors for the human condition. They feast on insects and plants and when they're old and wrinkled," he explained, "some of them are almost as large as a man or woman – and just as fat."

Davis eyed Williams with a mixture of revulsion and curiosity. Strange or not, he was a powerhouse name in the theater world. If she accepted his offer, it would mark the first time that Davis headlined in a New York stage production since treading the boards in Charles Sherman's musical revue *Two's Company* at the Alvin Theatre. That was in 1952. How wonderful, the aging luminary thought, if she could recapture that same magic.

Davis contemplated Williams' reflection next to hers in the dressing room mirror. "How interesting, the way you see things," she commented, and stood up, tugging at the waistline of her dress. Davis showed him to the dressing room door and they said farewell. When Williams had gone, she flung the door shut and leaned back against the wall. Then Davis opened her mouth and guffawed until her raucous laugh could be heard echoing through the empty corridors of the theatre.

Speeding along the Miami Overseas Highway in his shiny white Thunderbird convertible, Williams paused and took a swig of Kentucky bourbon from a silver flask he kept in the automobile's glove compartment.

He savored the taste of the sweet liquor, a look of blissful contentment on his moonlit face. In that quiet moment, alone on the highway, Williams felt blessed.

Hailed as the greatest living American playwright of his generation, Tennessee Williams had achieved that rare show business phenomenon: a meteoric rise from provincial obscurity to global prominence. The son of a Mississippi shoe salesman, Thomas Williams was sixteen when he began writing poems and essays. His first play *Cairo! Shanghai! Bombay!* was performed in 1935. Four years later, after moving to New Orleans, he changed his name from the banal-sounding Tom to the more lyrical Tennessee.

Williams was proclaimed a literary genius with his landmark play *The Glass Menagerie*, which opened on Broadway in 1945. His next groundbreaking triumph, *A Streetcar Named Desire*, won the Pulitzer Prize for Drama. The success of these two theatrical milestones turned Williams into an overnight celebrity and made him a wealthy man. But Williams was much more than a skilled writer of bold words.

From the start, his plays stirred up controversy with their sexual frankness and physical brutality. His shocking revelations of impotence, homosexuality, incest, rape and murder, stunned the nation's theatergoers and provoked the anger of the Roman Catholic Church. Despite winning a host of early accolades, he had not had a certified Broadway hit since *Cat on a Hot Tin Roof*, his second Pulitzer Prize winner, in 1955. So, in an effort to rekindle the fire, Williams turned his attention to Hollywood.

His screenplay for *Baby Doll*, a black comedy about a virginal thumb-sucking teenage bride, unleashed a howl of criticism. Two days before the film's release, the Archbishop of New York, Francis Cardinal Spellman, lambasted Williams from the pulpit of St. Patrick's Cathedral.

The Legion of Decency condemned the film, calling it immoral, and organized a national boycott of movie theatres. The resulting publicity tripled the film's earnings at the box office and pushed Williams' notoriety to unprecedented levels.

The pressure to dream up more sensational plays caused him to suffer a nervous breakdown, and in 1957 he began seeing a psychoanalyst. Although Williams kept trying to top himself, his most recent productions: *Orpheus Descending*, *Suddenly Last Summer*, and *Sweet Bird of Youth* were regarded as lesser works by an artist in decline. One disapproving critic, tired of Williams' unceasing prurience, called him a "dirty-minded dramatist who has long been losing hope for the human race."

Another equally repulsed reviewer wrote that "Williams now seems to be in a sort of race with himself, surpassing homosexuality with cannibalism, cannibalism with castration, devising new and greater shocks with each succeeding play." It remained to be seen if Williams, who considered vice his greatest virtue, could prove his accusers wrong.

THE NIGHT OF THE IGUANA had the longest gestation of any of Tennessee Williams' plays. It's creation spanned twenty years – almost half the duration of his literary career. Few people outside his small circle of friends and lovers knew of the play's obscure origins, nor the devastating effect that its writing had on his creative psyche.

Williams conceived the original story for *The Night of the Iguana* while on a trip to Acapulco in 1940. He was twenty-nine and, as yet, unknown. Almost broke from lack of funds, he checked into the Hotel Costa Verde, a small boardinghouse perched above a still-water beach named Playa Caleta. He stretched out in a canvas chair and ordered a Coco Loco – a potent cocktail of white rum, gin and tequila, served in a green coconut. To pass the time, Williams observed the hotel guests and made detailed notes about his surroundings.

At night, Williams huddled with other guests under the metal roof which reverberated like a timpani drum from the heavy tropical rainstorms. He noticed two Mexican boys catching an iguana and tying it below the verandah, where the lizard would be fattened for later eating. Such sights intrigued him. But Williams was more worried about scrounging up the money for food and lodging, than writing about drunken tourists and iguanas. Because of his precarious finances, it would be five years before he returned to Mexico. During that time, his life underwent a miraculous transformation. From an impoverished writer living on the fringes of society he became a rich and celebrated literary figure, whose name adorned theatre marquees in New York, London, Paris, and Rome.

Ever since it was first written as a short story in 1946, Williams had contemplated staging a theatrical version of *The Night of the Iguana*. He later incorporated the characters into a one-act play that premiered at the Festival of Two Worlds in Spoleto, Italy, in 1959. The positive reaction from people who saw its performance surprised him, so he set about expanding his libretto into a full-length stage play. But Williams was concerned about the play's commercial prospects. He needed a marketable box-office name to scare up investors, which is why he sought the participation of Bette Davis.

Once Davis was signed as Maxine Faulk, Williams turned his attention to finding an equally good actress for the role of the nomadic painter Hannah Jelkes – the play's moral conscience. His first choice was Miriam Hopkins, who had sparred so effectively with Davis in the 1943 film *Old Acquaintance*. Hopkins no longer had the stamina for playing strenuous roles, however, and turned down the part. He then approached Katharine Hepburn, whose star power and energy remained undiminished. But after thoughtful consideration she chose not to accept his offer.

Attempting to reinvent himself, Williams broke with his long-standing Broadway producer Cheryl Crawford, who had staged four of his plays. Her successor, Charles Bowden, had a showman's flair for grandeur, which Williams very much needed in 1960. He called on his longtime friend and collaborator Elia Kazan, who was considered a titan in American theatre, and asked him to direct *The Night of the Iguana*. Kazan was one of the founding members of the Actors Studio.

A daring and passionate interpreter of Williams' plays, Kazan gave spectacular life to the original productions of *A Streetcar Named Desire*, *Cat on a Hot Tin Roof* and *Sweet Bird of Youth*. Only now, when Williams needed him the most, Kazan said no, pleading overwork and exhaustion.

Williams turned to someone comparatively new on the theatre scene. Frank Corsaro had recently directed the Broadway hit *A Hatful of Rain*.

The sensitive drama about morphine addiction struck a deep emotional chord with Williams. Impressed with Corsaro's handling of the subject matter, Williams proposed they collaborate on *The Night of the Iguana*. Flattered, Corsaro read the unfinished play and encouraged him to finish it.

But Williams, who did not adapt easily to change, was bedeviled by writer's block and insomnia. He fretted about plagiarizing his own works and repeating himself in clichéd dramatic situations. Williams was now smoking two packs of cigarettes a day and drinking half a bottle of bourbon and vodka to alleviate the anxiety caused by his ever-present fear of failure.

In the mornings, when his fear was at its worst, he popped half a Dexamyl tablet to chase the blues away. Then he took two Miltown tranquilizers, the forerunner of Librium and Valium, to remain calm during the day, and swallowed 1½ Seconal pills to sleep at night. Williams didn't consider this to be habit-forming, he knew he could stop any time he wanted, but his mind and body needed the constant reassurance these drugs provided if his printed words were going to have any form or clarity.

After Corsaro agreed to direct *The Night of the Iguana*, a reading of the one-act play, which Williams had enlarged to eighty-one pages, was staged at the Actors Studio in Manhattan. Substituting for Bette Davis was Madeline Sherwood as the boisterous hotel owner Maxine Faulk. Rosemary Harris performed the part of the itinerant artist Hannah Jelkes, while Patrick O'Neal brought a sinister edge to his portrayal of the rebellious priest, Lawrence Shannon.

When the reading was over, Williams headed back to the peace and serenity of Key West, where he owned a Bahamian-style cottage on Duncan Street, a short distance from the beach. The modest three-room bungalow, which he purchased in 1949, was surrounded by a white picket fence and tall coconut palms.

The sturdy barrier deterred tourists from spying on Williams, who shared the home with Frank Merlo, his domestic partner, along with their two bulldogs, a talking parrot, and various stray cats.

There, behind the pink wooden shutters of their small frame conch house, Williams spent part of 1961 creating new scenes and dialogue for *The Night of the Iguana*. Each morning he arose early, brewed a pot of Stygian coffee and sat down at his Smith-Corona electric typewriter, where he worked until noon. In the afternoons, after taking a short nap, Williams dived into the large mosaic tiled pool that he built on the guest property adjoining his house and swam ten or twelve laps.

When Merlo began showing signs of ill health, his body weakened by the constant smoking that would result in his early death from lung cancer, Williams moved Merlo into the spare bedroom of the main house, where he became a semi invalid. Craving physical intimacy, Williams took a new lover. “He was a handsome blonde kid of about twenty-two,” described Williams, “with creamy skin and a very seductive backside which he was eager to offer.”

Behind the devil-may-care attitude that he wore like a protective shield against the world, Williams struggled with increasing bouts of depression. During moments of despair when his mind was overwhelmed by thoughts of hopelessness, he sought refuge in a church, where he lit a candle and asked God to forgive him.

Now Williams prayed for a miracle to save *The Night of the Iguana*, which he vowed, in an outpouring of self-pity, would be his last Broadway play. The strain of keeping up an artistic pretense, of trying to invent bigger and better tricks to impress the critics, was so emotionally draining that he intended never to do it again.

After a three-week European vacation, Williams felt sufficiently rejuvenated to write additional scenes for *The Night of the Iguana*. He rented a house in Cuernavaca, thirty-five miles south of Mexico City, where he wrote, on and off, for the next two months.

In the summer of 1961, Corsaro staged a second reading of the play, now comprising three acts, at the Coconut Grove Playhouse in Miami. "When he was working or reworking at this play," recalled Corsaro, "he was a genius, and he was inspiring to be with. You could see his understanding of people's pain, his compassion, his gentleness, his modesty in the face of the universe."

At the same time Williams was putting the finishing touches to his magnum-opus, the long and difficult search to find an actress to play Hannah Jelkes came to an end. Williams was thankful his prayers had been answered, though it remained to be seen what the other cast members, especially Davis, would think of the unlikely choice.

WEARING A GREEN WOOL SUIT, which flattered her blonde willowy figure, Margaret Leighton arrived by taxi in Manhattan at the beginning of October 1961, to start rehearsals for *The Night of the Iguana*. The cast had been told by director Frank Corsaro to assemble at the Shubert Theatre. On the car radio Frank Sinatra was singing *On the Sunny Side of the Street* as pedestrians walked briskly across intersections and along the sidewalks.

Leighton's mood was one of hopeful expectation and her jade-colored eyes took in the surrounding hotels, department stores and delicatessens as the yellow cab sped through Broadway on its way to the theatre district. The past five years had been a busy and rewarding time for the classically trained British star of stage and screen.

Leighton won a Tony Award as Best Actress in *Separate Tables*, a big hit of the 1956–57 Broadway season. This victory was followed by a meritorious performance as Beatrice opposite John Gielgud's Benedick in the 1959 revival of William Shakespeare's Elizabethan comedy *Much Ado About Nothing*.

Exuding an air of well-practiced confidence, Leighton, thirty-nine, alighted from the taxi outside the Shubert's white Venetian Renaissance façade on West 44th Street. In her handbag, which matched the color of her dress, Leighton carried a bound copy of Williams' play.

Inside the theatre, Leighton joined the cast from *The Night of the Iguana* on the empty stage.

Standing in the glare of the footlights was the bejeweled figure of Bette Davis. She wore a royal blue jacket over velvet slacks and was smoking a Chesterfield cigarette. Corsaro introduced the two majestic performers, who smiled warily at each other. “It is an honor to meet you,” praised Leighton. “I used to watch you at the Odeon in Leicester Square. You were wonderful in *The Little Foxes*.” There was an awkward silence.

Then Davis extinguished her cigarette in a standing ashtray and gave Leighton the fisheye. “I didn’t know you were that old!” said Davis, her voice dripping with sarcasm.

After their first encounter it was apparent that the two actresses did not get along, for each woman clearly regarded the other as her rival. Whereas Leighton was dignified, in keeping with her saintly character, Davis flounced across the brightly lit stage, shrieking and waving her arms. Her conduct surprised the other performers, who assumed she was either terribly nervous or very drunk.

Watching from the sidelines was Patrick O’Neal, sporting a Van Dyke beard, in the part of Shannon, and veteran British character actor Alan Webb as the elderly poet Jonathan Coffin, affectionately named Nonno. When it came time to recite her lines with the other actors, Davis tried to intimidate Lane Bradbury, who played the beguiling teenager Charlotte Goodall, and Patricia Roe as her chaperone Judith Fellowes.

During the next three weeks of rehearsals, the cast did their best to ignore Davis’ outbursts. In several scenes, Christopher Jones and James Farentino, who played Maxine’s maraca-shaking beach boys, had to dance around Davis in their bare feet. The boys constantly risked getting their toes stepped on by the sharp heels of her shoes. Director Corsaro tried to reign in the extroverted actress, but she would have none of it. Grinning maniacally, Davis grabbed Corsaro from behind and playfully rubbed her breasts against his back in a blatant attempt to undermine his authority.

Davis could not understand why Corsaro lacked a sense of humor, why he did not indulge her in the same deferential manner she had been treated by two of her favorite directors, William Wyler and Edmund Goulding, who played the piano and danced with her in Hollywood.

The problem, from the outset, was that Davis believed she was the play's main attraction when this was not the case. Having promised Davis billing above the play's title was a disingenuous trick that producer Charles Bowden employed to sell advance tickets but which Corsaro believed misrepresented her role in the play and would ultimately hurt its success.

"When she discovers that the play is not really about Maxine Faulk," a worried Corsaro told Williams, "we are going to have a great storm on our heads." The dark clouds gathered faster than expected.

No sooner had rehearsals started than Davis began voicing her dissatisfaction with the script. Fearful of what would happen if she quit, Williams promised to build up her part but Corsaro felt no such obligation.

Amid this threatening storm, the company left New York for two months of out-of-town previews, normally an occasion for celebration but which Williams remembered as "the longest and most appalling tour I've had with a play."

On November 3, 1961, the Iguana Theater Company arrived by train in Rochester, New York. Much to O'Neal's amazement, he found himself invited to a candlelit dinner with Davis in her stateroom. She greeted him wearing a silk robe heavily scented with violets – her favorite perfume, Le De by Givenchy.

When the thirty-five-year-old actor refused her advances, Davis picked up a heavy ashtray and hurled it at him, narrowly missing his head.

The enveloping sense of melodrama at the Auditorium Theatre was accentuated by the play's sharply raked set design by Oliver Smith. (One of the most prolific and imaginative designers in the history of American theater, Smith created the urban cityscapes that populated *West Side Story*, the Victorian backdrops for *My Fair Lady*, and the gilded palaces of *Camelot*. It was said that he could design anything, though musicals, not dramas, were his true forte.)

The feeling of impending doom, as thick as a winter fog, was compounded by the Costa Verde Hotel's wooden verandah, which jutted out from the stage and dangled perilously over the orchestra pit. The simulated flashes of lightning, thunder and rain that pounded the stage for two hours every night gave the impression of an approaching disaster.

At the opening night cast party, Davis was noticeably drunk. She fell on the stairs and sprained her ankle. But the pain of a swollen foot was nothing compared to the anger that Davis felt for Leighton, who had become smitten by O'Neal and him with her. Not only did they share the same stage together, they also had adjoining dressing rooms. Afterhours, Leighton coached O'Neal to help improve his acting, which raised suspicion they were having an affair.

The stress of the pre-Broadway tryouts almost pushed Williams to the breaking point. "It was a very difficult time," said Corsaro, "for him, for me, for the performers." Williams' uncertainty was not helped by his overreliance on liquor and pills, which dulled his mind when he should have been fully alert.

From Rochester, the speeding train continued to Detroit, Michigan, where *The Night of the Iguana* played a two-week engagement at the Shubert Theatre. The audience's unfavorable reaction to the rambling dialogue prompted Corsaro to shorten several scenes. When informed that her lines needed to be cut, Davis flew into a rage and threatened to quit.

The problems were not only psychological for Davis, they were also physical. Attired in a red wig, pink blouse, blue jeans and brown moccasins, she was required to maneuver a tea cart across the sharply inclined stage at each performance. Davis had to be careful not to lose her grip or the heavy cart, which was filled with liquor bottles and glasses, would careen over the edge of the hotel verandah and crash into the audience.

It was in Chicago, Illinois, where *The Night of the Iguana* was booked for a five-week run at the Blackstone Theatre that Davis finally rebelled. Having grown mistrustful of Corsaro, whom she suspected of reducing her role, so it would not overshadow the other parts, Davis began missing evening performances. Her absence sent disappointed ticket buyers storming the box office to ask for a refund.

From a commercial standpoint, producer Bowden knew her actions were justified. But on an artistic level her mutinous conduct was viewed as treason by the rest of the company. "I don't care!" Davis shouted, wedging a hand on her hips and blowing cigarette smoke into the air. Then, summoning all the power that her hoarse voice was able to muster, she pointed one arm at the defiant director, and screamed: "Get out!"

Refusing to take any more of Corsaro's direction, Davis ordered him barred from the theatre and a demoralized Williams had no choice but to acquiesce to her demands. His depression was not helped by lackluster reviews over the Thanksgiving Day weekend, when critics predicted that the play would be a massive turkey.

With no one else willing or available to supervise her, Williams took over the play's directing chores. "No, no," he called to Davis, his tone sweet but firm, "stand over there." Williams was high on booze and painkillers, and he cackled with delight at the comical sight of Davis strutting back and forth across the stage. When he sobered up, he conceded that part of the problem with Davis' performance was that she was trying to play to her screen image rather than adopting the personality of the character as he had written it.

"Bette," explained Williams, holding her hand. "Maxine was the wife of a great game-fisherman. Everything about her should have the openness and freedom of the sea. Time doesn't exist for her except in changes of weather and season. I can imagine she even smells like the sea. She moves with the ease of clouds and tides; her attitudes are free and relaxed." Davis became worried. "But Tennessee," she implored. "What about my fans? What will they think?" Williams smiled broadly. "Don't worry, baby," he replied. "The play is nearly sold out."

AFTER THREE TURBULENT MONTHS on the road, the cast of *The Night of the Iguana* arrived in New York City for the play's Broadway opening. Wearing a full-length ermine coat and trailing cigarette smoke, Bette Davis strode into the main entrance of the Royale Theatre on West 45th Street, where she was greeted by members of the press, who clamored for photographs and interviews. Davis savored her triumph like a prizefighter returning to the boxing ring.

On the evening of Thursday, December 28, 1961, when the curtain went up for the play's performance at the Royale, the stalls, boxes, mezzanine and balcony were packed with Davis's stanch followers, many of whom were lesbians and homosexuals. The moment the iconic Hollywood star swaggered out on the verandah of the Costa Verde Hotel at the beginning of the first act, a deafening thunderclap of applause reverberated throughout the theatre. People whistled and cheered, others stood up waving their hands in a feverish display of camp adulation and chanting "Bette! Bette!" Nothing like this had been witnessed in any of Williams' plays, and it was both exhilarating and unnerving for the other cast members.

Sitting in the front row was Tennessee Williams' mother Edwina, his younger brother Dakin Williams, Judy Garland, Helen Hayes, Lillian Gish, and the former first lady Eleanor Roosevelt. All eyes were focused on Davis, who sashayed and shimmied up and down the stage with malevolent glee.

Williams did not watch that night's performance of his play but nervously paced up and down outside the theatre like an expectant father. When Williams heard the rapturous reception that greeted the end of the third act, his eyes welled up with tears and he began to cry.

The next morning's newspapers attempted to make sense of Williams' damning prose in lengthy reviews that were both reproachful and conciliatory in tone. But several reviewers plainly enjoyed Williams' black humor. "Bette Davis, displaying an unbuttoned shirt, a shock of flame-colored hair, and the most raucously derisive laugh this side of a fish wharf, is marvelously brash and beguiling," wrote John McClain in *The New York Journal-American*. Walter Kerr in *The New York Times* wavered in his opinion of the play, finding fault with some of the characters and noting: "Nor is Miss Davis' role altogether substantial."

At that low point in his life, Williams could have cared less about the critics. Worn out by the stressful rehearsals leading up to the play's nerve-racking opening, he was winging his way across the Caribbean Sea on a British West Indian Airways flight to Kingston, Jamaica. There, for one week, Williams enjoyed his time sunbathing and swimming at the Silver Seas Hotel in Ocho Rios, surrounded by jungles, waterfalls and sandy beaches. He had no interest in talking about the theatre and wisely avoided any mention of iguanas.

On March 9, 1962, Tennessee Williams was featured on the cover of *Time* magazine. Inside, a six-page article revealed that Williams had earned more than $6,000,000, making him one of the wealthiest playwrights in theatrical history. "Williams is a gentle man who seethes with inner violence and something akin to self-hatred," divulged the publication. "I've always been obsessed that I'm dying of cancer, dying of heart trouble," he admitted. "I think it's good for a writer to think he's dying. He works harder."

Bette Davis had little concern for the playwright's welfare; she was more worried about her own health. The play no longer held any interest for her, and she had become tired of the repetition. Davis informed Charles Bowden that she was breaking her contract. No explanation was given, although it was later announced that she left the play because of dental problems. After her final performance on Saturday night, the cast gathered on stage for a farewell party.

Davis lit a cigarette and poured herself a glass of Scotch, which she downed in a single gulp. "I'm soooo happy that everyone thinks that Maggie is so charming, and Patrick is so brilliant!" she fumed, morphing into Margo Channing, the theater diva she played in *All About Eve*. "I'm sorry I had to irritate you for so long with my professionalism," she squeaked in front of the flabbergasted company. "You obviously like doing it your way much better. Well, now you can!" Then Davis turned on her heels and exited the theatre.

Facing the play's imminent closure, Frank Corsaro contacted Shelley Winters, who portrayed the anguished wife of the drug-addicted soldier, played by Ben Gazzara, in *A Hatful of Rain*. A flashy Hollywood starlet, Miss Winters, age forty-one, had been tutored in drama and speech by Lee Strasberg at the Actors Studio. Two years earlier she had been awarded an Oscar as Best Supporting Actress for her portrayal of a frightened Dutch mother in the movie *The Diary of Anne Frank*.

Corsaro handed Winters the script and told her to go home and memorize it. Twenty-four hours later, she was back on the stage at the Royale trying on costumes and makeup.

Though not in the same heavyweight class as Davis, who could wring the last drop of malice out of every line, Winters' interpretation of Maxine, which she imbued with subtlety and humor, was closer in spirit to the character's earthy personality.

Among the well-wishers who attended Winters' first performance in *The Night of the Iguana* on Monday, April 2, 1962, was the American pop singer Eddie Fisher. His backstage visit, recorded by television news cameras, coincided with the public announcement that same day of the breakup of Fisher's marriage to actress Elizabeth Taylor. Winters hugged him as news photographers snapped pictures of them standing together.

Like Davis, whose resignation from the play caused a hullabaloo, Winters was less inclined at the prospect of committing herself to a long theatrical run, and more concerned about the short-term exposure. After watching her from the wings, Williams seemed resigned to the play's fate as a commercially successful failure. "Winters has a fifth of Jack Daniels Tennessee sour mash whiskey in her dressing room and nips all through the show," he complained. "She never enters on cue." Whatever his criticisms,

Winters decided to stay with the play until the end of her six-month contract. Bowden's wife, actress Paula Laurence, played Maxine for the remainder of the play's run until it closed on September 29, 1962.

Despite its trials and tribulations, *The Night of the Iguana* was selected by the New York Drama Critics' Circle as the Best Play of 1962 – the fourth time Williams had won the award. Margaret Leighton received her second Tony Award for Best Performance by a Leading Actress in a Play.

By the time the news was released, Bette Davis was in Los Angeles, costarring with Joan Crawford in the macabre thriller *What Ever Happened to Baby Jane?* The film was directed by Robert Aldrich for Seven Arts Productions – the same company that financed the stage version of *The Night of the Iguana* and owned the motion picture rights.

BEVERLY HILLS, CALIFORNIA. The vestibule of Seven Arts Productions on North Canon Drive was a congenial meeting place for writers, directors and producers who gathered in the company's spacious offices to critique film scripts and discuss projects that were in various stages of development. Hanging on the walls of the reception area were framed posters of some of the recent films Seven Arts had financed: *The Misfits*, *By Love Possessed*, *West Side Story*, *The Roman Spring of Mrs. Stone*, *Lolita*, and *Two for the Seesaw.*

At the end of a short corridor, Seven Arts executive Raymond Stark was seated behind a large polished desk with a pretty view of the Santa Monica Mountains. His office was a model of contemporary interior design, augmented by Oriental-style furnishings and impressionist paintings. In the center of the room, spread out across a lacquered coffee table, in front of a plush leather sofa, were an assortment of newspapers and magazines: *The New York Times*, *Wall Street Journal*, *Los Angeles Times*, *Variety*, *Hollywood Reporter*, *Esquire*, and a well-thumbed copy of *Playboy*.

Wearing a pastel-colored business shirt, contrasting necktie, narrow-waisted trousers and horn-rimmed glasses, Stark was sifting through glossy eight-by-ten-inch photographs of Brylcreemed actors and bouffant haired actresses, some of whom showed more cleavage than was advisable for candidates with serious acting ambitions. A compact forty-eight-year-old Chicagoan with neatly trimmed flaxen hair, pale blue eyes and freckles, Stark looked more like a chartered accountant than a movie producer.

Perhaps it was the easy smile that people mistakenly trusted, because lurking behind his clean-cut image was a person with a killer's instinct. Stark glanced thoughtfully out the window at several miles of skinny palm trees that stood like giant pom-poms along Wilshire Boulevard. Then he pressed a small button on the side of his office telephone.

"Get me Eliot Hyman in New York," Stark asked his female secretary, who was typing a letter in the next room.

"Yes, Mr. Stark," came her efficient reply over the intercom. He leaned back in his chair and waited for the phone call.

Stark's salesmanship was the stuff of legend even before he produced a single film. "Flash back," as they say in movie parlance, to 1953. That was the year Stark joined Famous Artists Agency as the personal assistant to agency founder and company president Charles Feldman, whose firm represented some of the biggest stars and directors in Hollywood.

Working in the competitive agency business taught Stark how to gain the upper hand in business deals. He became adept at negotiating everything from a star's six-figure salary to buying the rights to a novel or play. But it also instilled in him the importance of having great personal style, which he learned at Famous Artists.

By the time Feldman retired his talent agency to concentrate on film production, there was no better deal-maker, it was said, than Ray Stark, whose friendly persuasion, whether it was kissing cheeks or twisting arms, would reach mythical status in Hollywood.

The intercom buzzed on Stark's desk. "Mr. Hyman is on the line," said his secretary. Stark picked up the telephone. "Eliot," he said cheerfully. "I'm ready to start pre-production on *The Night of the Iguana*. Do you have a signed distribution deal?"

Three thousand miles away in New York City, Eliot Hyman, the vice president of Seven Arts Corporation, was sitting in his plush office in the Union Carbide Building on Park Avenue. A dapper, fifty-seven-year-old businessman with receding white hair, a bulging nose and a blue pinstripe suit, Hyman exuded an air of well-practiced diplomacy that matched his calculated ambition.

"Yes, everything's been confirmed," Hyman spoke into the phone's receiver. "Seven Arts will pay for the production and M-G-M will distribute the film. The contracts will be ready tomorrow." Stark was jubilant. "That's good news," he beamed. "I'm glad we bought the rights."

Although separated by a vast distance both men were clearly elated by the outcome of these events. "It was a very popular play," said Hyman. "Anything Tennessee Williams writes makes money." That was certainly true for Warner Brothers, M-G-M, and Paramount, each of whom had raked in millions of dollars from their film adaptations of Williams' plays. Now it was Seven Arts' turn to have a roll of the dice. "Well, let's hope we have the same luck," Stark responded.

SEVEN ARTS PRODUCTIONS WAS the brainchild of Eliot Hyman and Ray Stark. The two men named their enterprise Seven Arts – homage to the cinema's reputation as "the seventh art," as well as a respectful nod to the seven board members who ran it. In 1960, Hyman and Stark unveiled plans to provide $17 million worth of financing for fifteen films with a total combined budget of $30 million. Seven Arts also functioned as Broadway angels, investing large sums of money in commercial plays in exchange for the film rights.

The company's first theatrical venture was *The World of Suzie Wong*, which opened on Broadway in 1958 and ran for two years. The movie version of the play, which Stark produced, was filmed in Hong Kong and London. When the play's troubled star France Nuyen suffered a nervous breakdown, her twenty-year-old understudy Nancy Kwan took over the role on stage and screen.

The World of Suzie Wong was Stark's greatest gamble – until *The Night of the Iguana* came along. A decade earlier, Charles Feldman had scored a triumph with his film adaptations of *The Glass Menagerie* and *A Streetcar Named Desire*, even though their impact was lessened because of strict censorship.

Stark felt reassured in his efforts to produce a movie of Tennessee Williams' latest play because of more favorable laws, though the blasphemous language and carnal lust in *The Night of the Iguana* were still considered objectionable subjects by the Roman Catholic Church.

Nonetheless, Stark was emboldened by the prospect of another commercial success. Over lunch, he informed newly-elected Seven Arts president Eliot Hyman that he wanted the project to be the company's next major release – not just another film, he insisted, but a major cinema event. "I thought it would make a wonderful picture," said Stark, "especially in Mexico."

The list of Hollywood directors capable of bringing their personal stamp to Stark's film was a long one: Joseph Mankiewicz, Nicholas Ray, Richard Brooks, Robert Wise, Stanley Kramer, Mark Robson, William Wyler, Otto Preminger, Mervyn LeRoy, Martin Ritt, and Robert Mulligan.

Stark didn't want any of them. The only director he actively sought was never on the list, he wasn't working in Hollywood, nor had he resided in the country for twelve years. Racetrack touts would have called it a long shot; Stark believed it was a surefire bet. On an impulse, the producer flew to Ireland to meet the man who most experts considered to be an outsider in the race.

Mellifluous of voice and sardonic in tone, John Huston specialized in making cynical movies that exposed people's vanity and avarice – with a touch of irreverent humor. Most of his plots revolved around nefarious groups of conspirators, who are done in by their own foolishness, others were insightful character studies about mismatched personal relationships.

Failure was a recurring theme of Huston's tales of greed and complicity that he adapted from popular novels by Herman Melville, C.S. Forester, W.R. Burnett and Dashiell Hammett. Huston was equally influenced by modern playwrights like Maxwell Anderson, Jean-Paul Sartre and Arthur Miller.

The results made for impressive, sometimes thrilling, entertainment: *The Maltese Falcon*, *Key Largo*, *The Asphalt Jungle* and *The African Queen*, which are frequently listed among his greatest films, along with *Moulin Rouge*, *Moby Dick*, and *The Misfits*.

Unlike other directors, who practiced their cinematic art on the air-conditioned soundstages and back-lots of movie studios, Huston wanted to paint his broad canvases against a more realistic backdrop – the four continents and seven seas of the world. There, amid snow-capped mountains, blistering deserts and surging oceans, Huston filmed mankind's struggle against mortality and, at the same time, indulged his fervent desire to hook a marlin, shoot a tiger, or bag an elephant.

Above all, Huston was a bold adventurer who viewed films as a continuation of his search for excitement. "I get no immediate satisfaction from directing," he confessed. "It doesn't gratify me in depth. When it's a good picture, it affords me satisfaction but not delight." When Huston expressed keen interest in a subject, however, there was no chance of stopping him, and he embraced a project that appealed to his sense of wonder with the same ardor that he lavished on a beautiful woman when trying to coax her into bed.

But truly gifted directors do not live by movies alone. Stark was also captivated by the director's wide-ranging interests, whether it was foxhunting, painting and sketching, or selecting a vintage Bordeaux wine. Huston was a charming and highly-motivated individual who could get things done, often under difficult circumstances. This, more than anything else, convinced Stark that he was backing the right horse.

Inevitably, the producer found himself being drawn into Huston's orbit where he witnessed another fascinating aspect of the director's personality: his encyclopedic knowledge of art and literature. For this reason, Stark considered Huston to be "the best read and the most knowledgeable man I've ever met, or that's ever been connected with the film industry. He was a Renaissance man, and everything he did was bigger than life."

Certainly, in both his flamboyant behavior and appearance, Huston was anything but conventional-looking. He had a large head, a long neck, bony shoulders and big hands and feet.

Soulful brown eyes peered out from deep pouches behind an aquiline nose, which had been broken by an opponent's fast jab in an amateur boxing match. The once youthful face was now lined and puffy and his wavy dark hair had turned gray.

Acutely fashionable, Huston favored theatrical costumes over street clothes. His sartorial tastes extended to fancy hats, riding capes, flaring tweed hacking jackets, stovepipe cavalry-twill trousers and two-piece safari suits that clung to his tall, skinny frame like a well-dressed scarecrow.

His favorite pastime of horse riding – a product of Huston's Midwestern upbringing that followed him from infancy in rural Missouri to adulthood in suburban California – benefited from an uncanny ability to communicate with people and animals, calming skittish horses and reprimanding barking dogs with a soft murmur of his voice or a gentle touch of his hands. This special gift qualified him to become an intuitive director of actors, tapping into their primal fears, as well as probing deeper, more complex emotions.

Huston had explored the subconscious mind in several films, most recently *Freud*, a biographical account of Sigmund Freud, the father of psychoanalysis. But this was the first time he had been asked to contribute his talents to a contemporary social drama by Tennessee Williams and which took place in Latin America. "John, of course, was the guru of Mexico," said Stark. "I just got him at a lucky time when he wanted to go back there."

As things turned out, John Huston didn't need much convincing to return to Mexico, the setting of his quintessential film, *The Treasure of the Sierra Madre*. "In the forties and fifties," observed Huston's biographer Lawrence Grobel, "it was the place that brought out the pirate in him, as he explored jungle-covered ruins and smuggled out precious pre-Colombian art."

The Treasure of the Sierra Madre, which Huston wrote and directed, was his most ambitious enterprise thus far. At the time it was an expensive undertaking; one of the first American films made almost entirely outside the United States. Huston based his screenplay on a scathing, anti-capitalist novel by the mysterious B. Traven – the *nom de plume* of Traven Torsvan, an elusive German writer who authored inflammatory political articles under the penname of Ret Marut.

When Huston went to see Traven in Mexico City he was met, instead, by a small thin man named Hal Croves, who claimed to be Traven's guide and translator. Huston wondered if it was a ruse to protect the writer's real identity.

Even Huston's Hollywood agent Paul Kohner, who represented Traven, but had never met him, was taken in by the clever deception. Kohner helped pull strings to get *The Treasure of the Sierra Madre* made in Mexico. Production was scheduled to begin in 1941 but was postponed until the end of the Second World War.

Huston's good friend Humphrey Bogart, whom he directed in six films, was his first and only choice to play the stubborn gold prospector, Fred Dobbs. The director's father, Walter Huston, a consummate stage performer, hammed it up as the old man Howard, who joins Bogart on his fateful quest. For the menacing role of Gold Hat, the bandit that attacks Bogart's camp, Huston chose the plump Mexican character actor Alfonso Bedoya. A few introductory scenes were filmed in the oil port of Tampico, where petroleum was drilled and pumped into barrels for export on cargo ships.

The bulk of filming took place in the hills surrounding the village of Jungapeo near San José Purúa in Michoacán. Between scenes, Walter Huston and his son smoked marijuana but Bogart preferred drinking Dos Equis – a popular local beer. Cast and crew stayed at the Agua Blanca Canyon Resort, a twenty-room hotel spa with two full-size swimming pools and hot mineral baths.

One evening, while having drinks in the hotel's dining room, Huston and Bogart glimpsed the vacationing Mexican movie star Maria Félix and her composer-husband Agustin Lara, who were seated at another table.

Félix was deeply tanned with lacquered black hair and heavy eye makeup. She took a small mirror out of her handbag and continually fussed with her appearance, oblivious to the presence of everyone around her. "Hey, I bet that dame doesn't even know who we are!" Bogart told Huston. The two men decided to play a practical joke on the conceited actress. Pretending to be tourists, they each went up to Félix's table, pestering her for autographs. Annoyed by the intrusion, she stormed out of the room, never knowing the names of her two smiling perpetrators.

Finally, after six months and a cost of nearly three million dollars, filming came to an end. Huston returned to Hollywood, but his mind was no longer occupied by work; he had fallen under a magic spell. Not only was he in love with Mexico, he had adopted a son: Pablo Albarran, a fourteen-year-old boy whom he befriended in Jungapeo and whose hand he now held as they walked through US Customs and Immigration at Los Angeles International Airport.

When it premiered in 1948, *The Treasure of the Sierra Madre* was highly praised by critics. *Life* magazine proclaimed it: "One of the few movies which genuinely deserve to be called great!" Bosley Crowther in *The New York Times* judged Bogart's performance to be "the best and most substantial that he has ever done." The film earned Huston two Oscars for Writing and Directing. His father deservedly won the Oscar for Best Supporting Actor. Bogart, surprisingly, went home empty-handed. He would have to wait three more years before he claimed the prize.

THE 1950'S WERE A TIME of tremendous upheaval in the life of John Huston. This marked the beginning of his international moviemaking phase as he went hopscotching across a dozen countries, directing ten films in as many years.

Part of the reason for Huston leaving Hollywood was the need for autonomy, an idealistic notion that appealed to him. At the time, US income tax laws allowed its citizens to earn up to $20,000 a year overseas and it was tax-free. In his bid for independence, Huston waged a risky gamble by taking on as his producing partner, Sam Spiegel, a quick-thinking, rotund man of outstanding salesmanship – but whose questionable ethics often landed him in hot water.

An illegal Polish immigrant with an extensive criminal record, Spiegel was a glib conman wanted for various crimes in several countries before he reinvented himself as a movie producer. Huston should have been wary of Spiegel. Instead, dazzled by the producer's conjuring tricks, he became a willing accomplice in the crooked scheme.

In 1948, Huston and Spiegel launched a production company named Horizon Pictures, which had been incorporated one year earlier – even though both of them were insolvent. Undaunted, Spiegel went out and raised the money for their joint production of *The African Queen*. This classic adventure story about a drunken steamboat captain, who falls in love with a prim missionary, came to define Huston's free-spirited style by plunking its two stars Humphrey Bogart and Katharine Hepburn in the hostile tributaries of the Belgian Congo and Uganda.

Incredibly, given its high reputation, *The African Queen* almost didn't get made. Spiegel's checks bounced and there was no money left to pay anybody. Financing eventually came from a British distributor, Romulus Films, which was owned by two brothers, James and John Woolf. The enterprising siblings guaranteed Horizon's production costs in return for the exclusive distribution rights for England and Europe; United Artists, who paid the stars' salaries, released the film in the United States and Canada. Bogart took home the Oscar for Best Actor, and the film became one of the most popular adventure stories of all time.

After location filming was completed on *The African Queen*, Huston returned to London where he rented a flat in Grosvenor Square with his fourth wife, American-Italian prima ballerina Enrica Soma and their two small children: a son named Walter Anthony and a daughter, Anjelica, who had been born while her father was away in Africa.

Huston, who was down to his last few hundred dollars and constantly worried about his finances, was elated when the box office returns for *The African Queen* began pouring in. When Spiegel saw the checks piling up he reverted to his old ways, cheating Huston out of his share of the profits.

Other directors would have threatened or sued, but not Huston. He knew he had been trumped by an expert trickster and graciously, if foolishly, conceded defeat. The film grossed nearly $9 million, which was a huge sum for the time.

Huston decided to wait things out abroad, hopeful that things would improve for him. What Huston did not explain was his motive for wanting to stay in Europe, a place that held endless fascination for him. Quite possibly, Huston's decision to remain there was not related to his desire to make movies, as he always maintained. More likely, it was the result of his unpopular political sympathies, which threatened his livelihood back in the United States.

Those troubles had begun a decade earlier. Angry over increased government control of the arts, he courageously took part in a public demonstration against the House Un-American Activities Committee (HUAC), which was investigating alleged Communist infiltration in Hollywood. The congressional hearings, which were launched amid a flurry of publicity in 1947, showed the dangers of ruthless politicians seeking personal glory at the expense of self-centered actors, proselytizing writers and authoritarian directors. But who among them would lead the rallying cry?

The most organized action group was the Committee for the First Amendment (CFA), founded by Huston, screenwriter Philip Dunne, and director William Wyler. On the eve of the first HUAC investigation, Democratic supporters of the CFA, including Humphrey Bogart, Lauren Bacall, Gene Kelly, John Garfield, Edward G. Robinson, Katharine Hepburn, Jane Wyatt, Marsha Hunt, Sterling Hayden, Danny Kaye and Frank Sinatra, flew to Washington with Dunne and Huston to protest the hearings. Instead of receiving a warm reception, they found the spotlight being turned on themselves and their motives questioned.

The *New York Herald Tribune* columnist George Sokolsky asked: “Who are Huston and Dunne? What is their connection with the Communist Party?” The media branded the protestors as troublemakers and they returned to Hollywood feeling betrayed.

During the nine-day public inquisition that followed, HUAC chairman J. Parnell Thomas heard testimony from forty-one subpoenaed witnesses. Some, like Walt Disney and Ronald Reagan, were considered “friendly.” Their patriotic beliefs and willingness to provide information to the committee led to the arrest and conviction of people who were suspected of being Communists. “In my estimation,” Huston lamented, “Communism was as nothing compared to the evil done by the witch-hunters.”

During these chaotic hearings, many subpoenaed witnesses, who were fearful of their own past political involvements, became stool pigeons. Thus, began the inglorious tradition of informing or "naming names."

When the second wave of HUAC investigations hit in 1951 and Senator Joseph McCarthy threatened to divulge the names of more Communists, Huston packed his bags and moved to Europe. Like the roving protagonists in his films, who often found themselves in strange towns, Huston seemed destined to become a wanderer – seeking shelter in whichever country offered it to him.

One of those early safe havens was in Ireland where he leased a country house near Kilcock in County Kildare. During his self-imposed exile, Huston did not make another movie for three years, preferring fishing and foxhunting to filmmaking. The anger he felt in Washington had not subsided, and he hid his bitterness by consuming large quantities of Irish whiskey and fine cigars, the thin smile on his face growing noticeably broader as the effects of the malt liquor and tobacco relaxed him.

Huston quickly grew to love the people and customs of Ireland and decided to put down roots there. Though he couldn't afford the added expense, he purchased St. Clerans – an abandoned estate with a leaky roof and no flooring.

The neglected property was tucked away behind a scraggly forest on a country dirt road, twenty miles east of Galway. Its centerpiece, a handsome Georgian manor house, built in the eighteenth century, appealed to Huston's sense of theatricality and he spent the next two years restoring it to its original splendor.

But the high cost of repairing the creaky three-story structure, laying down new hallways and buying period furnishings forced Huston to return to his chosen profession of making movies.

Always in debt, Huston signed a three-picture contract with 20th Century-Fox, and after finalizing the deal he departed Los Angeles for a six-week vacation in Ensenada, Baja California. It was in this quiet fishing community that he celebrated his fiftieth birthday while writing the screenplay for *Heaven Knows Mr. Allison*.

The following year, Huston rented a house in the town of San Miguel de Allende in Guanajuato, where he wrote the script for his next film *The Barbarian and the Geisha*.

At the same time Huston was busy writing scripts in Mexico, other exiled screenwriters were, coincidentally, rebuilding their lives there, including several members of the Hollywood Ten. One of them, Albert Maltz, who had served eleven months in jail, lived in San Angel, a suburb of Mexico City, where he continued writing scripts using a variety of pseudonyms.

Maltz's codefendant Ring Lardner, Jr., who had been sentenced to twelve months in Danbury prison, was his neighbor. Two of their peers, Dalton Trumbo and Gordon Kahn, who had also been blacklisted and spent time in prison, were residing in Cuernavaca.

Huston, of course, knew many of these people and had tremendous respect for the sacrifices they had made in defense of their liberty. Maybe that is why many people thought Huston was a Communist at heart. Film critic and writer James Agee put it in more equivocal terms: "He is, in short, rather less of a Communist than the most ultramontane Republican, for like perhaps five out of seven good artists who ever lived he is – to lapse into technical jargon – a natural-born anti-authoritarian individualistic libertarian anarchist, without portfolio."

This would explain why many of the films made by Huston during this unhappy time lacked conviction; he was fighting for his economic survival.

In spite of Huston's creative decline, Ray Stark's respect for the director was unwavering and their close personal bond, which was forged during the lengthy production of *The Night of the Iguana*, eventually led to them making four films together. But their long and profitable association may never have occurred if it weren't for the involvement of Frank Taylor, who brought these two human dynamos together. Taylor was formerly the editor-in-chief of Dell Books.

Huston and Stark first became acquainted on *The Misfits*, which Taylor produced for Seven Arts. Knowing Huston's career was in a slump, Taylor phoned him in Ireland, and offered Huston the job of directing a modern-day Western. The screenplay, written by Arthur Miller, continued the playwright's obsession with the failure of the American dream. It was an effectively simple premise: three disillusioned cowboys looking for love with different women eke out a meager living in the Nevada desert by roping wild horses and selling them to a slaughterhouse.

The Misfits was Huston's first production made in the USA after ten years spent living and working abroad. At a cost of $4 million, it was also the most expensive black-and-white movie ever produced up to that time. Like the film's demoralized characters, which lived each day of their lives in a drunken stupor, Huston had sunk into a temporary depression. He was intoxicated for much of the filming in Reno, where he gambled his money at the crap tables.

Often, Huston was so hung over that he fell asleep on the set and when he awoke he was unaware of having filmed the previous scenes. The film's saving grace was his love of horses, revealed in thrilling scenes depicting the lassoing of herds of galloping mustangs as they are chased across the salt flats by cowboys in speeding trucks.

The Misfits was released to helpful reviews but did only mediocre business, its message of hopelessness distinctly out of step with the optimism of America's Camelot – as the era of newly elected President John F. Kennedy, came to be called.

Huston needed a solid hit to get his career back on track, and so when Stark suggested he direct *The Night of the Iguana*, his second assignment for Seven Arts, Huston, now fifty-six, accepted the offer. “I had seen the play and liked it,” he recalled, “with reservations.”

JOHN HUSTON DID NOT BELIEVE in God. Nevertheless, when his best friend, Humphrey Bogart, age fifty-seven, died from esophageal cancer in 1957, it was Huston who read the eulogy at the actor's funeral, which was held at All Saints Episcopal Church in Beverly Hills, California.

One year later, Bogart's grieving widow Lauren Bacall, sold their two-story white French colonial mansion with its six bedrooms, eight bathrooms, four car garage, swimming pool, and tennis courts on South Mapleton Drive in neighboring Holmby Hills.

The home's buyer was Ray Stark, who cherished the memory of the late actor, but might have had an ulterior motive for owning the house. Now, he was able to indulge his dreams of success by living on the same street as Bogart and other members of the fabled Rat Pack, including singer Judy Garland, her husband Sid Luft, and composer Sammy Cahn, who gathered each week at Romanoff's – the most fashionable restaurant in the city – for cocktails and dinner.

Possessing Bogart's former home helped to legitimize Stark in the eyes of Hollywood. Seeking the approval of Huston, the actor's pal, was equally important to him.

"To be a tall, handsome WASP," ruminated Stark of his desire to be like Huston, "highly intelligent with a great wit and downright funny besides," was his primary goal. If Stark was going to meet that objective, he would have to win Huston over.

Before *The Night of the Iguana* ended its contentious Broadway run, Stark made a decision that had a resounding impact on the film. He commissioned Gavin Lambert, a studious-looking Englishman with a mop of brown hair and piercing blue eyes, to write a detailed synopsis or "treatment" of the play. An intuitive and perceptive writer, Lambert, thirty-eight, was well-acquainted with the works of Tennessee Williams, having adapted his racy novella *The Roman Spring of Mrs. Stone* to the screen in 1961.

What distinguished Lambert from many screenwriters, however, was his open homosexuality, which, like Williams, helped him empathize with the female characters he wrote about. When Stark summoned Lambert to his office, Seven Arts script editor William Fadiman, himself a writer and film critic, age fifty-three, took a keen interest in meeting the exotic, fair-skinned man in an open-necked sports shirt and tight-fitting slacks. Their ensuing three-hour story conference, held over a leisurely lunch, resulted in an exciting exchange of fresh ideas.

Fadiman and Lambert agreed that the popularity of *The Night of the Iguana* lay in its intriguing combination of sex and psychology, which, if adapted to the screen with care and imagination could result in a vivid and compelling film. Four weeks later, Lambert submitted an eighty-page treatment. Unlike Williams' stage-bound play, which took place entirely in the Costa Verde hotel, Lambert's version began with Shannon's mental breakdown in the pulpit of the Episcopalian church in Pleasant Valley, Virginia. The action then shifted to Guadalajara where Shannon is working as a tour guide and followed him and a busload of women to Acapulco where they check into the hotel.

Stark was initially pleased with the results. "I think he has done a damned good job in introducing new elements into the script," Stark told Fadiman after reading Lambert's treatment. "He has started the story early as I wished, and I think it is a good idea the way he has brought Hannah into the first few pages."

This aspect of the script was of crucial importance for Stark, who considered offering the role of Hannah to the Oscar-winning star Ingrid Bergman.

While Stark waited for Bergman's response, he approached the Greek actress Melina Mercouri to play the divergent role of Maxine. But as Stark maneuvered to find actors to fill the main roles he grew dissatisfied with Lambert's treatment, which he considered to be too mild.

To emphasize Maxine's flirtatiousness, Stark wanted a scene of her "unbuttoning Shannon's shirt and feeling him up; caressing him and putting her hand in his pocket; taunting, teasing and taking every physical advantage possible of Shannon, while he is tied up and they are alone together on the patio." Lambert incorporated several of these suggestions into the screenplay for *The Night of the Iguana*.

Lambert's 139-page script was written in eight weeks at his Santa Monica home above the bluffs of Palisades Beach. When he was finished, Lambert delivered the completed script to Seven Arts in Beverly Hills. On December 26, 1962, Stark airmailed a mimeographed copy of Lambert's screenplay to Huston in Ireland.

For the next seven days, Stark waited for Huston's response. On January 4, 1963, he dictated a second letter to Huston, stating his fervent desire for "a helluva lot more sexuality and excitement" in the script. Stark's possible intention was to use this tasty bait to entice the chiseled actor Kirk Douglas to portray Shannon. On the surface, it seemed like the perfect choice to have Douglas play a bellicose priest, but there was an unexpected snag. In a few months, Douglas would begin rehearsals for the upcoming Broadway play *One Flew Over the Cuckoo's Nest*, in which he had the central role and was also the producer. There was no way Douglas would be able to commit himself to both projects, so his name was crossed off the list.

Stark's dilemma was compounded by his absence of a suitable leading lady. In the weeks since he first considered hiring Bergman, she had accepted a costarring role opposite Anthony Quinn in *The Visit*, to be photographed that summer in Rome. Mercouri, meanwhile, had left Switzerland and was on her way to Turkey, where her husband Jules Dassin was about to start filming *Topkapi*. Inevitably, Stark would have to look around for other actresses.

After several more days of silence, a first-class airmail letter postmarked from Dublin, Ireland, arrived at the Beverly Hills post office. When Stark opened the envelope the tenor of its contents were far less enthusiastic than either he or Bill Fadiman had expected. "I'm not happy at all about the screenplay," was Huston's curt reply, which had been typed by his secretary Gladys Hill on January 7. "It doesn't bear out what promise the treatment seemed to offer. Rather," read the letter, "it shows up the latter's weaknesses. It's as though the screenwriter had been told to get as much 'sex' into the material as he possibly could, and, I must say," Huston's words bellowed with indignation, "he has laid it on with a trowel."

Stark's face turned red with anger. He picked up his copy of Lambert's script and flung it across the room. "Godammit," he complained to Fadiman, "the stupid faggot didn't have to use all my ideas!" Stark then ordered his secretary to call Lambert's agent and inform him that his services were no longer required.

"It's probably just as well," ventured Fadiman, after mulling things over, "because Huston will most likely want to rewrite the script anyway."

"Maybe," agreed Stark, his rage subsiding, "but I don't want to take the risk of losing him and having to find another director."

BACK ON THE EAST COAST, where the time in New York was three hours ahead, it was almost nightfall. Earlier that day, Tennessee Williams had attended rehearsals for his new play *The Milk Train Doesn't Stop Here Anymore* at Broadway's Morosco Theatre.

The play's elongated title contained the seed of a good idea: a rich ex-Follies star living in an Italian villa is visited by a handsome stranger, who is perceived to be the Angel of Death. The concept sounded almost as surreal as Williams' love life.

The previous summer, Williams became infatuated with Frederick Nicklaus, a twenty-four-year-old aspiring poet, whose talent he fostered in the hopes of launching his writing career. Williams had taken Nicklaus to Italy and Morocco, where they stayed at Paul and Jane Bowles' house in Tangier.

By the end of the year, Williams and Nicklaus were back in New York, cohabiting Williams' East 58th Street townhouse, while he readied *Milk Train* for opening night. The date was circled in red ink on Williams' calendar: January 16, 1963.

Impatient to make some headway on the screenplay for *The Night of the Iguana*, Stark cabled Williams to ask for his advice but Williams, who was preoccupied with the rehearsals of his play, didn't answer him.

Fortunately for Stark, a newspaper strike prevented theatre advertisements and reviews of *Milk Train* from being published and the play closed after only sixty-nine performances.

Awash in self-pity, Williams retreated to Key West, where he agreed to meet John Huston, who was arriving shortly from Ireland. It is not known whether or not Stark asked the director to intervene on his behalf. But Huston would not be traveling alone; he was bringing the screenwriter Anthony Veiller with him.

This turn of events occurred shortly after Stark dismissed Gavin Lambert and began searching for another writer. Veiller, whom Stark hired on Huston's suggestion, was a nearsighted, round-shouldered man. He smoked constantly and looked up glumly from his typewriter to contemplate the script on which he was working each day.

Like Huston, who came from a solid theatrical background, Veiller boasted an enviable pedigree: his father Bayard Veiller was a successful dramatist, his mother the British character actress Margaret Wycherly.

Politically well-informed with a strong social conscience, Veiller brought pithy dialogue to forty films, three of which starred Katharine Hepburn. Among his screenplays were *A Woman Rebels*, *Winterset*, and *Stage Door*, which netted him an Oscar nomination for Best Writing. Huston and Veiller previously coauthored the screenplay for *The Killers*, from a short story by Ernest Hemingway.

When Huston and Veiller, age fifty-nine, arrived in Key West at the beginning of March 1963, Williams was keeping house with the nascent poet Fred Nicklaus. At the same time, Williams' terminally ill boyfriend Frank Merlo languished in an upstairs room. "Suffering from lung cancer, Frank was deteriorating rapidly," said Williams' biographer Ronald Hayman, "and Tennessee was taking sadistic pleasure in flaunting other lovers in front of him." Williams selected a Billie Holiday long-playing record and turned on the stereo system. As Holiday's plaintive voice sang *I Only Have Eyes for You*, the dogs and cats growled at each other and a trained parrot named Laurita squawked noisily from her cage.

Williams mixed a pitcher of martinis, and the talk inevitably turned to *The Night of the Iguana*. Huston made it clear that he did not believe in God. "The truth is I don't profess any beliefs in an orthodox sense," he said. "It seems to me that the mystery of life is too great, too wide, too deep, to do more than wonder at. Anything further would be, as far as I'm concerned, impertinence."

Huston prescribed to a more tangible acceptance of the universe involving the main elements: earth, wind and fire. However, he found Williams' passionate debate about religion, which raised fundamental moral issues, dramatically compelling with its flawed characters seeking love and understanding. They discussed the film adaptation and the changes that would have to be made to the play.

Like Huston and Veiller, who abhorred censorship, Williams shared a healthy disdain for Hollywood. Huston sensed this feeling of mistrust and attempted to win over Williams by appealing to his writer's instincts. "Whatever happens," Huston told him, "my name will be on the script and so will yours, so we want what's best for everybody."

By the time the martini pitcher was empty, Williams felt reassured that Huston would make a commendable screen version of *The Night of the Iguana*. He thanked Huston and Veiller for coming and walked them to the front door. The three men bid goodnight. It was getting late, the pets were hungry, and Williams needed to check on Merlo's condition.

"Come on Freddy," Williams called to Nicklaus, who was sitting on the living room sofa reading a book. "It's time to go to bed."

Nicklaus batted his eyes. "But I'm not tired, Tennessee."

"I didn't say we were going to sleep," replied Williams with a mischievous cackle. "There's a crescent moon in the sky tonight and I feel like making love." Nicklaus stood up and gaily followed Williams to the bedroom.

After returning to Ireland, Huston and Veiller hunkered down at St. Clerans and began rewriting Gavin Lambert's script of *The Night of the Iguana*. The renovated three-story manor house functioned less as a family home and more like a hotel. Huston's wife Enrica, whom he called Ricki, raised their young children Tony and Anjelica in one of two lofts above the garage, and Huston used the other loft for his studio.

By this time the marriage had run its course and the couple was leading separate lives. Huston's personal assistant Gladys Hill, who resembled a bookish version of Grace Kelly with fluffy blonde hair, glasses and pale blue eyes, lived in the other cottage. Her duties included typing scripts and letters, paying bills, and making the director's travel arrangements.

Each morning, after a hearty Irish breakfast of bacon and eggs, black pudding, toast and marmalade, Huston and Veiller reviewed the previous day's writing. The framework of Lambert's first draft script, which began in the church, remained unchanged, though many additional sequences were dropped because they deviated from the plot.

Veiller dispensed with the scenes of Shannon taking the schoolteachers to a market in Guadalajara and eating lunch at a mountain café. The strolling mariachis, a marimba band, and an oceanographic tour on a glass-bottom boat were also deleted. A subplot involving German tourists, which had been a vital component of the original play, was eliminated.

Huston hoped to give his film a more uplifting finale. Williams promised to write a different outcome that didn't compromise the play's integrity.

On May 19, Ray Stark flew to Ireland to pick up the completed screenplay, which he had mimeographed and sent to Tennessee Williams in New York City before the playwright left for a vacation in southern Italy. Two weeks later, Williams cabled Huston and Veiller, expressing his delight at the improved script.

Stark, too, registered his approval of the end results. “I have finally had a chance to sit down and quietly read the script,” he wrote to Huston on June 4. “It is a damned good job, John, and I am most grateful to Tony and you for the time, effort and talent you have put into it.” Huston was grateful too; now, he could go foxhunting with the Galway Blazers, their galloping horses and riders leaping over the stone walls and steep ditches as yelping bloodhounds followed the scent of the small red prey.

THE THIRTY-FIFTH ACADEMY AWARDS, held on Monday, April 8, 1963 at the Santa Monica Civic Auditorium, was a typically star-studded affair. Frank Sinatra hosted the glittering three-hour ceremony, which was broadcast live on the ABC television network.

George Chakiris presented the golden statuette to Patty Duke for Best Actress in a Supporting Role as the deaf and blind girl Helen Keller, who learns to embrace life in *The Miracle Worker*. Rita Moreno awarded Ed Begley the trophy for Best Actor in a Supporting Role as the crooked politician "Boss" Finley in *Sweet Bird of Youth*.

That year's favorite nominee, Anne Bancroft, received the prize for Best Actress as Annie Sullivan, the tenacious governess who teaches the mute Helen Keller the power of speech in *The Miracle Worker*. Sophia Loren handed the statuette for Best Actor to Gregory Peck for his exemplary performance as Atticus Finch, the small town lawyer who defends a black man accused of rape in *To Kill a Mockingbird*.

The highlight of the evening occurred when David Lean won the award for Best Director, which was given to him by Joan Crawford, for his sweeping historical biography *Lawrence of Arabia*. Sam Spiegel, who had produced Lean's masterpiece, claimed the top honor for Best Motion Picture, which he collected from the demure leading lady Olivia de Havilland.

At the congratulatory party afterwards, Spiegel gulped Moët & Chandon champagne while chatting with well-wishers.

"It was amazing," said Ray Stark in a transatlantic telephone call to John Huston at St. Clerans in County Galway, Ireland. "There were so many people lining up to kiss Spiegel's ass it looked like they were waiting to use the rest room."

Five thousand miles away, Huston was puffing furiously on a half-smoked cigar. "Well, I hope everybody checked their pockets," he growled into the phone's receiver. "It wouldn't surprise me if Sam stole their wallets while they were shaking hands with him!"

Ten years after Spiegel embezzled the profits from *The African Queen*, Huston was still smarting over the loss of income. While he struggled against financial hardship, the crooked producer was wheeling and dealing his way to the top of the Hollywood pyramid.

Spiegel's 1954 film *On the Waterfront* broke box office records and won eight Oscars, including Best Picture. Three years later, *The Bridge on the River Kwai*, which he also produced, became one of the biggest hits of the decade, winning a total of seven Oscars, including Best Picture.

Huston sensed that *The Night of the Iguana* would be a defining moment in his career and decided to make the best of it. "Don't worry, John," soothed Stark on the phone, "we'll give Spiegel a run for his money." Huston had almost chewed his cigar down to the butt. "Nothing would make me happier," he snarled.

Huston instructed his agent Paul Kohner to negotiate very favorable terms, and asked Jess Morgan, his accountant, to invest his $300,000 salary in high-yield investments.

Once Huston's monetary compensation had been finalized, Stark turned his attention to the casting of *The Night of the Iguana*.

More than two months after beginning his search to find three major stars to play the anguished protagonists in his film, Stark had not engaged a single performer. One by one, various actors were proposed for their artistic merits and then rejected because they lacked commercial value.

No one escaped scrutiny, not even a star with an irrefutable reputation for brilliance. Marlon Brando had torn up the Broadway stage and seared movie screens with his ferocious portrayal of Stanley Kowalski in *A Streetcar Named Desire*. But success had quickly gone to the actor's head and he now appeared only in expensive films that frequently lost money. Yet he remained a consummate artist, capable of giving richly nuanced performances.

Huston thought that Brando would be an excellent choice to play the renegade priest. Stark disagreed with him. "I deeply believe that Marlon Brando is wrong for the role of Shannon," Stark wrote to Huston on April 9. When Huston pleaded his case, Stark stood his ground. A safer bet, in his opinion, was the dashing Irishman Richard Harris, who shared much of Shannon's rebelliousness.

Harris had won numerous plaudits for his vigorous performance as the rugby-playing hero in the British film *This Sporting Life*. Stark considered him "a fine actor and enough of an offbeat personality to be interesting." But Harris wasn't a bankable movie star in the USA at that time and so he had to forfeit the role.

Stark's third choice was definitely a star of the first rank, even if he was too old to conceivably portray a young reverend. The previous decade, William Holden had become an international heartthrob playing cynical loners in *Sunset Boulevard*, *Stalag 17*, and *Picnic*, which captured his virile qualities in abundance.

Unfortunately, Holden was undergoing a midlife crisis and had sunk into alcoholism, making him unreliable. Holden's recent film, *The World of Suzie Wong*, which he made for Seven Arts, was beset with personal problems. "I am afraid," Stark told Huston, "this will also be a headache."

Another worthy actor who merited Stark's consideration was Laurence Harvey, who hailed from England. Harvey's obsequious manner made him ideal to play abrasive social climbers in voguish "kitchen sink" dramas like *Room at the Top* and the film version of Williams' play *Summer and Smoke* opposite Geraldine Page.

Although Harvey possessed good credentials, Stark was disinclined to use him, "because of the many unsuccessful pictures he has made."

That left the unlikely possibility of hiring another foreigner: the noble Australian actor Peter Finch. The oldest and least well-known of the candidates, he was, however, among the best qualified. Finch had received widespread praise for playing compassionate heroes in the British films *Windom's Way*, *The Nun's Story* and *The Trials of Oscar Wilde*. But the consensus was that Finch's screen image lacked sex appeal, and Stark concurred with that decision.

An intriguing possibility was Jason Robards Jr., the foremost interpreter of the plays of Eugene O'Neill, though he lacked a defining screen presence in those years. The few film roles Robards had undertaken as jealous antagonists in *By Love Possessed* opposite Lana Turner, and *Tender is the Night*, starring Jennifer Jones, merely hinted at his future potential.

Cliff Robertson, best known so far for his heroic portrayal of John F. Kennedy in *PT 109*, which brought him critical respect and political favor, was also mentioned as a possible contender. None of these actors, however, satisfied Stark, who wanted a man who was not afraid to confront his "screaming demons."

As the countdown began to the start of filming, Stark found himself without a superior leading man, which he urgently needed if he was to attract a proper leading lady. He thumbed through a stack of Hollywood trade papers and inquired about the availability of a former client. In the spring of 1963 it was impossible to go anywhere without hearing the latest news about a boisterous thirty-seven-year-old actor named Richard Burton, whose name loomed large in newsprint.

A charming seducer, with untidy brown hair, intense blue-green eyes and a melancholy face that had been pockmarked since adolescence, Burton was devoid of traditional good looks. But this archetypal Welshman, whom *Time* magazine described "as pretty as a hill of granite" was blessed with something that was beyond special: a superlative voice that compelled audiences to listen to him. "His face can light suddenly with a smile," wrote journalist John McPhee, "but it always returns to its primal gloom."

Tall and broad-shouldered with a deep chest, Burton was already a familiar stage presence, having mastered both classical and modern acting styles. His talents ran from the brooding soliloquies of Shakespeare's *Coriolanus* and *Hamlet*, which he performed to great acclaim in London's West End, to the lyrical "sing-song" of Lerner and Loewe's *Camelot* that enchanted Broadway audiences.

Things had gone less well for Burton in Hollywood. Early on, he demonstrated his talent for emoting as the Roman tribune Marcellus, who undergoes a religious conversion in the first Cinemascope film *The Robe*.

Returning to England, Burton showed his versatility as the anguished jazz musician Jimmy Porter, who resents his middle-class life in *Look Back in Anger*. But, for the most part, Burton hated the cinema because it magnified his acne-scarred appearance. "In a film," he complained, "you are a puppet. On stage, you are the boss."

All of that was before the eruption of "*Le scandale.*" As Stark perused the social pages he found himself blinded by the orbit of a more brilliant star, whose name and sex loomed much larger than Burton – the man that was now constantly at her side.

A pampered cinematic attraction since childhood, Elizabeth Taylor was, in 1963, the most famous woman on the planet. She had literally grown up on movie screens, from a slender girl in *National Velvet*, to a busty debutante in *A Place in the Sun*, a playful wife in *The Last Time I Saw Paris*, and a Southern belle in *Raintree County*.

Amply endowed with the body of a Greek goddess, Taylor had luxurious black hair and thick brows framing large blue eyes that quickly darkened into violet. Her stunning complexion was compared to "a bowl of cream with a rose floating in it." Cameramen loved to photograph her, it was said, because she didn't have a bad angle.

Burton and Taylor fell madly in love while portraying history's most infamous pair of lovers, the arrogant Roman general Mark Antony and the ambitious Egyptian queen, who enslaves him in the gargantuan epic *Cleopatra*. In sheer size and scope, the logistics of this film have eclipsed every movie spectacle before or since, including such modern-day imitators as *Gladiator* and *Troy*.

At the time, *Cleopatra* was the most expensive film ever made, costing $62 million from start to completion. Its mammoth production, which spanned three years, involved the staging of four major army battles, the manufacturing of 26,000 costumes and the building of seventy-nine sets at Cinecittà Studios in Rome.

One thousand artists and technicians labored for ten months to recreate the ancient city of Alexandria on twenty acres of land on the coast of Anzio.

But this opulent film with its literate script and striking photography was more noteworthy for the electric sexual chemistry between its two headstrong stars.

The stormy relationship of Burton and Taylor, who were each married to other people before they began the film, dominated news coverage for more than eighteen months.

At first, Burton had no idea of the enormity of his involvement with Taylor, nor did he anticipate the negative reaction it would cause by cheating on his own wife, as well as breaking up his costar's marriage to the singer Eddie Fisher.

Today, leaving one's husband or wife for another spouse hardly causes a ripple, but fifty years ago, it was inconceivable that two people, especially celebrities, would engage in such disreputable conduct.

News cameramen staked out Taylor's rented Italian villa, where the actress was openly sharing her bed with Burton. Shocking photographs of the two lovers holding hands and stealing kisses were splashed across the front pages of the world's newspapers.

By violating the sanctity of marriage and disrespecting the vows of the Roman Catholic Church, Burton and Taylor incurred the wrath of religious leaders and politicians. For many observers it represented a breakdown in morality, a modern-day Sodom and Gomorrah.

When Burton tried to end the affair, and return to his wife, Taylor became hysterical. She took an overdose of Seconal tablets and was rushed to a Rome hospital. A short time later, Taylor suffered a black eye and facial bruises after she and Burton quarreled. The media reaction was explosive. The Vatican newspaper *L'Osservatore della Domenica*, which was read by 100,000 church leaders, accused Taylor of "erotic vagrancy" and being an "unfit mother."

In Washington DC, American Congresswoman Iris Blitch introduced a bill seeking to have Taylor and Burton, who were British citizens, barred from reentering the country on the grounds of undesirability. Congressman Michael Feighan asked the US State Department to revoke Burton's visa because his behavior "was detrimental to America's morals."

Looking back through the sieve of time it is difficult to comprehend the shocking impact of Taylor and Burton. Celebrity pairings have since become commonplace: Warren Beatty and Annette Bening, Michael Douglas and Catherine Zeta-Jones, Antonio Banderas and Melanie Griffith, Brad Pitt and Angelina Jolie, but none of such magisterial proportions as the conjoined phenomenon known as Liz and Dick.

In today's era of televised red-carpet arrivals filled with posturing celebrities and wisecracking announcers, stardom is taken for granted, as a consequence of which, fame has become discounted. Real stardom, the kind that blinds the eye with its brilliance, is a rarity.

"On their best days, Madonna or Tom Cruise has never seen the kind of attention that Elizabeth Taylor and Richard Burton got when they walked into a restaurant," affirmed the veteran screenwriter Tom Mankiewicz, whose father Joseph Mankiewicz directed *Cleopatra*. "By the time they'd finished eating there could be as many as 5,000 people in the streets."

Sitting in his Beverly Hills office, leafing through stacks of press clippings, Stark had an epiphany. In that shining moment of clarity, the producer realized that all his problems would be solved if he could talk Burton into accepting the starring role of Reverend Shannon in *The Night of the Iguana*. Top billing and the offer of $500,000 was certainly an inducement. But would the querulous actor go along with Stark's plan?

For all his bombast and bravado, Burton was far from being an easy catch. The loquacious thespian, who craved the spotlight as much as he craved a pint of Guinness, needed to be convinced that he was not being courted merely for his name value, important though it was to the film and to his immense ego.

Applauded for his commanding stage presence, Burton had been criticized for sleepwalking through films he disliked, often under the influence of alcohol. *Cleopatra*, in which he was required to speak his lines barelegged, wearing a pleated skirt and leather sandals, was no exception.

Every morning at breakfast, Burton drank six Bloody Marys to boost his confidence. He polished off two bottles of Krug champagne and several brandies at lunch. At night, to dull the back and leg pain caused by strenuous sword fights, Burton would retreat to the nearest bar or cocktail lounge, where he was joined by Taylor and the process of imbibing would begin all over again.

These marathon drinking sessions were not always a respite from work or a need for relaxation. Often, liquor was a safety valve to relieve Burton's sense of guilt over his squandered artistic talents, as well as the growing disgust that he and Taylor felt for their extravagant lifestyle.

One writer ruefully observed of Burton: "He chose Elizabeth Taylor over Shakespeare and the critics never forgave him." Another journalist took a cruel swipe at Taylor: "Overweight, over bosomed, overpaid, and under talented, she set the acting profession back a decade."

With all the unsavory commotion surrounding *Cleopatra*, Huston wondered if Burton's reputation would prove to be an asset to his film or a liability. The director stopped puffing on his cigar and glanced at Stark.

"Do we really need Burton?" asked Huston. "Well, he's a damn good actor," said Stark. "And no matter what happens he and Liz will give us a million bucks worth of free publicity."

So, Stark gave up chasing after inappropriate actors and concentrated his efforts on harnessing several thousand megawatts of star power to shine alongside Burton. He got a lucky break when two of Huston's favorite actresses, who were less inclined to work for other directors, agreed to bare their souls and midriffs next to the actor's soft belly.

JOHN HUSTON ALWAYS LIKED DEBORAH Kerr. He had admired her beauty since their paths first crossed at M-G-M, where he was directing two movies in 1950 and she was being promoted as the studio's successor to Greer Garson – the aristocratic English heroine, who endeared herself to wartime audiences. "Kerr... it rhymes with star!" shouted the advertisements.

A dedicated actress of quiet, determined courage, Kerr's most identifying quality was her aura of peace and serenity. She was at her best portraying outwardly vulnerable women imbued with great inner strength, what her biographer Eric Braun described as "moral fortitude concealed by a frail appearance."

This perceptive observation was confirmed with her starring role as the timid but resilient member of a dangerous expedition through Africa, searching for hidden treasure in the 1950 remake of *King Solomon's Mines*.

Graceful in her physical movements, the result of extensive training in ballet and drama, Kerr spoke with a rhapsodic lilt that concealed her natural Scottish burr. Her flaming red-gold hair and sparkling blue-green eyes were compared to a jewelry box – a fitting description since the movie was filmed in Technicolor.

Ultimately, Kerr would become more successful in less vigorous roles.

"I don't think anyone knew I could act until I put on a bathing suit," remarked Kerr of her breakthrough role as a US army captain's unfaithful wife – her hair cut short and dyed blonde – in *From Here to Eternity*. Her wet love scenes with an infantry sergeant, acted by Burt Lancaster, rolling in the Hawaiian surf, helped to bring about a new era of sexual permissiveness.

Capitalizing on her newfound cinematic reputation for adultery, Kerr appeared on Broadway in the daring play *Tea and Sympathy*. This provocative drama featured Kerr as a New England homemaker, who seduces an eighteen-year-old male student, much to the surprise of the boy's headmaster, who is also her husband. The play was so successful that Kerr reprised her role in the film version three years later.

Vivacious when she wasn't playing virtuous, Kerr showed her musical proficiency as a widowed Victorian tutor who sings and waltzes around the royal palace with Siamese monarch Yul Brynner in *The King and I*. She also shared a memorable screen kiss with Cary Grant at the top of the Empire State Building in the tearful love story *An Affair to Remember*.

After several failed attempts at working together, Huston finally got to direct Kerr in *Heaven Knows Mr. Allison*, the first of three films in which she costarred with Robert Mitchum. The pleasant experience prompted them to plan a reunion. For Kerr, it couldn't have happened sooner. At forty-one, her career as a romantic leading lady was in full flower; never again would it bloom so brightly.

In the preceding three years, since leaving Hollywood and settling in Europe, she had made only two films of any consequence: *The Innocents*, a ghostly tale of the supernatural, and *The Chalk Garden*, an adaptation of the suspenseful play about an emotionally disturbed child, which had riveted New York and London theatergoers.

In both movies, whose themes were murder and sexual repression, Kerr played governesses, which capitalized on her fame but did nothing to bolster her reputation. This, and the disappointment of having been nominated six times for the Academy Award for Best Actress only to lose each year, caused Kerr to doubt the wisdom of her artistic choices, and for that reason she preferred to stay at home. It was no loss to her. With an income of $250,000 per film, she could well afford the luxury of an indefinite vacation.

Secretly, Kerr yearned for another substantial acting role, one that would allow her to articulate the anger and frustration she often felt but was kept hidden under a mask of contentment. Huston understood the need to express herself. They had, after all, scratched the surface of these emotions once before, only now he would reach deeper into her core. Moreover, she trusted him, so when she heard his familiar voice on the telephone her face lit up. "John!" she cried, "what a pleasant surprise to hear from you after all this time."

Kerr was overjoyed when Huston offered her the chance to play Hannah Jelkes, who earns a modest living as a sketch artist. It was an inspired piece of casting that brought an added touch of authenticity to *The Night of the Iguana*. The role allowed Kerr to take advantage of her previously unknown talent as a watercolorist, which gave her many hours of quiet enjoyment. "I paint, rather badly," she declared, "but I love it."

During the time she took a short break from making movies, Kerr and her second husband, Peter Viertel, whom she married in 1960, resided in Switzerland, where they owned a chalet in the holiday resort of Klosters. They also maintained a villa in Marbella, Spain. A second-generation screenwriter and novelist, Viertel was the son of the Austrian poet-director Bertold Viertel and his Polish wife, Salka Steuermann, who was a close friend of Greta Garbo and had written screenplays for four of her films.

Intellectually gifted like his brilliant parents, Viertel, forty-two, possessed the tenacity of a pit-bull; he had an athletic physique with piercing blue eyes, and a petulant expression that concealed a quick wit.

In addition to having penned several films for Huston, the two men also shared a paternal connection: Bertold Viertel had directed Walter Huston in the biography *Rhodes of Africa*, about the life of Cecil Rhodes, who founded the diamond company De Beers and colonized the African state of Rhodesia. But the fathers never enjoyed the same prosperity as their sons. Like Huston, Viertel was as much a celebrity in his own right as his wife Kerr.

Even though the couple relished their privacy in the Swiss Alps, they were far from being alone. Many of their neighbors were friends from Hollywood. One of those colleagues, fortuitously, was Richard Burton. In 1957, to ease the burden of heavy taxes, which were draining Burton of one-third of his yearly income, the thrifty actor and his pregnant wife Sybil Williams purchased a country house in the village of Céligny, near Lake Geneva, where their first daughter Katherine, nicknamed Kate, was born six months later.

Burton christened his adopted home Le Pays de Galles because of its similarity to Wales. There were rolling green meadows with wildflowers, a fourteenth century church, and a storybook town square, where he could relax without attracting the judgmental stares of critics. On many days, Burton sat at a little pub drinking a bottle of wine until the sun went behind the mountain. Then he walked home, glassy-eyed, weaving his way across the dirt road that intersected the Geneva-Lausanne railway line.

Burton was not alone in his desire to live well and save money. In 1962, Elizabeth Taylor paid $346,500 for a gingerbread-style cottage in Gstaad, one of the most exclusive ski resorts in the country. This was where the glamorous actress went into hiding when news of her adulterous love affair with Burton was first made public and he filed for divorce. Gstaad became a suitable place for both stars to rendezvous in the coming weeks and months. Conveniently, Taylor's home was located one hour's drive from Burton's house.

The white-turreted Palace Hotel was the resort's toniest hangout, where European royalty, heads of state, and various actors and artists mingled. It was in the hotel's oak-paneled bar that Huston and Ray Stark arranged to meet Burton for lunch. Several weeks earlier, the actor had been baring his emotions in the high-flying romance *The V.I.P.'s*, his second onscreen appearance with Taylor, in which they played, appropriately, star-crossed lovers. After finishing their scenes at Pinewood Studios in England, the couple winged their way back to the snowfields, where they retired to Taylor's chalet.

On that brisk spring day in Gstaad, Burton was in high spirits and he enthusiastically shook Huston's hand in the hotel lobby. Burton was happy to renew his acquaintance with Stark, whose former agency Famous Artists represented him in Hollywood, where he was rapidly becoming the household name he had long wished. The three men settled into comfortable leather chairs in front of the fireplace and a waiter brought them a tray of drinks. Burton was wearing a tweed sports jacket over a green turtleneck sweater, corduroy pants and handmade Italian leather shoes. He was freshly barbered and bore the peppery fragrance of Vetiver by Guerlain.

Huston and Stark knew that time was of the essence if they were to get Burton's signature on a contract. His next film *Becket*, in which he played Thomas Becket, the Archbishop of Canterbury with Peter O'Toole as King Henry II, was about to commence shooting at Shepperton Studios in Surrey, England. There was only one week to negotiate his terms or Burton would be unavailable until the end of shooting in September. So they quickly got down to business.

This was the first of several auspicious meetings between the filmmakers of *The Night of the Iguana* and their prospective stars. "We went to see them," said Huston, "one after another. Richard, in Switzerland, promptly accepted, Deborah likewise in London. That took us to Madrid and Ava Gardner."

MADRID, THE SUNNY CAPITAL of Spain, was a teeming metropolis of startling contradictions. Rows of Medieval-style Castilian buildings, typified by their gray-slate spires and red-brick façades, stood in marked contrast to the grandiose French and Italian-influenced stone and marble palaces, museums, fountains and other monuments.

A popular meeting place for hundreds of years, Madrid was often referred to as "a city of outsiders" because the majority of its residents had migrated there from another city. Its pristine boulevards accommodated long lines of taxicabs and buses traveling at high speed on traffic-snarled streets radiating out from the city's hub like long spokes on a gigantic wheel. Each evening the darkening landscape came alive with smoky flamenco clubs and noisy discothèques that stayed open from midnight until dawn.

Ava Gardner was beautiful beyond belief when she first visited Madrid in the autumn of 1950. Photographs of her luminescent face, almond-shaped green eyes, high cheekbones, ruffled brunette hair and sensuous red lips peered out from magazine covers at newsstands on every street corner.

Entranced by the twinkling skyline from her room in the Hotel Ritz, Gardner went sightseeing and was seen dancing with handsome suitors at the best nightspots.

Then the actress departed in a whirl of excitement for the picturesque seaside village of Tossa de Mar, a crescent-shaped bay on the windswept Costa Brava, two hours north of Barcelona, where *Pandora and the Flying Dutchman*, her first movie in Technicolor, was to be filmed at a cost of $1.5 million.

At the time, Gardner was more acclaimed for her splendid physical attributes than her limited acting experience. Only David Selznick saw her true potential. "She is going to be a big star," he predicted with the accuracy of a clairvoyant. A mutual friend, Ernest Hemingway, helped to make that prophecy come true. The pugnacious author, who was also a Spanish loyalist, recommended Gardner for costarring roles in the film versions of his bestselling novels *The Snows of Kilimanjaro* and *The Sun Also Rises*. She gradually won the respect of critics for her ability to portray women with a troubled past, who, like her, frequently gave their hearts to one man while loving another.

Gardner was at her most seductive opposite Clark Gable in the African adventure *Mogambo*. Their steamy love scenes helped to secure her a Best Actress Oscar nomination. Behind the sexy image, however, was a shy insecure woman that lacked confidence and whose mind was filled with uncertainty. "Acting bores me," she admitted. "I like the simple life."

In 1953, Gardner returned to Madrid. This time, she was not there to make a film. Rather, her presence was requested at the inauguration of the Hotel Castellana Hilton – the first hotel built in Europe by American hotelier Conrad Hilton, whose son Conrad Jr., nicknamed "Nicky," was the first of Elizabeth Taylor's seven husbands.

When the festivities ended, Gardner rented a luxury suite at the hotel, where she lived for the next eighteen months while separating from her third husband Frank Sinatra, whom she had married two years earlier.

Their wedding was one of the most publicized Hollywood unions of all time, but the marriage was doomed. After many breakups and reconciliations between the hot-tempered singer and the embittered actress, they were now permanently estranged from each other, Sinatra venting his anger at newsmen, his soon-to-be ex-wife hiding from the cameras in Spain. "I'm living there," she told reporters, "because the journalists and photographers leave me in peace."

During this turmoil, Gardner went to Italy where she played her most famous role: a fiery gypsy dancer who becomes an international movie star in *The Barefoot Contessa*. The film was aptly named. Like its tragic heroine, Gardner rarely wore shoes – a holdover from her impoverished childhood on a North Carolina tobacco farm.

Gardner's highly-publicized involvement with the Spanish bullfighter Luis Miguel Dominguin made it impossible for the paparazzi to keep their distance. Tall and sinewy, Dominguin made love to Gardner with the same intensity as his famous sword thrusts brought cheering crowds to their feet at the Plaza de Toros in Madrid. His swordsmanship was so admired that many women fell in love with him.

Shortly after his romance with Gardner ended, Dominguin married the Italian movie star Lucia Bosé. Eight days after Dominguin's wedding to Bosé in Las Vegas, the tawny-haired Mexican actress Miroslava Stern, to whom he had pledged his love, was so heartbroken she committed suicide.

Gardner's feelings of rejection were consoled with a bottle of liquor instead of sleeping pills. In 1955, her divorce from Sinatra still pending, she purchased a villa named La Bruja in the suburb of La Moraleja, on the outskirts of Madrid. This peaceful setting was ideal for Gardner and her two corgis, Rags and Cara, whom she petted in front of the fireplace. But she hated living alone.

In her misguided search for love, Gardner befriended an assortment of playboys, college boys, writers and athletes, whom she followed everywhere with girlish devotion, wearing revealing skirts and tight blouses, doused in Tabú perfume.

By 1957, when she and Sinatra were officially divorced, Gardner's failed romantic exploits had reduced her name to a humorous cliché. Opportunistic producers exploited her fame in a variety of gaudy costume dramas that were more notable for their puns than their prestige. Stories about her non-stop drinking, playing flamenco records at all hours, and dancing in nightclubs made the rounds of newspapers everywhere.

Given her unlucky track record with men, it was no wonder that Gardner became an alcoholic, guzzling whiskey and tequila to dull her senses. She confessed not even liking the taste of alcohol, only its tranquilizing effect. "I was never a confirmed drinker," she maintained. "Once in a while I drank too much, only because I wanted to numb myself, forget myself, and feel lighter."

In 1960, her beauty fading but still intact, Gardner moved to an expensive duplex apartment in the leafy district of Colonia Cruz del Rayo in Madrid. Befitting her status as a cinema goddess, she resided in the same building as former Argentine President Juan Perón and his third wife Isabel Martinez, who had been offered political asylum by General Francisco Franco. Another political dissident, King Hassan II of Morocco, also lived there.

In her drunken revelry, Gardner became a woman of leisure, partnering various Spanish painters, interior decorators and designers, many of whom were homosexuals, to the theater and opera. Sometimes, the constant blur of parties tired the actress's health. She was hospitalized with a severe case of kidney stones while living in Madrid, and badly cut her face after being thrown from a horse at the home of Ángel Peralta, the famous *rejoneador* or mounted bullfighter from Seville.

But Hollywood producers kept calling her. In 1962, Gardner was offered the leading role of Alejandra del Lago in the film version of *Sweet Bird of Youth*. However, in an alcoholic fog, unsure of her ability to remember lines, she turned it down.

Perhaps the resemblance between the drug-addicted diva in Tennessee Williams' play, who takes a gigolo as her lover, and Gardner, the lush in real life, who was obsessed with younger men, was too close for comfort. If so, she must have regretted the mistake; the role netted Geraldine Page an Oscar nomination for Best Actress.

Determined not to make the same error twice, Gardner, age forty, was in a more receptive mood when John Huston called her on the telephone.

"Ava darlin'," spoke the director, his voice dripping honey. "We're in Madrid."

"Who's we?" she inquired suspiciously.

"Me and producer Ray Stark."

On the other end of the line, Gardner lit a Dunhill cigarette and relaxed on the tufted sofa in her apartment, which had been decorated by New York interior designer George Stacey in a mixture of eighteenth century French gilt furniture and modern upholstery.

"It's been a long time," purred Huston, softening her up. "What about a drink tonight? Show us the town."

Gardner brightened at the idea. "Sure, John, I'd like that."

They set a time and place to meet for dinner. Then she hung up the phone. "That goddamn son of a bitch!" she roared. "I'll show him the town!"

Drunk or sober, Gardner never forgot or forgave Huston for trying to take advantage of her. It was seventeen years ago, if she remembered correctly. One night, Huston invited Gardner to dinner at his ranch in Tarzana, a district of Los Angeles. After plying her with martinis, bottles of wine and cognac, the director propositioned her in the guestroom. She escaped his advances by running outside and dived headfirst into the swimming pool.

Now, Gardner enacted her revenge by taking Huston and Stark nightclubbing all over Madrid. The three of them stayed out every night, barhopping and flamenco dancing, for five days.

By week's end, Huston was almost comatose and Stark on the verge of a nervous breakdown, trying to get her to accept the role of Maxine Faulk. "When we left," said Huston, "poor Ray was a shattered wreck, but Ava had agreed to do the picture." It was her last chance at grabbing the brass ring, which she desperately needed to prevent her stardom from slipping away. But her self-doubt, and vanity, persisted.

Because Gardner was constantly nipping at the bottle her face had become bloated and she had difficulty memorizing dialogue. When intoxicated, her ladylike speech reverted to a thick Southern drawl.

Worried, Stark wrote to Huston, warning him of potential trouble. But the director was unconcerned by these ringing alarm bells. He knew Gardner's idiosyncrasies and was prepared to tolerate them because of his longstanding admiration and love for the actress. Stark decided to let Huston have his way, so long as the expert horse trainer kept Gardner, his prized filly, in the middle of the turf.

JOHN HUSTON AND RAY STARK traveled almost half way around the world to find the three principal stars – Richard Burton, Ava Gardner and Deborah Kerr – for the highly-anticipated movie version of *The Night of the Iguana*. Casting the secondary roles posed a similar challenge. For the part of Charlotte Goodall, the flirtatious Texas teenager whose romantic attraction to Lawrence Shannon lands them both in serious trouble, Stark and Huston debated the merits of several gifted actresses, ranging in age and experience.

Barbara Harris, a Tony Award nominee for the Broadway revue *From the Second City*, was, at twenty-seven, the oldest and, therefore, least desirable in Stark's opinion. In the middle was twenty-one-year-old Carol Lynley, who had caused a dramatic sensation on stage and film as the unwed pregnant teenager facing a moral dilemma in *Blue Denim*. That left the youngest performer.

Sue Lyon was a striking combination of beauty and innocence. Mature beyond her years, she had worked as a model in J. C. Penney catalogs and television commercials, helping to support her widowed mother, who moved Lyon and her four siblings from Davenport, Iowa, to Los Angeles following the death of their father, who owned an air-conditioning business.

Although Lyon had no dramatic training, director Stanley Kubrick chose the blonde-haired, blue-eyed youngster to play the title role in his controversial film *Lolita*, based on Vladimir Nabokov's salacious novel, which had been banned in some countries.

Lyon's screen debut as the lollipop-sucking teenager Dolores Haze, nicknamed Lolita, who wore frilly skirts and heart-shaped sunglasses, whipped up a hailstorm of alternate praise and criticism – and forever sealed her fate as a teenage sexpot. Only fourteen and still a virgin when she stepped in front of Kubrick's camera, Lyon exuded unusual poise and confidence as the object of desire of an English professor, played by the fifty-two-year-old actor James Mason.

A worldwide smash hit, whose impact would be felt for many years, *Lolita* grossed $4 million at the box office. Lyon, though, never shared in the film's monetary success. Despite winning a Golden Globe Award as Most Promising Female Newcomer, the budding starlet was snubbed at the film's premiere on June 13, 1962. The movie was given an "Adults Only" rating which meant that children were forbidden to see it. Lyon was fifteen at the time and, therefore, could not be admitted into the theatre.

Stark conveyed the news of Lyon's imminent casting to Huston at his home in Ireland. "She is a damn good actress," he said, "and I think she may give us some name value." Huston did not raise any objections. Lyon was screen-tested a short time later and the role of the precocious schoolgirl was hers – at a salary of $75,000. To celebrate the win, Lyon and her mother rented a new apartment in the residential community of Sherman Oaks in the San Fernando Valley.

In the spring and summer of 1963, Huston found himself traveling all over the map. He was in Dublin for three months, London for one week, and Rome for five days, where he unveiled his future plans for making *The Bible*. Then it was back to Dublin for another month of preproduction on *The Night of the Iguana*.

By August, the need to find actors and actresses for supporting roles in the film grew from an artistic prerogative to a vital requirement.

Huston hopped a Trans World Airlines flight from London to New York, where a chauffeur-driven limousine was waiting to take him from the airport into the city.

Seven Arts had leased bigger offices in the brand-new, fifty-nine-story Pan Am Building on Park Avenue, overlooking the Grand Central Terminal. This colossal structure, costing $100 million, was the largest privately-owned office building in the world when it opened in 1963.

"We are a big, important company," Seven Arts president Eliot Hyman told Huston, "so we needed somewhere that is big and important for us." The director was genuinely impressed. "Nothing but the best," grinned Huston as he helped himself to a glass of Chivas Regal whisky from Hyman's fully stocked bar.

For three days, Huston commandeered the offices of Seven Arts, where he interviewed more than forty actors for supporting parts in the movie.

Huston was assisted in his efforts by the Broadway casting director Michael Shurtleff. They flipped through heavy binders of studio headshots and made copious notes on yellow legal pads.

By sunset, the Seven Arts ashtrays were overflowing with cigar butts, the whiskey decanters almost empty. Huston couldn't resist the temptation for a joke. "Michael, this is worse than looking for a whore in a nunnery!" he complained. Shurtleff reached into the miniature haystack of photographs and held up a charming publicity shot. "How about this one?" he quipped. Huston stared at the woman's face. "Well," he frowned, "what is she, a mother superior or a madam?" Shurtleff shrugged. "Take your pick!" Huston roared with laughter.

The next day, Huston occupied the private screening room, where he sat in the middle of a row of leather chairs, the tip of his Cuban cigar like a glowing coal in the darkness.

The director watched reels of film clips and screen tests of hopeful actors and actresses, some of them complete novices, others showbiz veterans with familiar faces. He had to resist the temptation to give jobs to old friends or do favors for important people, no matter how beneficial it may have been for him and concentrate on what was best for the film.

In the role of Judith Fellowes, the overbearing chaperone, who tries to get Shannon fired from his job for seducing a minor, Stark favored Anne Bancroft, the winner of that year's Oscar for Best Actress. A forceful performer with large brown eyes and an expressive mouth, Bancroft was currently headlining in Bertolt Brecht's play *Mother Courage and Her Children*. "I don't know whether she is too young," said Stark, "but you may want to think about her."

When Bancroft showed no interest in taking the role, Stark was obliged to look further afield for somebody with the same intensity and charisma.

Shurtleff arranged for Huston to interview some fine actresses: Elizabeth Lawrence, Marian Winters, Jan Miner, Nancy Marchand, Lee Grant, Rosemary Murphy, and Jane Hoffman, whose reputations were rooted in theatre and television. But none of them satisfied his requirements.

Eventually Huston found what he was looking for in the sweetly sinister figure of Grayson Hall, whose wicked appearance – a mixture of small-town Capra and Fellini grotesque – made her stand out from more conventional actresses. Her teased red hair, slanted hazel eyes and a low, threatening voice, added to her insidious portrayals of neurotic women possessed with a mean streak.

Hall had played lead roles in the critically-acclaimed Circle in the Square productions of Arthur Schnitzler's *La Ronde* and Jean Genet's *The Balcony*. At age forty, she was now firmly entrenched in shrewish character parts, the latest of which was a non-singing role in the Broadway musical comedy *Subways Are for Sleeping*.

On the day Hall met Huston she was agreeable to his request for a reading but remained skeptical of the outcome. After twenty years in repertory, she was resigned to uncertainty. Still, the offer of a significant role in a major Hollywood film delighted Hall, who lived in a small apartment on Seventh Avenue, close to the theatre district.

When Huston congratulated Hall on her successful audition, the actress was thunderstruck. "Why did you choose me?" she asked, trying to hide her excitement. "Because you reminded me of a young Katharine Hepburn, and that was the quality I wanted," replied Huston with a broad smile. He may or may not have been influenced in his decision by the knowledge that Hall was a lifelong socialist.

Another of the roles that Shurtleff helped to cast from his vast repertoire of theatrical performers was that of Miss Peebles – one of the dyspeptic schoolteachers on Shannon's bus. Twelve established actresses were considered for the minor role, but only one of them was sufficiently interesting to Huston to merit her selection. Mary Boylan was well-known in New York's Off-Off Broadway theatres such as Caffe Cino and La Mama, where she played many parts, both large and small. She lived in a five-story apartment house on 9th Avenue near 52nd Street.

Although Boylan was fifty in 1963, she looked like a senior citizen; a genetic peculiarity gave her an elderly appearance. For that reason, she was frequently cast as women much older than her actual age. Theatre critic Walter Kerr called her "a canny actress who can handle just about anything" – and handle it she did.

Back in Hollywood, Stark and Huston searched far and wide for an actor to portray the assistant bus driver, Hank Prosner, who befriends Charlotte after she is rejected by Shannon. Because the subordinate role offered little in the way of dramatic potential, Stark's choices were limited to bland young men, whose only professional credits had been bit parts in films or television. Nevertheless, several interesting faces stood out from the rest.

Stark noted that a smiling, dimpled actor named Chad Everett "is very masculine and the right size for Burton." Huston also liked him, but nothing came of this suggestion, possibly because Everett was already committed to *The Dakotas*, a weekly TV series.

Instead, the role of Hank went to a rather obscure actor with the frivolous name of Skip Ward. Under Huston's tutelage, he would receive more respectable billing as James Ward in his first key role. Lean and muscular with bleached blonde hair, which was all the rage among California surfers that he resembled, Ward hoped this would be his lucky break after returning to civilian life from a stint in the US Army.

Ward's four-year military service record as an Air Force pilot stationed in Korea and Japan had opened several doors for him, one of which was studying method acting with Sanford Meisner at the Neighborhood Playhouse in New York. After arriving in Hollywood, Ward signed a seven-year contract with Warner Brothers. The studio was always looking for new talent, and Ward, who bore a strong resemblance to Troy Donahue, filled their requirements.

Ward quickly discovered that acting took a back seat to self-promotion, and he became fodder for the gossip magazines, which linked him to various starlets. In 1961, he tied the knot with a twenty-eight-year old lounge singer and dancer named Michelle Triola, but their marriage lasted less than a year. He didn't know which was worse: to file for divorce or unemployment.

Ward complained to Huston that he spent more time being screen tested instead of making movies. He saw his chances at stardom evaporating like a desert mirage and it scared him. “Look, Mr. Huston, I’m thirty years old,” railed Ward, a fire burning in his brown eyes. “It’s now or never.”

Huston reached out his hand and touched Ward’s shoulder like the Pope giving a benediction. “I know exactly what you mean,” Huston sympathized. He must have spotted a chivalrous quality in Ward’s battered ego that other directors had missed. Huston fixed Ward squarely in his sights and asked him the $64,000 question. “Tell me, son,” grinned the director. “Can you drive a bus?” Ward perked up. “If I can fly a plane, I can drive anything!” Huston nodded. “Good, then the part is yours.”

Perhaps the most vexing casting problem facing Ray Stark and John Huston in making *The Night of the Iguana* was choosing a suitable actor to portray Jonathan Coffin, the nonagenarian poet, who is also called Nonno. Huston made it clear that he didn’t want a middle-aged man wearing layers of greasepaint and a crepe beard, like you’d see in a Midwest summer stock production. He wanted a real geriatric person; whose face showed every wrinkle and furrow.

The symbolic role cried out for a great thespian like John Gielgud or Ralph Richardson, but Stark didn’t ask either of them. Instead, he tried to find a poet who could act or at least recite poetry. Pulitzer Prize-winning American writer Carl Sandburg was such a man. Much loved for his volumes of homespun verse, Sandburg, who turned eighty-five in 1963, was closer in looks and personality to the play’s elderly character. He was a star in his own right: droll, pithy, eloquent, but he was no actor.

There was one important detail, however, that Stark overlooked. Sandburg, who suffered from the infirmities of old age, didn't like to travel; in fact, it was virtually impossible to get him to budge from his beloved Connemara estate in Flat Rock, North Carolina, where he resided from 1945 until his death in 1967.

Could it be that Sandburg was disinclined to act in a film, or was Stark merely baiting the press with the notion of putting Sandburg, a national treasure, in front of the cameras? It is difficult to know, but after Sandburg declined Stark's offer, the producer was forced to look elsewhere.

Leaving no stone unturned, he mailed a copy of the screenplay to Raymond Duncan, the eighty-eight-year-old American poet. The elderly brother of the famous 1920's bohemian dancer Isadora Duncan, whose untimely death turned her into an icon, he was living out his final years in Paris. For a time, Stark also expressed his interest in the eccentric sixty-seven-year-old British writer Robert Graves, who resided in Majorca. Unfortunately, neither of these intriguing possibilities panned out.

Running short of time, Huston viewed tests of grizzled-looking actors, some of whom had once been matinee idols, others that were born looking old. One or two familiar faces caught Huston's eye. Henry Hull, age seventy-eight, had originated the role of Jeeter Lester in *Tobacco Road*. His voice crackled, and his eyes twinkled. Huston said he was "marvelous." Another great character actor, Frank Conroy, seventy-two, had created the role of Horace Giddens, the dying millionaire in *The Little Foxes*. Huston found him fascinating, but complained he was "not noble enough."

While casting agents wrote and telephoned Stark with more suggestions, Huston chanced upon the recent headshot of an actor that he recognized from his early days at Warner Brothers. The face was older, but the man's name was the same.

A spry seventy-four years old, Cyril Delevanti had made a lucrative career out of playing decrepit characters. His shrunken appearance, scruffy white hair, and sagging jowls belied his physical stamina and good health. It's hard to believe that Delevanti was once a juvenile performer in turn-of-the-century England. But that is where his career began, sixty years earlier, entertaining crowds with songs and jokes for a few shillings and pence.

The natural ease that Delevanti felt on stage and screen was not learned, however, it was ingrained. His younger sister was the Edwardian actress Winifred Delevanti, who appeared in a handful of British silent films with comedy star Lupino Lane. Like all truthful actors, Delevanti strove for recognition, and in 1920, the optimistic actor sailed from London with his wife Eva Peel and three children to New York, where he embarked on a busy stage career.

Delevanti made his film debut in 1931 as a newspaper reporter in the Ann Harding-Leslie Howard love story *Devotion*. His daughter Kitty became the second wife of Universal Pictures director Ford Beebe, who secured regular employment for his father-in-law as cab drivers, shopkeepers and butlers in many of the studio's fogbound thrillers and horror films.

Occasionally, he got to speak a few lines of dialogue, most recently as the faithful butler of Bette Davis in *Dead Ringer*, though not nearly as many words as he was required in his newest assignment.

"Cyril," beamed Huston, "you'll be perfect as a dying man."

"Thank you, Mr. Huston," replied Delevanti with a wan smile.

The role of Nonno in *The Night of the Iguana* was not a consolation prize for Delevanti – it was a deserving honor. The part was the first and only time in his movie career that he played an essential character. He was both delighted and slightly apprehensive by the magnitude of the reward.

Huston handed a copy of the script to the gnomish performer, who took it in a taxi from Seven Arts to his home in the Hollywood Hills. When Delevanti reached his tiny one-bedroom bungalow off Cahuenga Boulevard, he sat down in his favorite chair and opened the script at the first page. Then he promptly fell asleep and did not wake again until the next morning.

IT MIGHT HAVE BEEN MORE economical for John Huston to direct *The Night of the Iguana* in Acapulco, where Tennessee Williams based his original story. And, yet, even if the play had been filmed in Acapulco, it wouldn't have made the film any better – or easier. This Mexican beach resort, where thousands of vacationers frolicked on weekends and holidays, had changed radically since Williams first wriggled his toes in the wet sand.

Back in 1940 when Williams first resided in Acapulco it was still a sun-kissed land of primitive delights. This unbridled spirit of adventure tempted scores of peripatetic writers, who sought creative inspiration in the scenic mountaintops and nearby lagoons.

For Huston, who preferred the Mexican interior, the only reason to go to Acapulco was its excellent fishing. "That's what Acapulco is all about, honey," he told his onetime bride Evelyn Keyes, adding "all the rest is nonsense." Thankfully, his opinion did not deter Orson Welles from sailing into port in 1947 to direct sequences for his baffling conundrum *The Lady from Shanghai*.

With the advent of the jet age, Acapulco was transformed into a luxury playground for playboys and movie stars. Errol Flynn and John Wayne hosted parties on shiny motor yachts. Massachusetts senator John F. Kennedy and his second wife New York socialite Jacqueline Bouvier honeymooned at Las Brisas. Elizabeth Taylor and her third husband, Broadway and film producer Michael Todd, said their "I Do's" in an outdoor ceremony at Villa Scala.

By 1963, Acapulco was listed among the world's top tourist destinations – its skyline dwarfed by high-rise condominiums and luxury hotels. There were professional water-skiing shows with thrilling jumps performed by trained acrobats. The carnival atmosphere reached absurd heights with the film *Fun in Acapulco*, featuring Elvis Presley as a singing high diver serenading an assortment of bathing beauties.

To Huston, who frowned upon such commercialism, Acapulco no longer represented paradise; for him it was a Mexican Miami, overbuilt and overpopulated. "A dreadful place," observed the visiting American satirist S. J. Perelman, who labeled Acapulco "the epitome of touristic enterprise." Huston needed to find a quieter setting to make *The Night of the Iguana*. For a while, he considered the fishing ports of Ensenada and La Paz in Baja California, but technical limitations prevented him from making the film in either of those places at that time.

Huston consulted his library at St. Clerans, where he kept leather-bound volumes on history, art and travel. The inquisitive director opened a heavy atlas, flipped through its pages and found the spot he was looking for: a tiny harbor shaped like a horseshoe on the west coast of Mexico. The faraway destination, located in the state of Jalisco, where mariachi music, distilled tequila and broad-brimmed hats called sombreros had their origins, was literally a dot on the map, but it was the biggest dot Huston had ever seen.

The secluded port, where small waves crested to shore on golden beaches, was named Puerto Vallarta in honor of Ignacio Vallarta, the popular reformist and ally of President Benito Juarez – the country's first elected indigenous leader and a symbol of freedom.

The town's existence dated from 1851, though its geography was as old as the world itself. Thick clumps of vegetation covered the surrounding peaks and valleys, where mangoes, guavas, bananas, papayas and coconuts grew in wild abundance.

This tranquil setting reminded Huston of Acapulco twenty years earlier, only in Puerto Vallarta, time had practically stood still. "I first saw it about seven or eight years ago," Huston recollected in 1963, "and I remember thinking how very much like the South Seas it was."

Beyond the lines of breakers, framing the perimeter like a Gauguin painting, were tall skinny palm trees, grass huts, and rows of upturned *chiritos* or dugout canoes. In the background, clinging to the low hillside, were the terraced buildings of the town itself.

At first glance, the jumbled cluster of white adobe buildings and red-tiled roofs resembled French Polynesia – only its people spoke with the heavy cadence of Spain.

The classical architecture mirrored that cultural influence. High brick walls and stone balconies were fortified with iron grilles that protected the sanctity of life. Mosaic tile friezes and religious statues cast in alabaster and bronze paid tribute to revered Christian deities. Each morning church bells tolled in the village square, calling parishioners to mass in the Cathedral of Our Lady of Guadalupe. Pedestrians strolled along the *malecón* or waterfront, and couples sat on benches in the park.

On Sunday afternoons, a ten-piece band played waltzes in the *quiosco* or bandstand, where men in white linen suits and women in embroidered cotton dresses rendezvoused under fichus trees and danced until evening. Daily life kept an unhurried pace with the change of seasons.

In the spring and autumn months, cooling breezes rolled off the mountains, bringing relief from the heat and humidity. In the summer, heavy rainstorms turned the dry coastal plains into a lush green carpet.

Huston may have had another reason for choosing Puerto Vallarta as a movie backdrop: his lifelong study of whales. Huston was fascinated with the life cycle of these huge aquatic mammals, which migrated to the region every winter. Since the nineteenth century, boatloads of whalers from Boston had sailed to the Bahia de Banderas or Bay of Flags, in search of humpback whales. These graceful leviathans were such a common sight that vintage maps and nautical charts often referred to this part of the ocean, spanning a length of twenty-six miles, as Humpback Bay. Clearly, Huston relished the opportunity to go back there again.

oooooooo

As the man who was responsible for bringing *The Night of the Iguana* to the screen, Ray Stark needed little convincing about the merits of filming the story in Puerto Vallarta. The producer understood Huston's hankering for faraway places and indulged his desire to make the film in a remote setting – even if Stark felt more at home in an air-conditioned hotel room with hot and cold running water, instead of using a palm leaf fan and a rusty spigot.

For his part, Huston was not just being idealistic in his artistic preferences; he was also farsighted in his choice of geography. Where others saw only adversity in his selection of unreachable locales, Huston was quick to recognize the cinematic possibilities of filming in deserts and jungles, which gave his stories added veracity. But there were other practical considerations. Huston was always in need of money; consequently many of his friends were professional gamblers and speculators, whose financial advice he coveted.

One such man was the veteran Hollywood moviemaker Sidney "Sy" Bartlett. But this was no flashy producer with a cigar in his mouth and a pretty girl on his arm. Sy Bartlett was a decorated war hero, who had dined with five-star army generals. A sixty-two-year-old military expert with a receding crown of brownish gray hair, he had written several books and dozens of screenplays.

After being discharged from the army, Bartlett and Lt. Colonel Beirne Lay Jr., who eluded capture after his B-24 aircraft was shot down over Nazi-occupied France, published the bestselling novel *Twelve O'clock High*, which was based on their experiences stationed with the Eighth Air Force in England.

The factual story about the effects of shellshock on army personnel was turned into a gripping movie written by Bartlett and starring Gregory Peck. Its resounding success prompted Bartlett and Peck to form Melville Productions. Their company was named after the American writer Herman Melville, whose epic novel *Moby Dick* inspired Huston's classic film and gave Peck his most dramatic role as Captain Ahab.

In 1956, Huston began scouting locations for another Melville story, *Typee*, which he hoped to make with Peck, about a sailor held captive on a Polynesian island. Huston's search brought him to Puerto Vallarta, where he chartered a fishing boat that took him sixteen miles southwest to the tiny village of Yelapa. For added realism, he wanted to shoot his script on authentic jungle locations using the actual inhabitants, who were descended from four Indian families that originated in the neighboring community of Chacala.

But the film, as Huston envisioned it, proved to be too expensive and was never made. (A romanticized version of the same story, titled *Enchanted Island*, directed by Allan Dwan, and photographed in Acapulco, was released in 1958.)

In 1963, Bartlett, needing a respite, vacationed for two weeks in Puerto Vallarta, where he stayed at the Hotel Playa de Oro. Located on the northern outskirts of town, the modern accommodations comprised thirty new bungalows, a large swimming pool and a Tahitian-style bar.

Though it lacked the requisite trappings of larger resorts, the hotel held a strong attraction for Hollywood types, who posed for obligatory photographs with various wild pets: a baby boar, an ocelot kitten, and a playful anteater.

Bartlett was sitting in the beach pavilion, drinking a Planter's Punch and playing gin rummy, when the hotel's American owner Jack Cawood introduced him to a suntanned Mexican engineer named Guillermo Wulff. With his smooth black hair and neatly trimmed mustache he resembled a younger version of Clark Gable. "Are you an actor?" inquired Bartlett. "No, but people say I look like a movie star," beamed Wulff. They shook hands. "I spend a lot of time in Los Angeles," the engineer continued. "Next time I'm there I'll look you up."

The engineer's vanity amused Bartlett, who thought he was either conceited or star struck, possibly both. Yet there was an undeniable charm about him, and he seemed to understand the American mindset.

Wulff, forty-three, had traveled from Mexico City to seek his fortune in the flourishing building industry. Coincidentally, he arrived on the inaugural Mexicana Airlines flight to Puerto Vallarta in 1954. He boasted of having friends in high places and carried an impressive business card that he handed to prospective clients. "Everybody liked him," remembered Cawood, "he was just a great promoter."

It was Wulff who introduced the cupola, a small tiled dome, as an architectural flourish on the roofs of the many houses that he built throughout the city. The use of natural elements, such as adobe bricks, decorative river stones, and hardwood cut from the jungle, became his trademark.

Bartlett inquired if Wulff knew of any good real estate investments. "Yes, I do," he said, pulling up a chair. "Do you play gin rummy?" asked Bartlett. "I play poker," said Wulff. "Even better," smiled Bartlett, signaling the waiter. Wulff mentioned he had obtained a twenty-year lease on undeveloped land eight miles south of Puerto Vallarta in Mismaloya, a small bayside community, where travel was done by foot, canoe or on horseback. "It is my dream," he said, "to promote this paradise to the world." Bartlett was fascinated; he wanted to know more about the history of the land and its people.

Mismaloya, which takes its name from the Nahuatl word meaning "the fishing place," was a colorful footnote in the conquest of Mexico. When the Spanish explorer Pedro de Alvarado arrived at Mismaloya in 1541, he christened it Las Peñas – after three rocky islets with arching caves and grottos that lay offshore. Today, these huge granite formations are known as Los Arcos – the Arches.

In 1664, another explorer Bernardo Bernal de Pinadero discovered rich pearl beds in the surrounding bays and forced the local Indians to dive for this hidden treasure. The most hazardous part of the job was retrieving the pearl oysters from the black coral forests that were guarded by stingrays, moray eels, and octopus. The boys worked in relays, swimming hundreds of feet along an undersea platform that dropped perilously into a 1,800-foot abyss.

Three hundred years later, the village of Mismaloya, whose inhabitants numbered fewer than one hundred Tarascan Indians, remained unchanged, cut off from the world like a lost civilization.

In 1937, Mexican president Lazaro Cárdenas granted 3,000 acres of land to the indigenous residents of Mismaloya and Boca de Tomatlan. This land was to be shared equally by members of the community; it was not to be sold. Nevertheless, small parcels of land were now being offered for sale, which was attracting private investment.

Bartlett checked around and was told that Wulff had obtained permits from the Mexican president Adolfo Lopéz Mateos to develop a major investment in Mismaloya. Impressed by Wulff's diligence, the producer returned to Los Angeles, where he contacted Huston and arranged for him to meet the charismatic entrepreneur. Bartlett thought Wulff might be able to help Huston find suitable locations for *The Night of the Iguana*; perhaps they could buy some land together.

The moment Huston saw Mismaloya he was immediately struck by the beauty of the place. "There was a long, wide, sandy beach, and a jungly-overgrown tongue of land jutted out into the sea," he recalled. Behind the shore, some 300 feet above sea level, was a small mountain plateau. "The view from the top of this point – clear on three sides – was spectacular. It seemed to me perfect for shooting, and for keeping the motion picture company together. We could film most of the movie there and live there, too."

Convinced that he had found Eden by the sea, Huston persuaded Seven Arts that Mismaloya was the best of all possible locations, surpassing more scenic beaches, even those of Puerto Vallarta itself. But the site had one major drawback: it lacked essential services; there was no sewer system, electricity or running water. Everything would have to be built from scratch or transported and installed there.

"I don't know if that will be a problem," Huston told Wulff at the Beverly Hills Hotel. "You want to make a movie and I want to build a hotel," said the engineer, his eyes gleaming. "Why don't we do both?" Wulff offered to make Huston his development partner; they would split everything fifty-fifty and reap the financial benefits.

But Wulff, whose money was tied up in other projects, didn't have the available cash to build in Mismaloya. In addition to financing other construction jobs, he had recently purchased a women's dress shop for his wife, Nelly Galvan, who was the mother of his four children.

In his strong desire to succeed, Wulff was overextending himself, though no one seemed very concerned at the time, not even him. So, Seven Arts made him a tempting proposition: they would advance Wulff the money if he would discount his construction price. All they needed was a signed agreement.

Part of that agreement involved Wulff building the movie's set, along with a one hundred-seat restaurant with full-size kitchen and fifty bungalows for the cast and crew. It was planned to erect the hotel set above the beach with the accommodations in an adjacent cove (time constraints later reduced the number of bungalows to twenty-five). After the movie was completed, the buildings would be converted into a permanent resort and the day-to-day operating costs financed by American investors. Wulff christened the project Club Mismaloya.

Not for the first time was Huston's logic overwhelmed by his voraciousness. "The whole thing," he later commented, "certainly appealed to my sense of chicanery." What clinched the deal was Wulff's assurance that Huston would be given exclusive use of his own piece of land, to do so as he pleased, until the end of the lease in 1982. They shook hands and smoked two Montecristo cigars in celebration.

Huston would require a strong incentive, however, if his plan was to become a reality. "I decided the way to keep John interested in the picture was to let him build a house," said Stark. "It would be relaxation for him, since his mind always had to work on something." But this was no ordinary house, it was a small castle. The families that inhabited Mismaloya, growing subsistence crops and raising small livestock, had no idea that their lives were about to be turned upside down.

Eager to be the first person to own a modern home in Mismaloya, Huston pledged $23,000 towards the construction of a three-story residence overlooking the ocean. "You'll be a king in your own paradise," exclaimed Stark.

He was talking to Huston via overseas telephone from the new California office of Seven Arts, located in the eight-story modernistic Home Federal Savings & Loans Building on Wilshire Boulevard in Beverly Hills.

"Ray, you need to go and see Mismaloya," urged Huston from the living room of St. Clerans, his country estate in County Galway, Ireland. He was dressed in a scarlet hunting coat with gold colored buttons, black riding hat with chin strap, white shirt with cravat, white riding breeches and polished black dress boots. At his feet slept an Irish wolfhound named Seamus. "Don't worry," said Stark. "I'll be there next month." Huston was delighted. He hung up the phone and reached down to pet the dog's head. The wolfhound sat up and licked Huston's hand.

PART TWO:

20 DEGREES ABOVE THE EQUATOR

"It was the greatest single movie location in the history of movies."

– Ray Stark describing Puerto Vallarta

APRIL FOOLS DAY, 1963, was no joke for Ray Stark. After listening to John Huston's sales pitch about Mismaloya, Stark decided he wanted to see Puerto Vallarta for himself. He asked his secretary Lorry McCauley to call United Airlines and make two first class reservations for him and production manager Clarence Eurist, who would be accompanying him on the trip. A former US Marine with a strong physique that belied his age of fifty-seven, Eurist's job was to oversee the film's shooting schedule and stay within the approved budget.

When McCauley contacted the airline, however, she was told there were no direct flights from Los Angeles to Puerto Vallarta. The only company operating daily commuter flights was Mexicana Aviacion, whose fleet of reconditioned military aircraft flew out of four American cities: Los Angeles to Mazatlan, Chicago to Mexico City, and Dallas and San Antonio to Monterrey.

At Los Angeles International Airport, Stark and Eurist boarded a gleaming white de Havilland Comet 4C jet airliner with the name Mexicana trimmed in gold lettering on the fuselage and a replica of the Aztec stone calendar emblazoned on its tail. After a smooth takeoff, the plane zoomed south to Mazatlan, where it landed two and a half hours later.

Because of a heavy squall in the Pacific Ocean all connecting flights were delayed. One hour later, Stark and Eurist transferred to a smaller DC-6 that lurched and shuddered its way across the 9,000-feet-high Sierra Madres.

The plane encountered severe turbulence over the mountainous *barrancas* or ravines. The pilot was forced to take a detour before making his descent to Puerto Vallarta. In past years, light aircraft touched down on a dirt landing strip in the district of Santa Maria, several miles to the east. But since 1962, a newer airport, designed to handle the influx of regular visitors, had been constructed. The runway was adjacent to El Salado estuary, the marshy habitat of crocodiles, white ibis and blue herons. The airplane shook violently as it landed, wheels screeching, on the tarmac.

The entire journey lasted four hours, and Stark was relieved to put his Gucci loafers on the ground. As he exited the plane, Stark saw a herd of brown cows grazing next to the runway. A Mexican boy was leading a drove of donkeys with suitcases tied to their backs across the blacktop. The boy kept pace with the animals, hitting their backs with a *fuete* or whip. The convoy trotted past clumps of agave and stopped at the rear of the airport terminal, a low white stucco building that bordered the highway.

Passengers collected their bags from a long wooden table and moved through the customs and immigration hall, where their passports were stamped by Mexican officials. One by one, the weary travelers emerged at the front of the terminal and gathered at an empty taxi stand.

Wearing a straw-colored fedora, Stark quickly made his way to the head of the line, followed by Eurist in a blue porkpie hat. Because they had taken a different flight there was no one to meet them at the airport. Stark discovered there were only five taxis in the town – and all of them were occupied. The only alternative method of transportation was hitching a ride on one of the battered Volkswagens or rusty Chevrolet pickup trucks that occasionally sped by the airport.

"Whoever said that Puerto Vallarta was the unlikeliest resort this side of the Hindu Kush wasn't kidding," grumbled Stark. "I think it was Huston," remarked Eurist.

When Stark tried to buy a newspaper, he was shocked to learn there were no newspapers in Puerto Vallarta. To add to his chagrin there were no telephones or televisions either. The only form of communication with the outside world was a telegraph line across the street from the post office – a twenty-minute ride into town. Stark became exasperated. "Jesus Christ," he cried. "We're in the middle of nowhere!" Eurist was less perturbed. "Don't worry," he said reassuringly. "If there's a Walgreens drugstore within ten miles I'll find it!"

Quick-thinking and resourceful, Eurist had functioned as a production manager on scores of Hollywood movies. Eurist was a highly efficient overseer of film budgets and schedules, which is why Stark valued his practical experience. He knew the difference between making a cheap movie and how to make a good movie inexpensively.

The sun was sitting low on the horizon when Stark and Eurist checked in to the Hotel Rosita, the oldest of Puerto Vallarta's *posadas* or inns, which was built in 1948. The low, rambling structure with its four-sided red brick courtyard and circular fountain was located at the northern end of the boardwalk – beyond the sloping cobblestone streets with their colonial lampposts. Diagonally opposite the hotel was Park Hidalgo, a memorial to Miguel Hidalgo, the ordained priest and leader of the Mexican War of Independence.

On the sidewalk, Eurist waved goodbye to a swarthy man, who had given them a ride in his truck. As the truck sped away, a young bellboy carried the men's suitcases into the lobby. "Buenas noches," smiled the hotel's desk clerk, who handed Stark a letter. Scrawled on a sheet of folded paper was a message from Guillermo Wulff, telling them to meet him for drinks. They signed the guest register and were shown to their room.

It was nightfall when Stark and Eurist strolled up the darkening beachfront to the Hotel Oceano, located in the old Harbormaster's offices next to the lighthouse. Extensively remodeled in 1955, the four-story, whitewashed hotel with painted blue accents featured the liveliest bar in town.

The men walked up a flight of stairs to a large patio where groups of revelers were enjoying cocktails at rustic tables with chairs covered in pigskin.

Varnished wooden shutters and bamboo railings evoked the spirit of Ernest Hemingway. The flooring was constructed from the trunks of palm trees that had been cut into disks and set close together in cement to form a circular pattern. Framed paintings of swordfish and tropical birds adorned the walls. It was said that everything that happened in Puerto Vallarta – good, bad and indifferent – emanated from the bar of the Hotel Oceano.

Standing on the terrace, a frosty margarita in his hand and a friendly smile on his face, was Guillermo Wulff. Dressed in fitted beige slacks and a white polo shirt, he looked less like a hotel builder and more like an affluent country club member, which was, perhaps, his true aspiration.

Wulff had been eager to meet Stark, whose new movie was going to bring an influx of money to the town, providing employment to hundreds of people. He bid the Hollywood producer a hearty welcome, and the trio seated themselves at an empty table.

In a corner of the bar, a mariachi band began playing a festive song, their brassy musical notes filling the room with gaiety. "¡Oye, mesero!" gestured Wulff to an attending waiter. "Dos margaritas para mis amigos, por favor."

"No," Stark interjected, "I'll have a piña colada."

The waiter turned to Eurist. "Y para usted, señor?"

"Dame una margarita en las rocas con limon y sal."

Wulff was impressed. "I see you are familiar with our language."

"Somewhat."

A purposeful man not given to excess chatter, Eurist had spent the better part of a decade in Mexico, supervising American productions such as *The Magnificent Matador* that engaged Mexican technicians. Eurist knew his way around the country and spoke enough Spanish, he joked, to get him in trouble. "Clarence is one of the best production managers in the business," Stark told Wulff. "You'll find him very helpful."

The waiter brought a tray of drinks and set them on the table. "Tomorrow I will take you to Mismaloya," said Wulff. "There are many things I want to show you, and then we can get down to business." He raised his glass and intoned "Saludos amigos!"

The next day Wulff took Stark and Eurist in a Jeep to his office on Calle Juarez. Wulff showed Stark a small model of Club Mismaloya with papier-mâché rocks, tiny palm trees, and casitas made from matchsticks.

Eurist inspected a nearby workshop where employees were assembling tables, lamps and picture frames for his houses. "Furniture is a big industry in Jalisco," explained Wulff. "We use several types of wood – amapa, primavera, parota, cedar and nogal – which comes from the jungle, as well as two types of leather. Everything is handmade by our fulltime staff."

After leaving Wulff's office, the three men hopped in the Jeep and drove over the Cuale River on a new concrete bridge that connected the two sections of town. The vehicle bounced over the cobblestones, passing the Posada de la Selva or Jungle Inn, which was surrounded by mango orchards. At the end of the road was the ocean.

Wulff stopped the Jeep at Playa Los Muertos – Beach of the Dead. According to legend, this was once the scene of a violent massacre, when sailors transporting gold and silver from the Cuale mines, were attacked by local Indians.

A red-and-white speedboat was waiting near the shore to take Wulff and his guests to Mismaloya.

Youngsters in two canoes rowed the men out to the boat and they climbed up a rope ladder to the stern. The captain started the engine and the propeller spun to life, churning the water like an eggbeater.

It was an invigorating trip and Stark was impressed by the natural beauty of the coastline. He agreed with Wulff that the site was visually ideal. But figuring out the logistics of getting to and from the location required foresight and planning. There were no roads from Puerto Vallarta to Mismaloya in 1963, nor was a two-lane highway completed for another ten years. The only way in or out was by boat. Even that was a limited option because Mismaloya had no docks or piers.

Wulff didn't care; he was determined to succeed at any cost. He invited Stark and Eurist for lunch at El Dorado restaurant, which his family owned on Los Muertos Beach. The wine steward uncorked a bottle of French Chardonnay and poured three glasses. Smiling waiters served platters of fresh seafood. The men ate and talked.

Wulff said he wanted his contract with Seven Arts finalized by the beginning of May so he could start building the sets and accommodation. The proposed deadline was one hundred days or a little over three months.

Filming was scheduled to commence in Mexico City at the end of September and move to Puerto Vallarta in the first week of October. The estimated shooting time in Mismaloya was sixty days. "Normally, it takes three months to build one house," said Wulff. "If you want me to build the casitas, as well as the set for the hotel, we need to start now."

"Why?" asked Stark.

"Because June is the beginning of the rainy season," said Wulff.

Although hurricanes were rare in Puerto Vallarta, tropical storms still posed a real danger.

Wulff was justifiably concerned about the monsoon season, when twelve inches of water a day would be dumped on the mountainside. It made excavation and pouring concrete an impossible task, risking mudslides and collapsing foundations.

Stark valued Wulff's opinion but there were other pressing matters on his mind. At the same time that he was making *The Night of the Iguana*, Stark was also producing *Funny Girl*, based on the life of vaudeville star Fanny Brice, who was his mother-in-law. Her daughter Frances was Stark's wife. The problems of a Mexican engineer paled in significance to the trials and tribulations of putting on a Broadway show. "Don't worry," Stark said to Wulff. "My production executive will be coming here in a few weeks and he'll take care of everything."

After returning to Los Angeles, Stark flew to New York to meet with Garson Kanin, who was directing *Funny Girl*. Stark's choice for the lead role in his new play was a talented twenty-one-year-old performer, who had been discovered singing in a Greenwich Village nightclub. She could carry a song but, as yet, lacked dramatic experience. Her name, soon to be revealed, was Barbra Streisand.

On April 24, Wulff wrote to John Huston in Ireland, requesting a commencement date for breaking ground on the hotel set and accommodations for *The Night of the Iguana*. While Stark remained in New York, overseeing rehearsals for *Funny Girl*, Seven Arts production executive Abe Steinberg flew to Puerto Vallarta.

Steinberg's job was to finalize the terms of Wulff's business contract and seek the cooperation of local authorities, whose assistance was required in the making of the movie. A Hollywood veteran, Steinberg joined Seven Arts in 1961 after thirty-six years with 20th Century Fox, where he started in the property department and was promoted to assistant director. Two films on which Steinberg worked were based on short stories by Huston's friend Sy Bartlett.

In Wulff's office, Steinberg, age fifty-three, spent hours going over the architectural plans for the movie set. What he learned proved to be most illuminating. Based on a preconstruction budget of seven US dollars per square meter or ten square feet, the cost of labor and building materials for Club Mismaloya was estimated at $187,000 – a reasonable figure given the amount of work the project entailed. An additional $42,000 was earmarked for buying furniture, kitchen supplies and miscellaneous items.

A further $41,000 was allocated for the purchase and leasing of equipment, including $17,000 in car, jeep and boat rentals. Wulff was to be paid an advance of $8,000 plus $5,000 in personal expenses. That brought the total expenditure to $283,000 – the equivalent of 3.5 million Mexican pesos.

Satisfied with the breakdown of costs, Steinberg submitted his report to Seven Arts for payment. The task of disbursing funds was handled by Sidney Kiwitt, a thirty-five-year-old New York chartered accountant, who had been employed at Seven Arts since 1960. Kiwitt had full approval over the company's administrative spending and wrote the checks that were issued to contractors and other service providers.

Because of the protracted negotiations, Wulff was not paid until June 18 – three months after Stark and Eurist made their initial trip to Puerto Vallarta. If by procrastinating Seven Arts hoped to save money, they merely wasted valuable time that could not be recovered.

Despite this setback, Stark remained optimistic about the scheduled rate of progress. Wulff "has assured us that everything will be ready for shooting October 1," Stark wrote to Steinberg, instructing him "to make certain that the housing is finished even before the sets" because of the close proximity of the shooting schedule.

But Seven Arts drove a hard bargain. They demanded that Wulff build the streets twelve feet wide, put in additional roads, and make substantial changes to the cottages.

"What we originally had in mind was cement-slab or clay flooring, wattle walls and simple thatched roofs for the living quarters – with the conveniences of running water and electricity," said Huston. "The structures accordingly became cement-and-stone houses with red tile roofs, tile floors and expensive appointments throughout."

These were additional requirements that had not been included in the original budget, but which Wulff was now forced to provide without altering the cost. This was a fiscal impossibility. "Give up this foolish dream," Nelly Wulff told her husband. "No," he replied. "I will make my dream a reality."

While Huston regaled his Irish friends about his new vacation home in Mexico, Wulff sat in his office on Calle Juarez, composing a troubling letter. "John, we are having a problem," he wrote to the director on a hot rainy afternoon in July. "The company is paying us $1,400 for each bungalow we build, but we are spending a little more than $3,000 on each one. Of course, we are keeping the bungalows after the movie is finished, but we don't have enough money now to spend on your house."

When Huston read the letter, he became incensed. "The damned fool!" he hollered. "Where does he think I'm going to live, in a tree?" After thinking things over, Huston called Jess Morgan, his business manager, and requested extra cash. Morgan, however, advised him against investing more money in the venture. "Torn between his club and its contributors, his budget for construction from Seven Arts, plus a deadline for completion, Guillermo apparently over-extended," reflected Huston. "I think he simply promised more than he could deliver. In that lay the seeds of calamity."

JUNE 12, 1963, WAS a red-letter day in New York City. The faux Egyptian façade of the Rivoli Theatre at Broadway and 49th Street was illuminated by powerful searchlights for the world premiere of *Cleopatra*. Below the theater's marquee, 10,000 onlookers were corralled behind wooden barricades like herds of nervous cattle. Watching over the crowd was 500 policemen carrying holstered pistols and nightsticks. Television cameras followed the streaming procession of luminaries as they entered the theatre.

Among the invited dignitaries, whose arrival was snapped by waiting photographers, were the masterminds of *Cleopatra*: producer Walter Wanger, director Joseph Mankiewicz, and Darryl Zanuck, the president of 20th Century-Fox, whose studio was nearly bankrupted by the movie's astronomical expenditure. Joining them on the red carpet were British actors Rex Harrison and Roddy McDowall, who played Julius Caesar and his young heir Octavian in the film.

Inside the Greek revival-style auditorium, more than 2,000 guests in black-tie and evening dress had each paid $100 to witness the unveiling of this looming colossus, which *Life* magazine called "the most talked about movie ever made." Now, as this thundering spectacle of Egyptian soldiers, giant sphinxes, Roman warships, clashing armies, blaring trumpeters, Arabian horses, parading charioteers, ceremonial archers and snake dancers was about to be unleashed on moviegoers, the only two people missing from the proceedings were Elizabeth Taylor and Richard Burton, who had ignited each other's passions as Cleopatra and Mark Antony.

The world's most famous couple was 3,459 miles away, ensconced at the Dorchester Hotel in London, with a Rolls-Royce at their disposal. Since May, Burton had been filming *Becket*, which featured a royal coronation and long speeches that utilized his Shakespearean talents. But the only thing that people cared to talk about, then and for many months after, was *Cleopatra*.

The same day that this four-hour epic was unspooled for the public, another significant event was taking place. Alerted to the rising production costs of *The Night of the Iguana*, Stephen Grimes, the film's art director, who resided in a three-story house in the trendy London suburb of Camden, packed his suitcase with summer clothes. He grabbed a valise containing drafting paper, pencils and ink, and hailed a black cab which took him to Heathrow Airport.

After a brief stopover in New York, Grimes arrived in Mexico City, where he changed planes for the one-hour flight to Puerto Vallarta.

A soft-spoken artist with curly brown hair and a red beard, Grimes was Huston's aide-de-camp on twelve films. They first met when Grimes worked for Ralph Brinton, the art director on *Moby Dick*. "I immediately recognized a superior draftsman," said Huston, "and put him on the job."

Grimes, age thirty-six, had a discerning eye and a knack for choosing the correct materials and furnishings to ensure complete accuracy. But he was painfully shy.

"If you addressed him directly," said Huston, "a great blush would spread over his face. It's a good thing he could draw, because he could hardly speak." Shy or not, Grimes was never idle. Happily married, he had two sons, three daughters and numerous liaisons with women of various nationalities.

At this busy period in this life, Grimes may have wished for an easier project than *The Night of the Iguana*, which took him far away from home.

In addition to transferring the visual style of Tennessee Williams' play from stage to screen, Grimes had to contend with hundreds of Mexican laborers, who spoke little or no English. The biggest challenge facing him in the months ahead would be replicating the play's sharply angular set design on the windy slopes of Mismaloya.

Since an actual hotel was required, Grimes had to fabricate an entire structure from bricks and mortar in the jungle. It was a time-consuming chore but one that he performed without complaint. Grimes made sketches of the main set, using the movie script as his blueprint.

The next step was to build a scale model that gave miniature form to Anthony Veiller's typed words: "It is a low, rambling building, completely surrounded by a wide verandah, and surmounted by a roof of palm fronds. It is mounted on stilts so that the verandah is almost at eye level. A flight of steps leads up to it."

Not only was Grimes required to design the set, he had to find an efficient way to get everything he needed sent to the film location. It was like planning a small military invasion, right down to anticipating the best weather conditions. With the onset of the rainy season in July, the hours of daylight were reduced to six hours, afternoon temperatures climbed to 87 degrees Fahrenheit and humidity rose to sixty-five percent.

"However, I feel that if we accept this factor right from the start and make intelligent provision," Grimes advised Seven Arts, "there needn't be much headache on this score."

The headache to which Grimes was referring involved the tricky maneuvering and installation of noisy electrical generators that supplied power to a huge array of technical apparatus: bulky Mitchell movie cameras, heavy Chapman cranes, portable dollies, sound recording equipment, arc lights and sun lamps.

Grimes had to figure out where to put the electrical generators, so the whirring sound of the motors would not disrupt filming. Initially, the machinery was going to be stored on a pontoon near the shoreline. But the possibility of tropical storms nixed that idea. "I don't think the suggestion of keeping the generators on a barge is practical," warned Grimes, adding "even a short squall could land us in plenty of trouble." He decided to hoist the electrical units up the Mismaloya hillside and place them on a recessed ledge below the actual set.

Before any work could commence, however, large boulders that obstructed the peninsula had to be dynamited by Guillermo Wulff and his construction crew.

On a bright sunny day, as villagers roasted fish on small charcoal fires and children played on the sand, the earth beneath their feet shook with the sound of exploding dynamite. There were three loud detonations in quick succession. Thick jets of fire and smoke shot upward, splitting trees in half and eviscerating fleeing birds. Broken rocks rained down like hailstones on the beach and small tremors rippled across the bay.

Curious residents ran to the shoreline, where dogs were barking and injured seagulls lay floating in the water. A few minutes later, two motorboats filled with workmen carrying machetes, axes, picks and shovels, rounded the headland to begin the process of clearing away the debris.

No sooner had work commenced than news of this audacious enterprise was relayed with the speed of tom-toms all the way back to Los Angeles.

"Houses are hastily being built for the cast and crew," Louella Parsons informed readers in her syndicated weekly column in the *Los Angeles Herald-Examiner*. "Every man in the village is being employed with extra labor being brought in to add restaurants and cantinas to the little village."

Within a month, nearly three hundred men and one hundred burros were pressed into service, bringing the total workforce to almost four hundred. The foundations of a stone temple began rising from the remains of desiccated tree stumps. Although Abe Steinberg had observed plenty of construction around town, there was no shortage of manpower or building materials. (That same year, the city's newest attraction, Hotel Posada, with its towering cone-shaped *palapas*, and featuring 125 rooms and 12 suites, each with its own terrace, was nearing completion.)

Almost from the outset it was apparent that local contractors were taking unfair advantage of Seven Arts, overcharging them for goods and services. It started with the cost of a bag of cement that sold for 17 pesos in Puerto Vallarta and was delivered to Mismaloya for 33 pesos. The inflation went on from there, driving up the cost of water, food, liquor – even cigarettes. Likewise, the daily wage of 20 pesos for unskilled labor in Puerto Vallarta rose to 25 pesos plus a 12 pesos food allowance – presumably because of the extra travel distance to Mismaloya.

"In this happy land of unrestricted free enterprise," Steinberg wrote to Ray Stark, "it seems that the price charged for any commodity is based upon the purchaser's immediate need of it."

Whereas the standard rate for master carpenters and stone masons in Puerto Vallarta was fixed at 35 pesos a day, in Mismaloya the payment jumped to 40 pesos plus meals. Humans were not alone in this apparent price fixing; even animals demanded more money. "The burros have a very strong union," said Steinberg, "and they wouldn't go up those hills for less than $1.60."

Many of these monetary decisions were not made by disgruntled workers or their burros but were advocated by representatives of the Confederación de Trabajadores de Mexico or Confederation of Mexican Workers (CTM), who monitored the pay and working conditions of its members.

The nation's largest trade union, CTM was closely aligned to the Partido Revolucionario Institucional or Institutional Revolutionary Party (PRI), which ruled Mexico for more than seventy years.

The union had strong ties to the Mexican Communist Party, which helped President Lazaro Cárdenas prevent a threatened political coup and opposed industrial layoffs and strikes. Clearly, the union was not to be trifled with, for they had the power to bring company bosses to their knees.

But in Mismaloya, politics took a back seat to economics. As work progressed, Grimes became dismayed at the lack of control Wulff exercised over the project. Although he had agreed to provide Seven Arts with "bungalows of first class construction" the casitas that Wulff designed were conspicuously small with no living rooms and, worse, no kitchens. It was irrational, inexplicable, and infuriating.

"I spend hours talking Guillermo into putting the extra window in here and there – and so on down the line," said Grimes, who feared the only results would be "a set of superbly designed foundations to show, come October" when the cast and crew arrived in town for the start of filming.

In the middle of construction, Wulff drove eight hours from Puerto Vallarta to Guadalajara and back to buy beds and accessories for the unfinished casitas, instead of getting what was needed in the way of cement, tiles and lumber. The engineer's thirty-nine-year-old assistant, Luis Favela, was put in charge. "The first three months we did the houses for the artists, but it was really six months of pressure," he said.

Wulff's spending spree made no sense; it depleted his supply of cash and forced him to ask for credit, resulting in local merchants charging him even higher prices. "Privately, I don't think he is equipped for such an undertaking," wrote Grimes, adding "he spends too much time and energy trying to make the odd peso on that or the other clause of the contract."

Regardless of these difficulties, the Costa Verde Hotel, which sat like a shrine on the exposed hilltop, gradually evolved from a pencil and ink rendering into the three-dimensional centerpiece of Williams' story.

At the same time Grimes supervised the hotel set, he was also designing Huston's coastal villa. Grimes crossed his fingers and hoped the director would approve of the alterations, which eliminated fancy details such as patios and balconies to conserve money for the other accommodations.

Built on concrete stilts, the evolving twenty-five cabins on the other side of the peninsula, where the cast and crew were going to be billeted, would eventually be turned into hotel suites.

Grimes alternated one day at his drawing board in the Seven Arts production offices in the five-story El Dorado building, located behind Wulff's restaurant, with a day in Mismaloya – trying to make the results work.

By the end of September, when construction of the hotel was nearly completed, the cost for skilled workers had risen to almost 100 pesos a day.

"With about fifteen thousand-man days of peon labor and ten thousand-man days for expert craftsmen," Steinberg calculated of Wulff's extra spending, "he was in for an average of something over forty thousand dollars."

Memo from Ray Stark to John Huston dated June 18, 1963: "I have taken the liberty of hiring a very bright man by the name of Sandy Whitelaw as an assistant to me to take care of certain follow through details. I hope that you will find him intelligent and pleasant, but if you don't, I will have no problem putting him on another project."

Tall and fair-haired, befitting his boyish nickname, Alexander Whitelaw had already worked for several top Hollywood producers on foreign locations. He previously functioned as Harold Hecht's representative on *Taras Bulba* – a sixteenth century epic about fighting Cossacks that was filmed in Argentina.

On June 25, Whitelaw found himself in a Puerto Vallarta hotel room, unpacking his travel bag containing resort beachwear. His assignment was taking Polaroid photographs of middle-aged and elderly American women for bit parts as the schoolteachers on Shannon's bus. He talked to customers at the central market and interviewed residents. One frail lady asked Whitelaw to carry a bag of groceries to her home. A heavyset woman invited him to lunch, and a rich widow propositioned him.

Whitelaw was also instructed to find two good-looking Mexican beach boys for roles in the film. He decided to stake out Playa Los Muertos, where youngsters offered skin-diving trips for $1.60 in their canoes, and professional tour operators rented deep-sea fishing boats for $30-50 a day.

One muscled young man, who was giving water-skiing lessons to a female tourist, caught Whitelaw's eye. He took a snapshot of the bronzed instructor and wrote down his name on the back of the photo. Then he checked his wristwatch and decided it was time to get some lunch.

EVER SINCE JOHN HUSTON BEGAN making *The Night of the Iguana*, Seven Arts had been happy to indulge the impetuous director, but his desire to build a hotel resort development in Mismaloya was putting a strain of the film's $3 million budget. Granted, it was not an exorbitant figure, but the added costs still posed a financial risk. "Ray Stark is a gambler," said Huston. But the fact was that Stark was gambling with Eliot Hyman's money – not Huston's. Naturally, his first responsibility was to protect that investment, so Stark had to find another way to save money on the production.

"Before we began filming, Ray and I discussed whether *The Night of the Iguana* should be black-and-white or color. Ray wanted color; I wanted black-and-white," remembered Huston. "I thought that color – especially of sea, sky, jungle, flowers, birds, iguanas, beaches – would be distracting. Black-and-white would place the emphasis where it belonged – on the story." His explanation, while plausible on the surface, concealed a different truth. Although Huston preferred black-and-white over color, especially for psychological dramas, he was not averse to the concept of using color – far from it.

Earlier in his career, Huston had experimented with color to achieve striking results. His most innovative films – *The African Queen*, *Moulin Rouge*, *Moby Dick* – were filmed using different color processes, and he would continue exploring the realms of color in films like *The Bible* and *Reflections in a Golden Eye*.

Nevertheless, filming in color was, at that time, a cumbersome and expensive procedure. The camera required immense amounts of light, which was often difficult to accomplish in the jungle. This meant that it took considerably more time to photograph each scene, adding to the length of the shooting schedule, which increased the film's budget. Huston was keenly aware of these drawbacks, and wisely deferred to his producer before making any decisions.

A brief time later, Huston stood in the hallway of St. Clerans, holding a typewritten letter from Stark: "You and I talked about using color for *Iguana*, John. Therefore, today on the phone I wanted to go overboard in stating that both Eliot and I feel very strongly that we want to give you everything possible to make this a helluva motion picture. I only brought up the black and white to you today as what might be a needed expediency in the event we run into budget problems."

Stark went on to explain that he had always been afraid of the lush green quality they would get from the rain forest, believing "it would photograph just about as phony as blood does." Huston didn't agree with him. He always approached the color schemes of his films with a painter's eye, choosing the palette that was best suited for the story. Besides, plenty of color films had been photographed in the tropics, often with stunning results.

The reality was that Stark was only concerned with the bottom line. To recoup the added expenses of filming in Puerto Vallarta, he wanted to apply for financial assistance under the Eady Levy – an act of British Parliament passed in 1949 that imposed a small tax on the sale of cinema tickets in England.

The revenue from ticket sales was used to help finance the production of British films that otherwise might not have seen the light of day. The incentive was a boon for American directors like Sidney Lumet, Richard Lester and Stanley Kubrick, who made some of their finest movies in England.

Consequently, Stark hoped to do the same thing with Huston. "The idea started when I realized that we had Deborah Kerr, Richard Burton, you, Grimes, the sound men and several other people who could have been credited as an Eady Plan labor cost," said the producer. If *The Night of the Iguana* qualified as an English picture, the cost of production would be subsidized by the British government, saving the company as much as $100,000 – roughly half the total cost for labor in Mexico. This meant that the film could be photographed in color.

Naturally, Huston, the artist, had his heart set on making the film his way. All the same, Stark's explanation caught Huston by surprise. He wanted to make the film in color and, now, the producer was calling his bluff. The only stumbling block was Eady's insistence on using a British cameraman, which meant they could not hire Huston's first choice: Gabriel Figueroa. Hailed as the greatest cinematographer in all of Latin America, Figueroa's glistening panoramas of Mexican revolutionaries and armed bandits on horseback framed by giant maguey cactus were a longstanding cinema tradition. A veteran of more than two hundred films, his career began in the 1930s and eventually spanned half a century.

Figueroa's camera captured rare moments of beauty and terror; it revealed hunger in peasants' faces and murder in soldiers' eyes. His lens recorded the chipped texture of stone and marble churches and the soft glow of burning candles as women knelt before the Virgin Guadalupe in humble prayer. These sharply contrasted chiaroscuros were triumphs of artistic composition.

Outside of Mexico, Figueroa, age fifty-six, was best known for his superlative photography on such poetic films as *Maria Candelaria*, which was awarded the Grand Prize at the Cannes Film Festival, and *La Perla* – winner of a Golden Globe Award for Best Cinematography by the Hollywood Foreign Press Association. Another of his widely commended films, *Macario*, was nominated for an Academy Award as Best Foreign Film.

However, Figueroa was more than a pictorial diarist; he was someone who expressed himself through cinematography. "I am certain that if I have any merit," he said upon receiving the Mexico National Arts Prize, "it is knowing how to make good use of my eyes, to guide the camera in its task of capturing not only colors, lights and shadows, but the movement of life itself."

The brilliance of Figueroa's cinematography was matched by his aristocratic appearance; he had a large forehead with penetrating brown eyes and a thin mustache. His films were not only applauded for their excellence, he was greatly admired for his personal style. For these reasons, Huston had wanted to work with Figueroa for many years. Only now it looked as if the opportunity was going to be taken away from him because Figueroa was Mexican.

To qualify for the Eady subsidy, an English cinematographer like Freddie Young, Jack Cardiff or Oswald Morris would have to be substituted. Morris was the best qualified, having already photographed five films for Huston. They were a formidable team – pushing the acceptable boundaries of moviemaking in their pursuit of art. A gifted innovator, Morris had filmed the French can-can sequences in *Moulin Rouge* using fog filters, smoke and colored lighting to simulate the chalky lithographs of Toulouse-Lautrec. On *Moby Dick*, he de-saturated the Technicolor pigment through a special dye transfer process, creating a silver-tinged pastel image reminiscent of old etchings and whaling prints.

In light of the benefits that Eady provided, Stark viewed Figueroa as an unnecessary extravagance, as well as a potential liability. In the same way that Huston had brought unwelcome attention with his political activities, Figueroa also courted the hostile Mexican press. In 1945, during his interim term as head of the Manual and Technical Section of the Sindicato de Trabajadores de la Industria Cinematográfica or Union of Cinema Industry Workers (STIC), Figueroa accused Salvador Carrillo, the secretary-general, of fostering corruption within the union.

Figueroa's brave stand won him many admirers from the rank and file, but it also made for some powerful enemies, who took revenge against the outspoken cinematographer. He was labeled a Communist and prohibited from working in the USA. Not only was Figueroa's politics considered to be questionable by Hollywood standards, the Mexican unions, who controlled national film production, were demanding that their workers get paid for sitting idle while American movies were made on Mexican soil employing foreign casts and crews. These financial ultimatums weren't caused by greed; they were the result of economic necessity.

By 1963, the Mexican film industry was experiencing a crisis; only forty-one domestic features were produced that year compared to seventy films just twenty years earlier. Even a range of protectionist policies and tariffs instituted by the federal government to keep the film industry afloat had failed to improve things. As a consequence, Hollywood producers making films in Mexico were required to pay for "standby" Mexican film crews, whether they used them or not.

Stark told Abe Steinberg: "Mexican unions will not reduce their crew demands and a full crew consists of 50 people and the salaries alone of this crew of 50 without housing, meals or transportation amount to approximately $6,000 per week including fringe benefits." Since it took anywhere from eight to ten weeks to shoot a feature film, this meant a budget increase of more than $50,000.

That's when Stark seized on the opportunity to make *The Night of the Iguana* using an English crew with money from the Eady Levy, stating "this gives us a perfect out not to use Figueroa." If Huston had agreed to replace him, the film would undoubtedly have been made in color.

For some reason, maybe prejudice, Stark presumed that Figueroa was only accustomed to working in black-and-white. He had, in fact, photographed Mexico's leading actress Maria Félix in three vibrant color films – *La Cucaracha*, *Juana Gallo* and *La Bandida* – between 1958 and 1963.

Huston's yearning to make *The Night of the Iguana* in Puerto Vallarta hinged largely on the abilities of Figueroa, who was a master of light and composition. Stark, however, was just as happy to forgo these considerations in favor of British investment. He told Huston he would offer Figueroa the promise of future employment "so that we will have his goodwill." Huston refused. He wanted his film to be a true Mexican experience and felt that Figueroa was the only cameraman who could achieve that feeling.

Having reached a temporary impasse, Stark and Huston resolved to find a compromise that would not jeopardize the quality of the film. The producer had no choice but to abandon his moneysaving plan in order to keep his director satisfied. "If 28 English crew louse up the situation for you," said Stark, hiding his disappointment, "then I am perfectly happy to forgo any further discussions on Eady."

Huston's victory was bittersweet. He was granted his wish to keep Figueroa, but color was no longer an option. The film did not qualify for British financing, and, therefore, without the benefit of additional capital, it would have to be made in black-and-white.

Meanwhile, Anthony Veiller's script for *The Night of the Iguana* still begged attention. The need to rewrite was twofold: as was his bent, Huston liked to fine tune dialogue until he had just the right choice of words, but the film's denouement, as yet unfinished, still bothered him. In Williams' play everybody was damned at the fadeout. The movie could not finish on such an emotional low point. There needed to be some kind of moral redemption for the characters. "Not a happy ending," as Huston put it, "but a more acceptable one than already existed."

More urgent was the need to head off a brewing controversy over the film's racism and blasphemy. The Mexican censors had contacted Seven Arts script editor William Fadiman and were withholding their final approval until two scenes of Mexicans lying drunk on the street and smoking marijuana were eliminated.

"What a stupid comment," scoffed Huston after reading Fadiman's report. "Of course, Mexicans get drunk and smoke marijuana! The next thing the censors will tell us is that all Mexican girls are virgins!"

The censors also complained about the repeated use in Huston's script of the phrase Montezuma's revenge, which they considered to be a humorless cliché. Huston paused and lit a cigar. "Everybody gets the shits, what's wrong with that?" he asked.

"Well, dysentery is no laughing matter," said Veiller.

In Hollywood, the screenplay's morality raised similar concerns. In 1962, the Motion Picture Association of America (MPAA), a self-governing body of representatives which controlled movie censorship, had refused to give the Seven Arts film *Lolita* a seal of approval unless the original script about pedophilia was changed. Now, it appeared the same fate would befall *The Night of the Iguana*, whose lead character had carnal knowledge of a minor.

These restrictive guidelines dated back to 1934 when the movie industry's watchdog, the Production Code Administration (PCA), began regulating the content and exhibition of movies. Eventually, those rules were revised, allowing for the depiction of previously forbidden subjects such as miscegenation, abortion, childbirth, and drug addiction.

By 1959, virtually any subject except homosexuality could be presented in PCA–approved films as long as a moral conflict provided the proper frame of reference. But the code still presented many obstacles for liberal-minded filmmakers such as Huston.

Many producers and directors were secretly relieved when Eric Johnston, the longtime president of the MPAA, suffered a stroke in Washington, DC, on June 17, 1963. For two months, Johnston lingered in a coma; he died on August 22, age sixty-six.

The PCA vice president Geoffrey Shurlock, who was no less tolerant of sexual aberration, found several objectionable scenes in Huston's script. He requested the deletion of cuss words such as "son of a bitch" and "mother grabbing," and would not permit a scene with male and female characters dancing on the beach in their bikinis, calling it "too suggestive."

Angered by Shurlock's insensitivity, Huston balked at making any further changes to the screenplay until he talked to Tennessee Williams, who had final script approval. To appease the censors, Stark proposed hiring additional writers to restructure problematic scenes and substitute new dialogue.

This practice is known in the movie business as "doctoring" or "polishing" a script. However, most writers that Stark approached, including the pedantic English dramatist Peter Shaffer, and the seditious American playwright Paddy Chayefsky, wanted no part of it.

Chayefsky was candid in his assessment of the script: "I would suggest to whoever will be doing the rewriting that he compress the action to in and about the hotel, using the variety of that particular location to achieve the mobility expected in films."

With the script's problems still unresolved, Stark tracked down Williams to Miami, Florida, where he was staying at the Carlton Towers. Williams told Stark that he believed the script was fine, and only needed help at the very end. The playwright was more concerned about the health of his longtime companion, Frank Merlo, who was undergoing cobalt treatments for cancer. But Stark persisted.

When Williams kept dodging Stark's phone calls, the producer tried to entice him with the offer of a speedboat as an inducement. So Williams, who had gone on a vacation, unpacked his portable Royal typewriter, fixed himself a martini, and reluctantly went to work. His scenes, typed on the back of hotel stationery, described Charlotte dancing wildly in a beach cantina with the two beach boys.

Williams wrote to Huston: "Stark has been after me to write this bit in the Ramada. I think I like it but it is more important that you should... This little speedboat that Stark promised me has now grown to the size of Sam Spiegel's yacht. When the picture is finished, sail with me on it to Avalon or Xanadu or Tahiti. We would be sensational in muu-muus. Love to all, especially to Ava. (The letter was signed in blue ink) 10."

ON AUGUST 5, 1963, John Huston, his secretary Gladys Hill, screenwriter Anthony Veiller and a small group of friends and neighbors gathered at the director's manor house in County Galway, Ireland, to celebrate his fifty-seventh birthday. The main entrance of St. Clerans was flanked by two medieval lions carved from stone. Visitors entered through the hallway and walked outside to the garden.

In the courtyard, a cast-iron figure of Punchinello looked out across the manicured lawn, where a long table of Irish linen, Georgian silver and Baccarat crystal had been set for the guests. (Huston's wife Ricki, their thirteen year-old son Tony, and his twelve-year-old sister Anjelica were away in London.)

There were homemade porkpies, goose liver pâtés, and assorted cheeses. A liveried butler poured Bollinger champagne and an Irish folk band played traditional songs.

After two hours of cheerful imbibing, Tony Veiller called everyone's attention by ringing a silver bell. "Today we honor a great man who has been a good friend to us all," Veiller enthused about his longtime collaborator.

The tipsy well-wishers, which included the actress Suzanne Flon and Veiller's teenage son Philip, raised their glasses and toasted Huston, who beamed with gratitude. "May the good Lord take a liking to you," said Veiller amid the exuberant laughter and applause of guests, "but not too soon!"

Three days later, Huston boarded an Aer Lingus Irish International passenger flight at Dublin airport. He was dressed in the manner of a country squire: a tailored hound's-tooth jacket, corduroy slacks, boots and a felt cap to protect him against the early morning chill.

Huston was accompanied by Hill, who sat next to him, inhaling his favorite cologne Acqua Di Palma with its classic scent of lemon, bergamot and English lavender. The director felt a tinge of melancholy as the Boeing 720 jet with a bright green shamrock on the tail fin sped down the runway and lifted off, its conical metal nose pointing in the direction of New York.

In the plane's cargo hold were ten Mark Cross suitcases containing Huston's summer clothes, bundles of scripts, hardbound books, paper files and two portable typewriters. He would not return to St. Clerans until the end of the year, an absence of five months – the longest time he had spent away from his adopted Irish home.

Huston lent back in his seat and contemplated the long journey that lay ahead. He was not overly sentimental. Any trace of sadness he felt upon his departure was quickly replaced by a pang of excitement and his face took on a cheerful repose. The stewardess brought a large glass of Greenore Single Grain Irish Whiskey and placed it on the plastic seat tray in front of Huston. He smiled in appreciation and his gaze followed the soft contours of her body as she continued down the aisle.

Huston took a long swallow of the amber liquid and was reminded of the many circuitous trips he had undertaken, like a wayward papal emissary, to Europe, Africa and the Far East, in his quest to make movies. Mostly they had been happy occasions, brimming with artistic accomplishment and financed by indulgent producers. This time, however, his motivation was to build a rustic villa in the Mexican jungle – thousands of miles away from modern-day civilization.

Despite his acquired primitivism, Huston remained a committed jetsetter. His last few days in the USA were spent in carefree indulgence.

Arriving in Los Angeles, Huston and Hill checked into the Beverly Hills Hotel, where they had reserved two bungalows.

On August 28, he watched the CBS television broadcast of Martin Luther King, Jr. delivering his inspirational "I Have a Dream" speech to 200,000 civil rights supporters at the Lincoln Memorial in Washington, DC.

Although he was a confirmed atheist, Huston found himself transfixed by the Baptist minister's impassioned rhetoric. Seeing the familiar faces of pipe-smoking director Joseph Mankiewicz, actor Charlton Heston and novelist James Baldwin, who attended the rally, reminded him of his own activism.

The following morning, Huston lit a double corona cigar, put on his eyeglasses and read the script for his next film *The Bible*. Did Huston undergo a spiritual conversion, or was he merely intrigued by the dramatic possibilities of filming the Book of Genesis? He sent a cable to the film's producer Dino de Laurentiis in Rome: "Bible script magnificent Will Do Yes repeat Yes." The three-hour religious epic, which Huston directed the following year in Egypt and Italy, would become the single biggest achievement of his long career.

On his last day in the City of Angels, Huston got a haircut and a massage. And then, the primal call of Mexico beckoned him. He put the script in his briefcase and Hill called the hotel porter, who arranged for a taxi to take them to the airport.

Up in the sky, Huston experienced the sensation of weightlessness that is common to air travelers. Gradually, the clouds parted and he felt the pull of the earth's gravity.

Arriving in Puerto Vallarta, Huston took up residence at Casa Don Cuco, a two-story house on Calle Cuauhtémoc, overhanging the banks of the Rio Cuale, which was shaded by acacia, tamarind and willow trees.

Huston's temporary digs had two bedrooms, two baths, a decorative tile kitchen, and a three-sided living room – the fourth side open to the river. Built by Guillermo Wulff, the brick and tile residence was located in the hilly district of Gringo Gulch. The area derived its name from the large numbers of expatriate Americans that lived there.

Huston's secretary occupied Casa Avilla on the same street. The rent was $300 a month including a maid and all utilities. The choice of address was dictated by price as much as it was by selection. Before leaving Dublin, Hill had inquired all over Puerto Vallarta for suitable accommodations. However, her options had been limited by the upsurge in tourism. "What with the movie company coming in and the swarm of tourists this year," Mary Frances Tremear, a local real estate agent, informed Hill, "we fill up so fast. September will not be a problem but beginning in November and thru April our houses are already reserved."

It was good news for Puerto Vallarta. After years of uncertainty, Mexico's faltering economy was improving, spurred by strong foreign investment and a high exchange rate. In 1963, trade between the USA and Mexico reached a record high of $1.5 million, helping to make Mexico the most profitable and stable country in Central and Latin America. Puerto Vallarta, though it remained isolated, was feeling those economic benefits with the creation of hundreds of new construction jobs – especially in Mismaloya.

The next day, Huston arose early. He drank a cup of black coffee while reading some correspondence and smoked a cigar on the balcony.

At midday, after changing into a freshly pressed white linen suit, Huston was collected by his driver Juan in a Land-Rover and taken across the bridge to Playa Los Muertos. Despite its funereal name, the beach was teeming with life. Swimmers were diving into the waves, and local boys were fishing from nearby rocks.

A popular vacation spot since the 1920s, the long strip of finely granulated sand stretched south from the section of beach known as Olas Altas, meaning high waves, to a small cove named Las Pilitas or small reefs, where lovers rendezvoused at sunset. To the east rose the steep mountainside. To the west stretched the infinite blue glaze of the Pacific Ocean.

On the upper shore, tourists reclined on woven palm mats under shady *ramadas*. Families ate homemade *tacos* – tortillas filled with shredded beef and pork, seasoned with diced onions and cilantro, or munched on *ceviche* – finely chopped fish, marinated in lime juice and served on crunchy tostadas.

By the time of Huston's visit, the present was already receding into the past. The Hotel Tropicana, which opened in 1958, was the first modern hotel built on the beach. A marvel of engineering design, the nine-story concrete tower and 166 guestrooms were erected on solid bedrock. The bedrooms had sea-green headboards, rose-colored walls, hot showers and Kohler flushing toilets.

The following year, La Palapa restaurant began serving barbecued ribs to customers on Calle Pulpito. The Polynesian-style décor was made from tree trunks, the palm-fronded cores tied with lianas and accented with bamboo. Competition to entice more diners was inevitable and two years later a second restaurant, El Dorado, opened on the same street. Both restaurants were built by Guillermo Wulff, who also constructed fourteen beachfront apartments, which Seven Arts leased as their production offices on the corner of Calle Amapas.

Huston ambled down to the sand, past the umbrella tables, mariachis and food sellers, where he took a waiting *panga* – a twenty-foot outboard – to Mismaloya. Sergio, the boatman, started the motor and turned the wooden bow into the oncoming waves. Huston sat in the stern as the tiny craft bounced its way across the ocean. The noise of the gas engine prevented audible conversation so thirty minutes passed without either man speaking a word.

When they reached the movie location, Sergio turned off the motor and the boat glided silently to shore. On the beach, Huston breathed in the fresh air, lit a cigar and puffed on it thoughtfully.

To the native Mexicans, the sight of Huston loping towards them in his white suit was an apparition nearly as startling as the Spanish conqueror Hernan Cortés, when he encountered ancient Mayan and Aztec tribes. Wherever the American director went he was followed by inquisitive villagers, mostly barefoot children, who gazed up in awe at him. He shook their tiny hands and passed out shiny pesos, which made Huston smile nearly as much as the boys and girls who ogled him.

At the construction office, Huston talked to Stephen Grimes about the progress of Club Mismaloya, which had been slowed down by bad weather. That year, Mexico was hit by eight tropical storms – among the highest number on record. The first, named Emily, struck the southern states on June 30, followed by more storms and flash floods along the west coast that summer.

To make up for lost time, Guillermo Wulff was working twelve-hour days and hiring extra labor. "But when Grimes saw him using the sand from the beach to make cement, he advised him against it, because the beach sand had too much salt and would weaken the cement," said Lawrence Grobel. "They argued about it and Wulff wound up using the beach sand for the housing project, and less salty sand for the set."

Now, after lengthy delays and cost overruns, construction of the Hotel Costa Verde was almost done. With the agility of a mountain goat, Huston scampered up the hill to the set. Workers pushed wooden wheelbarrows of sand; others were laying bricks and carrying mortar in five-gallon lard tins. The sounds of sawing, chopping and hammering echoed through the jungle.

Huston arrived in time to witness the hotel's centerpiece: a polished thirty-seven-foot rectangular wooden beam, which held the roof in place, being hoisted into position. The laborious procedure had taken hundreds of man-hours – merely a split second in the evolution of time. In the preceding weeks, Indians employed as boatmen, masons, carpenters and bearers had chopped down a large tree in the jungle, trimmed it, and miraculously edged it down into the sea. Since the trunk weighed four tons and wouldn't float, engineers buoyed it with empty gasoline drums and towed it to shore.

Huston and Grimes stood on the hotel verandah watching the workers lifting the heavy lumber into the air using ropes and pulleys. In the middle of all this commotion Wulff was yelling instructions in Spanish to his fatigued workers. Steadily, through a series of anguished grunts and groans, the center beam was lowered into place on top of the hotel walls. Long after the filming was over, and the participants gone, that timber slab would remain there, a testament to the modern colonization of Mismaloya.

IN AN EXPANSIVE MOOD, John Huston shortly left Puerto Vallarta for Mexico City. The night before his departure he had a vivid dream. As he slept, his mind traveled back in time. He imagined that he was an eagle circling the sky. Below him was a vast patchwork of forests, rivers and fields. He looked down and saw his bird legs dangling over a huge crater.

The snow-covered 17,802-foot volcanic cone of Popocatepetl – or Smoking Mountain in Nahuatl language – cast its ominous shadow across the Valley of Mexico. To the naked eye, the mountain's frozen whiteness formed an impenetrable barrier.

At noon, when the sun was at its highest, a harsh symphony of drums, conch horns and flutes could be heard in the distance. Still dreaming, Huston flew towards the light, his ears alert to the shrill sounds.

Forty-five miles northwest of Popocatepetl was the Aztec metropolis of Tenochtitlan or "cactus on stone" – one of the marvels of the Ancient World. This immense geometric configuration of lavishly decorated pyramids, plazas and canals occupied five square miles of land on the west shore of Lake Texcoco. Bigger than most European cities, the population of Tenochtitlan numbered 300,000 men, women and children. Daily life revolved around the Templo Mayor or Main Temple with its twin pyramids dedicated to the rain god, Tlaloc, and the god of war, Huitzilopochtli.

But there was a dark side to Tenochtitlan involving ceremonial human sacrifice, which the Aztecs practiced ensuring the continued fertility of the earth and safe passage of the sun. Each year, the king's warriors abducted hundreds of young men from the surrounding villages. These men were drugged and placed on altars in front of chanting masses. Then, priests with obsidian knives cut open the heaving chests of their screaming victims and removed the beating hearts. During these gruesome festivals, rivers of blood flowed down the steps of the temple in tribute to the Aztec gods – the same idols that would, ironically, bring about the city's destruction.

In 1521, Tenochtitlan was leveled by an explosion of cannon fire that left its complex infrastructure in ruins. Spanish soldiers dismantled the heavy masonry and broken statuary that had stood for two centuries in triumph to the various gods. On top of the demolished public forums and religious temples was erected a lasting monument to Spanish colonization that dominated the country for the next four centuries: The Baroque clock towers, church steeples and copper domes that characterized modern-day Mexico City.

It was this timely reminder of the country's brutal history that greeted Huston upon arrival in the nation's capital for the Independence Day celebrations on September 15, 1963.

Seven Arts had provided the film director with a generous expense account: $1,000 a week, which brought him a regular supply of Montecristo cigars and Château Mouton Rothschild. He was accustomed to living well and never varied that habit, spending lavishly on food, entertainment, and gifts.

Huston was eager to take part in the annual festivities celebrating Mexico's liberation from Spain, when thousands of angry militants, rebelling against 300 years of injustice, had risen up against their oppressors. Only nowadays, men and women commemorated these events by swilling bottles of tequila instead of firing guns in the air.

Huston wanted to join the throngs of cheering revelers waving flags in Plaza de la Constitucion when Adolfo Lopéz Mateos, the country's twenty-eighth elected president, walked out on the balcony of the National Palace shortly before midnight, rang the Bell of Independence and uttered the defiant cry: "Viva Mexico!"

At Benito Juarez International Airport, Huston hailed a lime green 1958 Chevrolet *taxi cocodrilo*. The crocodile taxi derived its odd nickname from the sedan's painted triangular white markings that resembled rows of crocodile teeth. There were other, more modern, taxis waiting in line, but the reptilian appearance of this particular vehicle appealed to Huston. He climbed into the passenger seat and the driver set off along Airport Boulevard on its nine-mile journey to the city.

The taxi traveled southwest along the main boulevard, Paseo de la Reforma, passing trams, buses, sports cars and delivery vans. Huston glanced out the taxi's window at El Caballito, the equestrian statue of King Charles IV of Spain, who once had total dominion over Mexico. Another landmark that caught Huston's eye was the majestic figure of Cuauhtémoc. This spectacular monument to Mexico's pagan heritage portrayed the omnipotent Aztec emperor in full regalia accompanied by eight bronze leopards with feathered headdresses.

These statues paled in significance to the Angel of Independence – a stunning 115-feet-high Corinthian stone column topped by a twenty-two-foot golden-orbed Winged Victory. This tremendous engineering accomplishment, unveiled on the one hundredth anniversary of Mexico's Independence in 1910, was surrounded by a huge circular plinth with four statues representing Peace, Law, Justice and War.

When Huston arrived at the Hotel Bamer on Avenida Juarez, he was met by his production manager Clarence Eurist, whose lugubrious expression brightened into a welcoming smile.

While bellhops attended to Huston's luggage, Eurist escorted him into the pillared lobby with its circular ceiling alcove, recessed lighting and modern furnishings.

The Bamer was the most well-appointed hotel in the city when it opened ten years earlier. Breakfast was served every day on the hotel's fifteenth floor roof garden, overlooking Alameda Central, the city's oldest park, where tourists snapped photographs of the Juarez Monument – an imposing semicircle of ten white marble columns with an outsized statue of Benito Juarez holding aloft the Mexican Constitution of 1857.

Because the hotel offered sweeping views of the city and surrounding mountains, it was a popular choice for foreign visitors, many of them Hollywood executives. In the bar, Huston and Eurist ordered two Stolichnaya vodka martinis.

"So, what's the plan?" asked Huston.

"We have a tentative starting date of September 23," replied Eurist.

"Perfect," nodded Huston. "You know, I haven't seen this city for more than ten years. Let's do some sightseeing."

Eurist was tickled. "Are you sure you won't get bored?"

Huston smiled. "Not a chance!"

Leaving the hotel, Huston and Eurist walked east along Avenida Juarez toward the Torre Latino Americana or Latin American Tower – Mexico's tallest skyscraper, which glinted in the sunlight.

Reminiscent of the Empire State Building, the tower offered a dazzling 360-degree panorama of the valley and its two mythologized volcanoes Popocatepetl and Iztaccihuatl from a public observation deck on the forty-fourth floor.

Famished, Huston and Eurist headed over to Sanborn's restaurant in the world-famous Casa de los Azulejos – House of Tiles. A palatial eighteenth-century mansion covered with Talavera blue-and-white tiles, this famous eatery had long been a popular dining spot with politicians, writers, and revolutionaries. On the main wall of the dining room was a large peacock mural by Romanian artist Pacologue.

Huston selected a quiet table for him and Eurist in a bright corner of the courtyard. A wine steward uncorked a bottle of French Burgundy and the waiter brought them menus offering a choice of tasty regional dishes.

Their appetites sated, Huston and Eurist crossed the street to the Italian-style Palacio de Bellas Artes or Palace of Fine Arts with its distinctive Beaux-Arts white marble exterior and Art Nouveau bronze-domed roof.

On the promenade, Eurist hailed a *calandria* or horse-drawn carriage to take them eight blocks to Constitucion Plaza – popularly known as the Zócalo. A gathering place for Mexicans since ancient times, the plaza was twice the size of Red Square in Moscow, and four times larger than Trafalgar Square in London.

Huston's gaze took in the immense quadrangle with its fluttering pigeons and multitude of tourists. The knowledge that a primitive civilization once flourished there filled him with awe and fascination.

Entombed beneath the concrete pavement were the bodies of thousands of Aztecs, who died in defense of the city when their emperor Moctezuma was captured by Hernan Cortés and his soldiers. For a time, the director even contemplated making a film about this ignominious chapter from the past.

"The heart of the Aztec world still beats with a strong passion for life," said Huston as he reached down and touched the ground. "If you listen closely you can hear their anguished voices calling from the depths."

When the Spanish built Mexico City over the ruins of Tenochtitlan, they neglected to change the layout of the old temples and streets. Pyramid stones were used to construct the northern area surrounding the Metropolitan Cathedral, once the largest building on the American continent. Construction and decoration of the huge church, made of basalt and grey sandstone, took nearly three centuries. The final elements, bell towers and domed cupola, designed by the Spanish neoclassical artist Manuel Tolsa, were completed in 1813.

To the east stood the National Palace, the center of modern government, which was erected on the former site of Moctezuma's palace, where Cortés took up residence after snatching power from the Aztecs. At various times, Spanish viceroys and Mexican presidents occupied this splendid fortress with its immense 650-foot long façade built of reddish *tezontle* stone.

Huston and Eurist climbed the varnished stairways to marvel at the superb collection of frescos painted by Diego Rivera on the second floor. Rivera's capricious artistry was never better than his colossal triptych, "The Epic of the Mexican People," depicting his ancestral history from Quetzalcoatl to the Spanish conquest, the Reform period and Revolution. It was, Huston commented to Eurist, "absolutely splendid."

Unfortunately, the same thing could not be said for Mexico City's sunny skies, which had abruptly turned cloudy. On September 16, Hurricane Cindy, the third tropical storm of 1963 and the first hurricane to form in the Gulf of Mexico since 1960, caused $12.5 million damage and three fatalities as it swept through Texas and Louisiana with fierce winds of eighty miles per hour.

Two days later, a fifth tropical storm hit Baja California, causing heavy rains on the Pacific west coast. In between organizing travel and filming schedules, Eurist was keeping a concerned eye on the meteorological charts. "If this keeps up we can forget shooting anything for another week," he said.

Huston frowned. “Well, it had better not rain tonight,” he warned, “because Emilio Fernández is having a big party at his house.”

“You mean El Indio?” inquired Eurist.

“The one and the same,” said Huston.

THAT EVENING THE STARS CAME out, both earthly and celestial. Wearing a camel's hair sports coat over grey flannel trousers, John Huston took a red and white taxi to an exclusive address in the upper-class borough of Coyoacán – "the place of coyotes" in Indian parlance. On Calle Ignacio Zaragoza, a long line of snazzy coupés was parked outside Casa Fuerte del Indio – Indio's Fortress.

This was the bastion of Emilio Fernández, the single most important figure in the history of Mexican cinema. Egotistical, eccentric and emotional, Fernández, age fifty-nine, was fiercely loyal to his family and friends, which occupied every level of society.

For three decades, Fernández wrote and directed richly symbolic films that evoked the raw beauty and violent machismo of Mexico. His stories always had a strong, nationalistic flavor. In such influential movies as *Flor Silvestre*, *Maria Candelaria*, *Enamorada*, *La Perla* and *Maclovia*, he depicted the plight of his fellow countrymen in honest, if not always sympathetic, terms. "The cinema is like a magnifying glass," he said, "you can get close to anything you want and put an emphasis on what is important."

Audiences reveled in these mystical Indian fables and heated passion plays, whose heroes were political dissidents and social outcasts. Cinematographer Gabriel Figueroa collaborated with Fernández on dozens of movies. Their fifteen-year partnership created some of the most beautifully photographed classics in Mexico's epoca de oro – the golden age of cinema.

"Emilio Fernández had an incredible sensibility for all things Mexican, especially for those having to do with country life," said Figueroa. "He had a knack for selecting Mexican songs and dances and had an extensive knowledge of military life."

But Fernández's talents were not limited to recreating the past, he was equally adept at depicting modern-day corruption and social injustice in such significant films as *Salón México*, *Victimas del pecado*, *Islas Marias* and *La Rosa Blanca*.

These and other compelling movies firmly established his reputation as a master storyteller and helped to make him a rich and powerful man in his own country, as well as a highly-respected figure in Europe.

From the outside, Fernández's three-story house resembled an impenetrable bunker with high stone walls made from volcanic rocks. Designed by architect Manuel Parra, who was responsible for the art direction on nine of Fernández's films, this was more than just a fort, as the name implied – it was a castle.

A coveted meeting place for artists and intellectuals, Fernández's home was a reflection of his own creative brilliance. The Spanish-style citadel featured wood-beamed ceilings, arched doorways and polished floors.

From the moment Huston crossed the threshold he knew he had entered a special place. Passion and creativity emanated from every room. Floor-to-ceiling shelves displayed his large collection of books and leather-bound scripts, along with pre-Hispanic artifacts, numerous awards and signed photographs of army generals, politicians and movie stars.

In the living room, Huston was admiring a life-size portrait of Fernández's second wife, the shining actress Columba Dominguez, when a tall, robust man with smooth black hair, eyes the color of ebony, and a thick mustache, strolled up to him.

"Isn't she beautiful?" commented Fernández in his heavy accent. He was wearing pleated trousers, a navy-blue blazer, open-necked white shirt, and red silk cravat.

"Emilio, you old devil!" cried Huston. They embraced like long-lost comrades. "Welcome, John. It's good to see you again," said Fernández. "Come on, I will get you a drink."

The two men strolled through the house, where various guests sat talking to each other. The enormous Puebla-style kitchen was a beehive of activity. Chefs were preparing authentic Mexican food in copper pots and pans on gas-burning stoves. Steaming *pozole*, a traditional stew made from hominy, meat and vegetables, was being ladled into decorative Talavera pottery. Oaxaca-style tamales stuffed with pork, chicken and fish were placed in Michoacán dishware, which waiters carried to the dining room and set down on a large table set for twelve people with starched white linen and embroidered napkins.

On the moonlit terrace, bartenders were fixing cocktails and pouring champagne. The fragrant scents of Royal English Leather, Shalimar, and Arpege mingled in the air. Huston spotted Gabriel Figueroa, looking dapper in a grey herringbone jacket and black turtleneck sweater. "Finally, we are going to work together!" said Figueroa, shaking the director's hand. "I am looking forward to it," smiled Huston.

The beautiful, sloe-eyed actress Katy Jurado walked up to the bar. She was wearing a blue chiffon cocktail dress and matching earrings. Huston and Jurado exchanged pleasantries. "I discovered her when she was sixteen," said Fernández, "and she still looks wonderful." An attractive woman in a frilly blouse and long skirt passed them by. It was Lola Beltrán, the queen of mariachi music, wearing her trademark *rebozo* or shawl.

Standing next to a stone fountain was the glamorous movie star Maria Félix, whom her admirers called La Doña. Félix wore a shimmering Christian Dior gown adorned with a necklace of emeralds and diamonds.

Her escort was the handsome, grey-haired actor Ernesto Alonso, who was dressed in a white dinner jacket and black trousers. He took a gold case from his pocket, offered her a Raleigh cigarette and then lit it. She blew a column of smoke from her pursed lips.

"Maria, darling," announced Fernández. "This is John Huston." Félix extended her bejeweled hand. "We met many years ago in Jungapeo where I was making a movie with Humphrey Bogart," said Huston. Félix flashed her large brown eyes. "I'm sorry," she replied. "I don't remember you. I meet so many men!" There was scattered laughter.

In the garden, two *cocineros* or cooks wearing long aprons were roasting *barbacoa*, barbecued lamb in maguey leaves, over a fire-pit. Huston watched the men hauling the cooked meat out of the burning coals. Fernández took a gleaming saber, pierced the lamb, and waved the moist blade in the air. "Dinner is served!" he announced with a flourish. While the guests slowly filed into the house, eight strolling mariachis playing guitars, trumpets and violins performed *La Negra*, which was one of their host's favorite songs. It was followed by *El Rey*.

As to be expected from such a fascinating group, the conversation was lively and stimulating. Huston shared his memories of directing Marilyn Monroe in both her first and last films. "She took so many sleeping pills to rest that in the morning she had to take stimulants to wake her up," he explained, "and this ravaged the girl."

In February 1962, Monroe visited Mexico City hoping to adopt a child. Fernández invited Monroe to his home, where she was photographed sipping tequila. Unable to proceed with the adoption, she returned to Los Angeles and died six months later.

After dessert was served, Dolores del Rio arrived from the Teatro Insurgentes, where she was appearing in Jerome Kilty's play *Dear Liar*.

The romantic comedy was first performed on Broadway in 1960 with Katharine Cornell in the starring role. The Mexican première had been a sensation and was sold out through October. When Del Rio entered the room, she looked ravishing in a pink Givenchy pantsuit and cultured pearl necklace.

"Ah! Dolores," smiled Fernández. "I'm glad you could make it." She offered her cheek to him and he kissed it tenderly. His nose detected the aroma of her favorite perfume: Youth Dew by Estee Lauder. There was an intimacy between them that went beyond normal friendship. It was said that she was his true love; they had known each other for thirty-five years – a lifetime in the movie business.

One famous actor from their shared past, however, was conspicuously absent that night. "If only Pedro Armendáriz could be with us," commented Del Rio, her face a vision of saintliness. The couple had appeared together in seven memorable films. Fernández had known the gallant actor with the insolent grin since 1942, when they made the first of nine movies together. "How well I remember those green eyes and fiery temper," said Huston, who directed Armendáriz in *We Were Strangers*. "Emilio called him the cat!"

Four months ago, Armendáriz had been diagnosed with lymphatic cancer. The 51-year-old actor was undergoing tests at the UCLA Medical Center in Los Angeles, when he chose to end his life. On June 18, 1963, Armendáriz shot himself in the heart with a .357 Colt magnum revolver. His Mexican homecoming in a funeral casket was a tragic end to a glorious career.

When the other guests had left the party, Fernández and Huston sat in the study sipping Courvoisier brandy and smoking cigars.

Behind the bravado, Huston sensed that Fernández was not a happy man. He was chased by demons, like many artists, and was trying to fight them off. In the dim light of an art nouveau table lamp that reason would soon be revealed.

"I am going to tell you something that I have never told anyone else," said Huston.

Through the shroud of cigar smoke, history replayed itself like an old newsreel. It was the evening of September 27, 1933. Huston was driving a Buick convertible along Sunset Boulevard in Los Angeles. A young female pedestrian ran in front of his car. He slammed on the brakes, but she fell under the front wheels.

Huston took the injured woman to Hollywood Receiving Hospital. He nervously waited outside the room, his hat in his hands. One hour later, a doctor told him the woman had died. The victim was Tosca Querze, a beautiful twenty-three-year-old starlet. Brazilian heartthrob Raul Roulien, who crooned the romantic song *Orchids in the Moonlight* in the musical *Flying Down to Rio,* was her husband. The film's star was Dolores del Rio; Fernández was a dancer in the same film.

The smoke in the room cleared. "Did you love her?" asked Fernández. "We were having an affair and I told her it was over," Huston admitted. "She wanted to talk to me but I didn't stop the car in time."

The tragedy was hushed up by M-G-M as a favor to Walter Huston, who had two new films scheduled for release by the prestigious studio. At the Los Angeles Coroner's inquest, his son was absolved of any responsibility in the deadly accident, but he never again drove an automobile. Shortly after, Huston moved to England, where he lived for several years. "Maybe that is why I've never felt comfortable in Hollywood," he said.

Fernández took a swig of brandy. "I also have a secret," he confessed to Huston, who listened attentively.

In 1943, two years after the art director Cedric Gibbons and Del Rio were divorced, Fernández asked her to marry him. Del Rio was flattered but turned him down. There were too many suitors banging at her dressing room door, she told him, for her to make up her mind.

Fernández went crazy with jealousy. "I wanted vengeance," he said. So Fernández took an unknown actress, Columba Dominguez Alarid, who was sixteen, and groomed her for stardom. They were married in 1949. He showcased her in eleven movies, hoping to make Dominguez as famous as Del Rio.

Sadly, the golden era of Mexican moviemaking was drawing to a close. Fernández was unable to duplicate the same glamour, and the quality of his films declined. He suffered a loss of critical prestige and often fought with producers who were unwilling to accede to his demands.

During one fierce argument Fernández shot a producer with his revolver. He was boycotted from directing films for six years.

When Fernández was unemployed, Huston threw him a lifeline as second unit director on *The Unforgiven*, which was filmed in Durango. Fernández was subsequently hired as the assistant director to John Sturges on *The Magnificent Seven*. In 1961, Fernández completed his probation and was reinstated to the director's chair.

In the coming months, Fernández would prove useful as Huston's associate director on *The Night of the Iguana* – mediating between Seven Arts and the powerful Mexican trade unions. But it almost didn't happen. Fernández had already accepted an invitation to be a judge at the seventh San Francisco Film Festival. Luckily, it took him all of five minutes to change his mind. The bottle of brandy now empty, Huston bid good night and returned to his hotel for a few hours' sleep.

A flurry of news coverage heralded the influx of Hollywood personnel that descended on Mexico City for the start of principal photography on *The Night of the Iguana*.

Prophetically, the arrival of the film's cast members coincided with the yearly Aztec ceremony, Teotleco – Arrival of the Deities.

Before the intervention of the Spaniards, this pagan custom had been observed every September, which was the twelfth month of the year on the Aztec calendar. According to tradition, the youngest deity Tlamazincatl, who represented fate and destiny, arrived first with the oldest, Huehueteotl, symbolic of fire, arriving last.

Now, after a span of four millenniums, the actors from the movie would repeat history as if it was preordained. The first star to be spotted disembarking at Benito Juarez Airport was Sue Lyon, who arrived on a Western Airlines flight from Los Angeles on Saturday, September 21.

Sexy and provocative with shoulder-length silvery blond hair, Lyon was escorted into the V.I.P. lounge by James Harris, the balding, thirty-five-year-old producer of *Lolita*, who had signed the actress to a long-term contract. Luis Pasquel, the Mexican representative from Western Airlines, welcomed Lyon to Mexico, while bunches of photographers, deployed by veteran publicist Ernest Anderson, aimed their Minolta, Nikon and Olympus cameras at the film's teenage protagonist.

Although Lyon was seventeen and legally a minor, her sexual allure was evident. "Lyon wore an elegant blue suit that made her blue eyes look even bluer," observed Mexican journalist Jaime Valdes, who was waiting in the reception line. "When she arrived at the immigration room," he commented, "she took a seat and crossed her legs in a sexy pose," prompting an explosion of flashbulbs.

Reporters called out in both Spanish and English. "Hey, Sue!" "Lolita!" "How old are you?" "Are you married?" "Do you like Mexico?" Lyon's response demonstrated uncanny maturity for a teenager. "I'm very happy to be here... This is only my second film... I still go to school... I want to be a good actress..." She patiently answered the stream of questions and posed for photographs.

Ernie Anderson was pleased. His talent was getting people's names in newspapers when needed, as well as keeping them out if required. Emilio Fernández, Columba Dominguez, and their twelve-year-old daughter Jacaranda were at the airport to greet Lyon. Grinning from behind his mustache, Fernandez received her affectionately, covering Lyon's head in a big charro hat. "On behalf of the National Association of Actors, I welcome you to Mexico!" he announced. Dominguez offered Lyon a bouquet of red roses and Jacaranda presented her with a white dove – the traditional symbol of peace. Lyon was overjoyed. "Thank you," she giggled.

"We have another surprise for you." said Fernández.

"What is it?" she asked excitedly.

"Tomorrow we will take you to the bullfights."

"Wow," said Lyon. "That's great!"

IT WAS SUNDAY, 4:30 P.M. The traffic outside Plaza Mexico, located five miles south of the city center, was heavily congested. Forty-one thousand spectators were streaming into the world's largest bullring, where numerous aficionados, tourists and celebrities had converged to watch the time-honored event that Ernest Hemingway described piquantly as "death in the afternoon."

What Yankee Stadium was to New York baseball fans, the Monumental Plaza de Toros was to sports-loving Mexicans, who flocked *en masse* to the giant saucer-shaped arena every weekend during the bullfight season. To enthusiastic supporters of this grim contest, as well as the morbidly curious, the plaza was hallowed ground.

Manolete, Luis Miguel Dominguin, Antonio Ordóñez, Silverio Pérez, Carlos Arruza, Luis Procuna, Manuel Capetillo and Paco Camino were among the famed matadors from Spain and Mexico who had triumphed in the 16,000 square-foot ring.

If not a fanatic of Hemingway's class, John Huston was, nonetheless, a keen spectator. Purchasing a ticket to one of the many weekly *corridas*, as Huston often did, was a memorable experience.

Visitors entering the plaza's main gates were greeted by a stupendous sight: straddling the frontispiece of the stadium was a fifty-foot long bronze sculpture of twenty-four running bulls and horsemen, created by Manuel Tolsa.

Inside the vast arena were colorful advertisements for Corona, Dos Equis, Bacardi, Cinzano, Benedictine D.O.M., Coca-Cola and Delicados cigarettes. Sellers walked up and down the stairs carrying trays of beer, soft drinks, cigarettes, popcorn, and *churros* – fritters sprinkled with chili and lime.

As latecomers took their seats, the plaza's orchestra, Banda Taurina, conducted by Genaro Nunez, began playing *Cielo Andaluz* – a sprightly three-minute march that heralded the coming spectacle. The walls resonated with the blaring sound of French horns, tubas, trumpets and trombones. At the music's conclusion, there was vigorous applause.

In the orchestra pit, trumpeter Rosalio Juarez stood up, pressed the mouthpiece of the brass instrument to his lips and blew a loud fanfare.

At the opposite end of the bullring a large wooden gate opened and two *alguacillos* – ceremonial bailiffs, dressed in sixteenth century Spanish costume with red plumed hats – rode out on a pair of white horses. They stopped in front of the box of the *president* – the official judge of the bullfight – and doffed their hats. Then the bailiffs rode back to their starting point.

A rustle of anticipation spread through the crowd. Nunez lifted his baton and promptly led the orchestra into the opening bars of the customary overture *La Virgen de la Macarena*. This bombastic tune, punctuated by banging drums, clashing cymbals and clicking castanets, introduced the *paseillo* or parade – the time-honored procession of the bullfighters.

Every set of eyes in the arena was focused on the main gate of the bullring. Three athletic matadors in traditional bullfighting costume, each with a black *montera*, cloth cap, on their heads, strode into the sunlight, their measured steps coinciding with the persistent beat of music.

The first matador was Joel Téllez, billed as "El Silverio," who hailed from Monterrey in Nuevo Leon.

A brave and dominating bullfighter, Tellez took his nickname from the beloved Mexican matador Silverio Pérez, whom he resembled.

The second matador was Antonio Duarte, known as "El Nayarit," because he originated in that western state. The third was Victor Pastor from Merida, Yucatan. The matadors walked side by side, their jeweled dress capes furled and wrapped around their left arms. They moved across the 140-foot diameter ring with a loose-hipped stride, their heads aloft, looking towards the president's box.

Each matador wore a specially made *traje de luces* or suit of lights, which referred to the dazzling red, blue, or green sequins and reflective threads of gold and silver that were embroidered into the costume. The suit consisted of a short jacket, a waistcoat, white shirt, thin necktie, and knee-length skintight trousers of satin and silk. Completing the outfit were fitted leg stockings and black *zapatillas* – leather slippers secured with a bow.

Marching behind each of the matadors, in three columns, was his *cuadrilla* or bullfighting team: three *banderilleros* – running toreros that placed two barbed wooden darts in the bull's neck muscles – and two *picadors* – lancers armed with long metal spears – on horseback.

The picadors were dressed in a gold-and-silver brocaded jacket, wide sash, bowl-topped hat, and thick buckskin trousers that covered the steel leaf armor over the right leg.

The horses were blindfolded and wore thick padding on their chest and belly to protect them against the charging bull. When the matadors reached the box of the *juez* or judge, they bowed and lifted their caps.

Next, the matadors removed their parade capes and passed them to the *ayudantes* or helpers to spread along the front wall behind the painted red fence of the bullring.

Each matador selected a *capote* – heavy percale fighting cape – that was pink on the outside and yellow on the inside with a wide stiffened collar.

The crowd watched the matadors practicing some bullfighting passes, testing the weight of the cape against the breeze. Seated in the first row of seats, behind the *barrera* or barrier, was John Huston, Emilio Fernández, Columba Dominguez, James Harris and Sue Lyon. "Spanish bullfighters are like ballet dancers, they perform with grace and dignity," explained Fernández. "Mexicans are daredevils. They are gay, suicidal, and dramatic."

Lyon studied Téllez, paying close attention to his wide shoulders, trim waist and muscular thighs. Her eyes observed his smooth olive skin and shiny black hair, which he wore in a *coleta* or short braided pigtail with a *mona*, silk-covered button, at the base. "Each matador has fifteen minutes to kill the bull," said Huston, noticing Lyon's interest in the young bullfighter. "If he has not killed or wounded the bull in that time he is in disgrace."

Téllez, in turn, was fascinated by Lyon's pale, doll-like features, and dedicated his bull to the smiling actress. He acknowledged her presence with a short wave of his hand, then turned his body away from her and tossed his *montera* backwards into the air. Lyon leaned forward and caught the cap with both hands. There was spontaneous applause.

"I've always wondered what bullfighters get paid for risking their lives," Harris asked Fernández. "A good bullfighter earns about four thousand dollars for killing two bulls in a single afternoon," replied Fernández. "If he works hard, he can make 160,000 dollars a year." Harris was impressed. "That's almost as much money as a movie producer," he joked.

Suddenly there was a loud commotion from behind the red gate of the *toril*, where the bulls waited to enter the ring. The gate swung open and a fearsome black bull, weighing almost 1,000 pounds, ran out of the chute.

The animal impatiently circled the fence, snorting angrily and testing its sharp horns on the *burladero* or wooden shelter that protected the toreros. Téllez waved his cape back and forth, provoking the bull to charge him.

The Banda Taurina struck up the first bars of *Espana Cani* – a fiery paso doble that added to the excitement. Standing with his feet together, Téllez demonstrated a *veronica* – a classic pass of the cape using two hands – which brought the bull running towards him.

The crowd yelled "Olé!" He then performed a *chicuelina* or pirouette as the bull ran past him. There was a second "Olé!" The bull made a semicircle and charged at him again. Téllez dropped to his knees and made a dramatic pass with his cape, called a *rodillazo*. There was a third "Olé!" The crowd burst into applause. "I fought a bull once in Madrid," Huston told Fernández. "It was ten years ago. The damned thing could have killed me."

"You were lucky," said Fernández.

"No, I was drunk," admitted Huston.

When it was time to kill the bull, Téllez exchanged his cape for a *muleta* – a heart-shaped scarlet cloth – that was folded and draped over a tapered wooden stick with a sharp point at the end. This deadly ballet between man and beast continued for several minutes. Téllez took a sip of water from a metal cup and then asked his *mozo de espada* or sword handler for the *estoque* – a special bullfighting sword with the thirty-inch silver blade curved downward at the tip.

The orchestra ceased playing music, and an audible hush fell over the tense crowd. Téllez made the final series of passes known as a *faena* and maneuvered the bull into a submissive position. When the bull was standing directly in front of him with its head lowered, Téllez thrust the sword over the bull's horns and plunged the sharpened steel into its sleek back, directly between the shoulder blades.

"Bravo!" yelled Huston and Fernández. Lyon shrieked and grabbed Harris, who stared at the polished sword handle protruding from the bull's hump.

The crowd roared their approval, and the animal collapsed on its front legs, blood pouring from the nose and mouth. As it lay dying on the ground, a *puntillero* or point man took a dagger and stabbed the bull in the base of the skull, severing the spinal cord. The judge awarded one ear as a trophy to Téllez, and ecstatic fans whistled and cheered in celebration.

While the two mules were dragging the lifeless body of the last bull out of the Plaza de Toros, a different kind of drama was about to unfold at Terminal 1 of Benito Juarez Airport. An Aeroméxico flight from Montreal, Canada, was beginning its descent to Mexico City.

In the cockpit of the Sabena Boeing 707, the pilot received his last-minute instructions from the control tower. Below the airplane, in the darkening twilight, a labyrinth of crisscrossing streets stretched out in long ribbons and a large blinking rectangle, which was the airport runway, suddenly rose into view.

Shortly after eight o'clock the plane landed with a thud on the tarmac, wheels screeching, and taxied along the blacktop past a line of red and blue lights of police cars, fire engines and ambulances, to the main gate of the terminal. Painted on the plane's illuminated tailfin was the distinctive head of an Aztec *cuāuhtli* – or eagle warrior. Inside the pressurized jet, the seat belt sign was extinguished, and the second and third of the Teotleco festival's arriving deities awoke from their long slumber.

In the first-class cabin, a pair of violet eyes looked out the small elliptical window. The image resembled a cameo portrait framed in a locket. Elizabeth Taylor wore a black Chanel suit with a natural pearl necklace and gold bracelets. Her black hair was cut short above the neck, with a black velvet bow on top of her head.

From her window seat, Taylor could see thousands of people massed behind wooden barriers outside the terminal. There were television news crews and pressmen carrying Graflex Pacemaker Speed Graphic cameras with flexible bellows and interchangeable lenses. A cordon of uniformed policemen armed with handguns stood nearby.

Behind the plane's window, Taylor nervously fondled the heavy bangles on her left wrist. She had been well-advised by her insurance company, Lloyd's of London, not to wear any valuable jewelry, so those items remained locked in a safety deposit box.

During the making of *Cleopatra* in Italy, Richard Burton paid $100,000 to the jeweler Gianni Bulgari for a sparkling 18.61 carat emerald-and-diamond necklace with a detachable 10-carat diamond pendant, which he offered to Taylor as a token of his love. The expensive gift topped her thirtieth birthday present: a pair of yellow-diamond pendant earrings, a brooch and a matching ring that Eddie Fisher gave her in 1962. She sighed at the bittersweet memory. The happiness of that moment was long gone, replaced by a nagging uncertainty.

In the past year, the furor over Burton's ongoing affair with Taylor had eclipsed all other news – it surpassed the Cuban Missile Crisis and outshone American astronaut John Glenn's historic orbit around the earth. The press was still seething when Burton and Taylor arrived in Mexico to continue their lovemaking in the summer of '63.

The actress took a gold compact mirror from her handbag and applied thick black eyeliner and bright pink lipstick. Then she dabbed Chanel No. 5 on her neck and wrists and drew in the heavy floral scent. Peering into the semidarkness, Taylor spied a group of protesters standing near the tarmac holding painted signs that read: ADULTEROS! FUERA DEL PAIS! VAYANSE DE AQUI! – ADULTERERS! LEAVE THE COUNTRY! GET OUT OF HERE! She turned her head away, as if trying to will the disturbing apparition to disappear from view.

In the adjacent seat, a second pair of eyes, blue-green and bloodshot, peeked over her shoulder. The object of Taylor's obsessive love, Burton was dressed in a brown wool blazer, white shirt, royal blue tie and light brown slacks. He leant over and kissed her on the cheek. "It's time to go, love," he said, patting her hand. "I don't want to go outside," she replied. "Don't worry," he smiled. "Everything will be alright."

Burton wanted to leave the plane immediately, but Taylor was frightened. "I've never seen anything like this in my life," she told him. "Oh, Elizabeth," he teased. "They're only a bunch of star-struck fans waiting to see the most beautiful woman in the world." Taylor shook her head. "No, Richard, this is a mob. I don't like it." Neither did some of the other passengers.

On the same flight was Burton's dapper agent Hugh French from the Famous Artists Agency. French, fifty-three, wore an Ergo-weave corduroy jacket, slacks, and trilby hat. An astute dealmaker, he had accepted Burton's offer of a Mexican vacation as a respite from his busy work schedule. After *Cleopatra*, French raised Burton's salary to $500,000. In time, he became Taylor's agent as well, demanding $1.1 million for her plus 10 percent of the gross, and $750,000 for Burton for their fourth film *Who's Afraid of Virginia Woolf?*

Accompanying French on his holiday in the sun was Taylor's second husband Michael Wilding in a dark wool suit and necktie. Urbane, witty and charming, Wilding had once been a popular leading man in British movies, partnering Anna Neagle in a string of frothy musical romances produced by Neagle's husband Herbert Wilcox.

In 1952, Wilding met and married Taylor, who was twenty years his junior. The marriage lasted five years, during which time her star waxed, and his star waned.

In spite of their divorce, Taylor and Wilding remained good friends. Now, at age fifty-one, he was attempting to reinvent himself as French's assistant, while drawing a hefty salary as Burton's press agent.

An anxious child in the seat behind Taylor started jumping up and down. It was her six-year-old daughter, Liza Todd, from the actress' third marriage to producer Mike Todd. The girl had large blue eyes and short black hair and wore a ruffled pink dress with buckle strap shoes. "Mommy," she asked, sensing danger, "is this something about the police?"

Burton picked up the child in his arms and held her against his jacket. "No, no," he shushed, "your mommy is perfectly safe." Taylor turned to him with growing panic in her eyes. "Do something for god's sake before we all get murdered!" A stewardess calmly approached them. "We're waiting for permission to disembark," she said. "It will only take a few minutes." Liza started crying. "My daughter is upset. I think she needs to go to the toilet," said Taylor.

Burton turned angrily to the stewardess. "We need to get off this plane now!" he bellowed. Under the circumstances, his anger was justified. The previous day they had flown from Geneva to Paris. Deplaning in Montreal, Taylor and Burton had been engulfed by an angry mob. Reporters penetrated airport security, thrusting microphones into the couple's faces and inundating them with personal questions: "Miss Taylor, do you plan to get a divorce in Mexico?" and asking Burton: "Are you going to sleep with Ava Gardner?"

The media practically chased the two actors through the airport. "The press in Montreal is the rudest and dirtiest-minded in the world," Burton raged. "The British press can be gentlemen, the French press is not too bad, and the Italians terrible, but not as bad as they are in Montreal."

Now, Burton feared a repetition of these events in Mexico. On the airport tarmac, ground crews were maneuvering portable metal stairs into place at the front exit doors of the plane, while fans and photographers pushed against the flimsy barricades. "Get those doors open!" yelled Burton to the cabin crew.

The plane's copilot emerged from the cockpit and hurried down the aisle. "We are waiting for extra security," he said. Suddenly the front door was unlocked from the outside and a large Mexican dressed like a gaucho ran up the stairs and onto the plane. He was wearing a black sombrero and brandished a Colt .45 semiautomatic pistol.

The man, who looked oddly familiar, grabbed Taylor by the arm and cried "Follow me!" She pulled free of him, screaming in terror. "Get this bloody maniac off the plane before I kill him!" roared Burton. "I am Emilio Fernández!" the man protested loudly. "I was sent here by John Huston to escort you to the hotel!" Burton was aghast. "We need some real policemen here, not a god damn actor!"

Fernández straightened his hat. "I am a director!" he proclaimed with righteous anger. "Stop it, both of you!" interjected Taylor harshly. Fernández's outrage turned to embarrassment. "I am sorry," he apologized. "I was not expecting this kind of trouble." Burton regained his composure. "Neither were we," he said sheepishly.

They decided to seek safety in the terminal before the barriers were trampled underfoot. Taylor put on a white wool coat and gave her trembling daughter to Burton. "Stay close to me," said Fernández reassuringly.

The couple cautiously followed their protector down the metal stairs to the tarmac, where hundreds of press cameras were pointed at them like loaded bazookas. From behind the barriers came angry shouts, whistles and jeers. On the ground, the prominent trio was blinded by exploding flashbulbs.

Raising his revolver, Fernández cleared a path for Burton and Taylor through the squirming hordes. The threat of a deadly stampede became a chilling possibility as thousands of people waved their hands and shook their fists. Even the resolute Fernández was a trifle scared.

Burton carried the whimpering girl in his arms, her head buried in his chest, while Taylor clung to him, one arm clutching her handbag. The surging crowd pushed and strained against each other to get a better view of the two superstars as they made their way into the terminal. When Fernández reached the main doors, he flung them open and Burton and Taylor darted into the building.

Ten policemen in blue uniforms and peaked caps arrived and escorted the frazzled pair through a hallway to the Immigration Room. As they turned a corner, an unexpected sight stopped them dead in their tracks. Waiting for the duo was a gauntlet of reporters from Mexico City's nine daily newspapers and 150 magazines that had converged on the airport. As the startled actors looked around them it was apparent they had been ambushed.

The surrounding corridors were packed with journalists from the USA, England, France, Germany, Italy, and Spain, who were following the exploits of Burton and Taylor. "Outside Rome it was their first real taste of the mobbing they were to receive from now on, for years, wherever they went," said the BBC interviewer Melvyn Bragg.

Taylor instinctively covered her face for protection against the blast of white-hot flashbulbs. When she opened her eyes again, Burton and Liza were gone, swept away by the sea of outstretched hands. Burton tried in vain to reach Taylor, pushing against the swelling tide and howling "Elizabeth! Elizabeth!" Rapidly his body became submerged in the human torrent. The sensation was similar to being tossed underwater by a huge wave and then surfacing again.

There were anguished shouts and screams; arms flayed about and microphones whipped back and forth like deadly rapiers. "A press agent was kicked and in retaliation took a swing at a couple of photographers," wrote the journalist Helen Lawrenson.

One woman standing in front of Taylor reached up and tried to steal her necklace. "Don't you dare!" hissed Taylor, grabbing the woman's hand. Burton was shoved and stepped on, and Taylor lost her shoes and handbag in the mêlée.

An impatient interviewer confronted Burton over his inflammatory remarks about the Canadian press. Burton snarled "I made no such statement!" and punched his accuser in the face, sending him sprawling backwards amid the terrified screams of onlookers. Even Fernández, with his reputation for directing crowd scenes, was unable to control the violence. "Elizabeth was manhandled badly," recounted Bragg. "Burton fought back, bare knuckles, lashing out." Somehow, Fernández rescued Taylor's daughter and carried her on his back to safety.

After a few precious minutes that seemed like an eternity, police reinforcements, deployed by the airport commandant, arrived to break up the fight. The officers accompanied Taylor in her stockings and Burton with the shocked child clinging to his torn jacket through Mexican customs. The pair were joined by Huston's publicist Ernie Anderson, who was badly shaken up, and taken out a side door to a waiting black Cadillac limousine. On the curb, an elderly Mexican woman holding a beaded rosary looked at Taylor with pity in her eyes. "Pobrecita!" she exclaimed, meaning: "You poor thing!"

A police motorcycle escort was waiting in front of the terminal to take Burton and Taylor to their hotel. When the limousine was ready to leave, a siren sounded, and the motorcade sped off, lights flashing, on the nine-mile ride to the city. The procession followed the same route taken by President John F. Kennedy on his three day visit to Mexico City in June 1962. But instead of two million people cheering from office windows and throwing confetti, as JFK had experienced, Burton and Taylor were subjected to a frenzied pursuit by the paparazzi. Even though they had traveled across three continents in the past two days, the promise of some much-needed privacy and rest was still one hour away.

"I'm going to soak in a hot tub and not come out for twenty-four hours," sighed Taylor, lighting a Philip Morris cigarette in the back of the limousine. She glanced over at Burton in the next seat and noticed he had already fallen asleep with her daughter on his lap.

"I feel like I've been through a tornado," said Anderson, who was sitting across from them with an ugly abrasion on his forehead. Taylor handed him a Kleenex tissue to clean the wound. "When the Germans bombed London during the war, my brother and I hid under the kitchen table," she remembered. "The only thing we could hear was the sound of explosions."

Anderson opened one of the sliding compartments and discovered a newly-filled decanter of Scotch. "Would you like a drink?" he asked. "Hell, yes," smiled Taylor, adding "better make them doubles." Anderson poured two large glasses of whisky and they drank in silence as the car hummed along the highway, police lights blinking in the darkness.

As usual, Burton and Taylor traveled in grand style. They occupied the 19th floor penthouse and three adjoining suites of the Maria Isabel Hotel – conveniently located next door to the United States Embassy. Financed at a cost of $12 million by the Bolivian tin magnate Antenor Patiño, and decorated with modern art and antiques, this 600-room palace was the biggest hotel in Latin America when it opened in 1962.

Although Taylor did not have an active role in *The Night of the Iguana*, Seven Arts had agreed to pay the cost of her visit – estimated at $50,000. A giant-sized fruit basket wrapped in cellophane with a blue velvet ribbon was sitting on the entryway marble table. There was a large card printed with the words: WELCOME TO MEXICO. It was signed: Ray Stark. Taylor laughed when she saw it. There were also jars of Brazil nuts, macadamias, and cashews, as well as boxes of Swiss chocolate, almond nougats and bonbons. She unwrapped one of the candies and popped it in her mouth.

In the Burton-Taylor entourage was their majordomo Richard Hanley and his partner John Lee, who took care of the domestic needs. Taylor's makeup man Ron Berkeley made sure she always looked perfect, and Burton's valet Bob Wilson laundered and pressed his wardrobe. Two male secretaries, James Benton and George Davis answered the couple's daily correspondence.

As the staff was unpacking, there was a loud knock on the penthouse door. John Huston and a waiter entered the room with a silver ice bucket, two frosted glasses and a chilled bottle of Maison Veuve Clicquot vintage champagne. "I hope you find the accommodations to your liking," smiled the director. "Maria Isabel is the finest hotel in the country."

"What a charming name," said Taylor.

"Yes," replied Huston. "The owner's eighteen-year-old daughter died of a cerebral hemorrhage, so he named the hotel Maria Isabel in her memory."

"How very touching," remarked Burton, eyeing the champagne. "We can now drown our sorrows."

Later, Anderson released a statement to the press from Taylor, glossing over the unfortunate incident at the airport. "I have always wanted to come back to Mexico," she said, rekindling happy memories of Broadway producer Mike Todd, whom she married in Acapulco. Taylor reiterated her optimism by stating: "I've always liked Mexico." But Burton's remarks, which he penned himself, had a more pessimistic tone. "This is my first visit to Mexico," he announced with his usual gravitas, adding "I trust it shall be my last."

A FEW DAYS LATER, another high wattage Hollywood star flew to Mexico City. Unlike Elizabeth Taylor, whose appearance caused a great commotion, the arrival of Ava Gardner went unnoticed. Hiding her famous visage behind Italian dark tortoiseshell sunglasses, Gardner slipped under the radar of the paparazzi. As preordained by Aztec custom, she was the fourth deity to attend that year's Teotleco ceremony.

Although 1963 held out the promise of better things for Gardner, her mind was filled with regrets. It had been ten years since the restless cinema idol announced she was divorcing her third husband Frank Sinatra, after a tempestuous two-year marriage and two abortions, even though they remained good friends. Ten years had also passed since Gardner had fallen in love with the Spanish matador Luis Miguel Dominguin – an unfulfilling romance, which propelled her love life back into the gossip columns. And ten years had elapsed since the Italian comedian Walter Chiari first signaled his romantic intentions for Gardner but deserted her for another woman.

Gardner's personal anxieties were not helped by sensational reports about her lack of sobriety and self-destructiveness. Ray Stark arranged for his right-hand man Sandy Whitelaw to be her bodyguard. "I was supposed to keep an eye on her, go over her lines with her, and get her ready," he said. "We went to this place in Mexico, where people went to dry out and get in shape." A chauffeured limousine drove them to the state capital of Toluca, which was surrounded by Pre-Columbian villages and archaeological sites.

From there the trio headed south to the town of Ixtapan de la Sal or "place of the salt," where Gardner checked into the Hotel Spa Ixtapan – an exclusive health resort famed for its thermal springs and beauty treatments. For five days, the enervated actress underwent a rigorous schedule of facial masks, body massages, and calisthenics to firm up her arms and legs. She submerged herself in the 100-degree hot mineral baths, took ice cold showers and ate low calorie meals in the spa dining room on the hotel's fifth floor.

Whitelaw was paid to stay in the background and make sure no harm came to Gardner. When they had met the previous year in Madrid, Whitelaw said she had tried to seduce him. But the film executive did not want to mix business with pleasure. At first, Gardner took offense at his rejection. "Why are they always sending faggots to see me all the time!" she complained to Stark. "Sandy's not a faggot," he replied. "He was Jane Fonda's boyfriend!" Gardner took a gulp of champagne and snorted: "Phooey!"

Gardner's beauty may have been catnip to roaming Casanovas like Mario Cabré and Dominguin, but her allure was lost on Whitelaw. "When she drank, she became very paranoid," he said. "She had all this hostility and fear. She was very fussy about the strangest things," adding "she could turn nasty."

After returning to Mexico City, Gardner registered under an assumed name at the El Presidente, one of ten hotels owned by Cesar Balsa – dubbed "the Conrad Hilton of Mexico." Located in the heart of Colonia Juarez, the 128-room hotel featured a handsome lobby with marble floors, wood paneling and heavy drapes – the perfect hiding place for a reluctant star who was trying to regain her confidence. For several days, Gardner stayed in her luxury suite, with the curtains closed, watching television and drinking champagne and cognac. It's unlikely she ever saw the abstract murals by Spanish artist Salvador Dali that welcomed hotel diners to the Jacaranda Room. But inevitably she was recognized.

When Gardner asked the switchboard operator to place an international phone call to her ex-husband Sinatra in Las Vegas, someone tipped off the media. Journalists began calling her room and leaving messages under the door. According to a hotel employee, Gardner did not want to be photographed because of recent plastic surgery to remove the puffy bags from under her eyes, though it could have been from the skin peels she had in Ixtapan.

Furious at the breech in hotel security, Gardner threatened to leave Mexico. She truly despised the press, even though they were a necessary part of the film business. Stark found her behavior intolerable. After all, he had only hired Gardner on Huston's recommendation. When she demanded that no photographers be allowed on the set, Stark told Huston that it was impossible. "We would like someone besides the people at Puerto Vallarta to know the picture is being made," Stark informed him, "so I hope once she gets there she will become reasonable."

Not wanting to lose his favorite star, Huston went to Gardner's hotel room to try and calm her down. When he arrived, she was sitting on the Oriental rug, a champagne glass at her elbow. Huston poured himself a drink and joined Gardner on the floor. The strong aroma of L'Air du Temps perfume with its rich scent of gardenia, jasmine and sandalwood, clung to her skin. "Ava, honey," cooed Huston, "you are a beautiful woman and people want to see you."

"Bullshit!" she cried. "I don't know why I let you talk me into doing this stupid movie," she said. "Ray Stark is just using me. I don't want to do it."

Huston looked at Gardner like a disapproving father. In the soft light of two Chinese porcelain lamps that shone like glowworms on the living room table she resembled an Indian princess. "Come on, Ava," he said sternly, "that's quite enough of this now. You're going to do it, you've got to do it, and I don't want to hear one more word about backing out of it!"

Gardner stared at him. “Are you finished?” Huston nodded. “Yes.”

“Well I have something to say,” she said.

He frowned. “What is it?”

Gardner smiled and raised her glass: “Bottoms up!”

The next morning, Gregory Morrison, the chief of publicity for Seven Arts, sent out embossed invitations to the Mexican press. The words were written with his characteristic efficiency:

“THE NIGHT OF THE IGUANA”
PRESS CONFERENCE
BEETHOVEN ROOM – HOTEL REFORMA
TUESDAY, SEPTEMBER 24, 1963
5:30 P.M.

There were rumors that Burton and Taylor would be there, which were probably started by Morrison. Expectations were running high for the film, and he wanted a show of unity. “Your attendance will be appreciated,” he added in a handwritten postscript on each letter that was sent to the film’s cast and crew. He concluded by saying: “We will make the meeting as brief as possible.” To Burton, however, the word “brief” meant not at all. “I have no intention of being pawed and prodded,” he said. “It serves no purpose other than to infuriate me. I might hit somebody, or worse, Elizabeth might spit on them.”

Once known as the place where dukes and movie stars drank champagne out of beaded slippers, the Hotel Reforma was the most fashionable establishment in the city. In the foyer, a glittering French chandelier, copied from the main gallery in the Palace of Versailles, dazzled onlookers. Guests dined on filet mignon at Longchamps restaurant and danced the rumba at Ciro’s nightclub on the mezzanine floor.

The club had the biggest bar in town, where waiters in bright green jackets served cocktails to wealthy politicians, bankers, and celebrities.

The press conference for *The Night of the Iguana* brought a touch of Hollywood glamour back to the hotel, which had been extensively remodeled after the 1957 Mexico City earthquake. In the Beethoven Room, a painted banner with the words NIGHT OF THE IGUANA PRESS CONFERENCE was strung across the back wall. Below the sign was a long banquet table and chairs for the filmmakers, along with a rostrum and microphone.

On either side of the table were two easels displaying advance one-sheet movie posters, measuring twenty-seven inches in width and forty-one inches in height.

The poster's eye-catching title motif: a half-man, half-iguana lying horizontally across an inverted figure of a naked woman, is often credited to the famous graphic designer Saul Bass.

The actual poster was created by Howard Terpning – a thirty-five-year-old New York commercial artist much admired for his magazine illustrations and paintings of Native Americans. From 1961 until 1974, Terpning designed original poster art for eighty-five movies. Seven of these designs were for various dramas starring Richard Burton, including four with Elizabeth Taylor – most notably *Cleopatra*.

In the center of the room were ten rows of seats for journalists and photographers. Sitting in the front row were interviewers from the Mexico City radio stations XEW, Nucleo Radio Mil, and Organización Radio Centro. English-speaking reporters from the conservative Mexican newspaper *El Universal* and its liberal competitor *Excélsior* occupied the second and third rows.

In the fourth row of seats was the show business reporter Jaime Valdes – a fifteen-year veteran of *Novedades de Mexico*. His thirty-year-old apprentice Raúl Velasco was preparing a list of questions on a shorthand pad.

In the fifth and sixth rows were columnists for the Mexican tabloid *La Prensa* and the English language daily paper *The News*, along with officials from various Mexican trade unions representing film industry employees. At the back of the room, television news crews from channels 2, 4, and 5 were busy setting up their cameras.

Ray Stark stepped up to the microphone and cordially welcomed everybody. He was wearing a Glen Urquhart checked wool suit that offset his light complexion. "Today marks the beginning of a movie milestone," he stated. "This is a very prestigious film for Mexico, and one of the most important films ever made."

Stark spoke briefly about his role as a producer, while members of the press wrote down his remarks. "Now I'd like you to meet some of the talented people that are going to bring this wonderful film to life," he said. "It is my great pleasure to introduce you to one of the finest directors in the world today, John Huston." There was spontaneous applause and the loud popping of flashbulbs.

Stark turned the microphone over to the grinning director, who was dressed in a black leather jacket and matching pants. "Forty years ago, I fell in love with Mexico. I've already made two films here," said Huston. "Now I am going to make another one. This is a special opportunity for me to tell a wonderful story by the brilliant playwright Tennessee Williams with a superb international cast. As you know, Richard Burton, Ava Gardner and Deborah Kerr are the big stars of the movie. Regrettably, they cannot be here tonight. But you will meet them all in the weeks ahead."

Another round of flashbulbs popped when Huston introduced the "ravishingly beautiful" Sue Lyon, "handsome newcomer" James Ward and "talented stage star" Grayson Hall, who were seated on either side of Stark at the table.

Damian Garcia of the *Excélsior* raised his hand. "Is it true that Sue Lyon is going to steal Richard Burton away from Elizabeth Taylor?" Huston seemed surprised. "I don't think so. No."

A second reporter spoke up. "Is there any jealousy between Ava Gardner and Elizabeth Taylor?" There was a moment's disquiet. "None that I am aware of," Huston answered truthfully. "So far as I know they have always been good friends." Jaime Valdes called out to the director. "What is your opinion of Richard Burton?" The crowd murmured expectantly. "He is one of the finest actors in the world," replied Huston. "I have nothing but the highest respect for him."

Raúl Velasco rose from his chair. "There are many people that believe your film will glorify sex and depravity. What do you say to them?" Huston chuckled. "To the contrary, this is a compassionate story about lonely people who are looking for love. The only thing I might be guilty of glorifying," he joked, "is one or two iguanas." There was scattered laughter.

Then Jaime Pericas from *Cine Mundial* posed a sensible question. "What do you think of the Mexican cinema?"

Huston reacted with delight. "I am a great admirer of Mexican filmmaking. One of my wishes has been that Gabriel Figueroa will do the photography in some of my movies because his work is recognized around the world." He handed the microphone to Figueroa, who received strong applause.

“I am very proud to be associated with this film La Noche de la Iguana,” said Figueroa, “because it gives me the chance to work with two great directors, John Huston and my good friend Emilio Fernández.” Huston lent into the microphone. “And I want to tell you that Emilio and I have been friends for a long time. “That is true,” said Fernández. “We are the three amigos!” They shook hands and smiled for photographers.

That evening, the film’s cast and crew celebrated the start of filming with a party at Mexico’s premier nightspot El Patio. Renowned for its first-class cabaret, the club was located in the neoclassical-style Hotel Regis – opposite Alameda Central Park.

The club’s headliner made his entrance and sang a medley of songs. When the lights came up, the head waiter brought large menus over to Huston’s table where he was seated with Stark, Morrison, Figueroa, and Fernández. The set of choices was extensive: Russian caviar, imported smoked salmon, suckling pig, filet mignon, English roast beef, grilled red snapper, and Maryland-style chicken.

Following dessert there was music and dancing. Ward and Lyon took off their shoes and did an uninhibited version of the Twist, earning the adoration of Huston, who applauded vigorously at the end of the number. After the party broke up, the director walked back to the Hotel Bamer. He stopped under an amber streetlight to light a cigarette, and a lady with Mayan features approached him. She was just the type of woman that appealed to him: dark, exotic and young.

“I’m going to my hotel,” he mentioned. “Would you like to join me?”

“Yes, I’d be delighted,” she answered, and they strolled up the street.

AFTER SIX MONTHS OF EXTENSIVE preparation, *The Night of the Iguana* began shooting at Estudios Churubusco on September 25, 1963. Vivid reenactments of important events from Mexican history were an integral part of the studio's lavish output of costume dramas, musical romances and slapstick comedies in which Pedro Armendáriz and Dolores del Rio loved, Maria Félix frowned, Cantinflas laughed and Pedro Infante sang. Masked avengers chased monsters across the back lot and children's fairy tales were colorfully brought to life on the miniature forest and lake.

From the air, the broad configuration of metal hangars and painted barns resembled an airplane factory. On closer inspection, there was a three-story administration building, ten soundstages and two film processing laboratories, a script and art department, makeup and dressing rooms, costume and music departments, a commissary, machine shop, and lumberyard. An electrical substation generated 20,000 volts of power for the twelve-acre industrial complex.

The high operating cost, along with a downturn in the nation's economy, prevented the studios from making a profit. Facing bankruptcy, Churubusco was acquired by the state of Mexico in 1958. No longer was it a private enterprise; henceforth, the offices and soundstages were decreed a government entity – ensuring its economic survival. Eventually, a new administration took over the studio.

But, in 1963, Churubusco's general manager Carlos Toussaint still clung to vestiges of the past. Ten new films, mostly collegiate musicals and storybook romances, were in various phases of production. However, the pious characters and trite dialogue, which were staple ingredients of Mexican cinema, had little in common with the tangled world of Tennessee Williams.

The soundstages at Churubusco were humming with carpenters, electricians and grips when John Huston arrived there at nine o'clock on Wednesday morning. Art director Ramón Rodriguez Granada and his assistant Agustin Ituarte had spent three weeks recreating the full-size interior of an Episcopal church for the film's dramatic prelude: a rainy Sunday sermon in West Virginia.

To the casual observer it appeared that church services were actually being conducted that day – such was the realism of the furnishings. There were six brass chandeliers, eight stained glass arched windows with corresponding wall sconces, a gilded altarpiece with a decorative retable for holding candles and flowers, a two-tiered pulpit with lectern, and twenty mahogany pews.

Richard Burton strode onto the set. He was dressed as Reverend Shannon in his church vestment – white cassock, black stole, and gold pectoral cross. In front of the pews, Huston conferred briefly with Burton, speaking in whispered tones. At the back of the church, seated on a twelve-foot high Chapman dolly crane, was cinematographer Gabriel Figueroa – a viewing filter suspended from a leather cord around his neck.

Figueroa peered through the eyepiece of a Mitchell 35-millimeter soundproof motorized camera that was mounted to the platform of the crane. He was carefully framing the widescreen image, so that it would appear Burton was delivering a real sermon. The five-minute scene would be shot in four different setups, from long shots and medium shots to close ups and reverse shots.

After several minutes, Huston announced to the assembled technicians: "We are ready." Burton climbed the steps of the pulpit, lost in his own thoughts. It appeared as if he was entering a trance and when he spoke his voice resonated with growing fury. "Today's sermon is from Proverbs, Chapter 25, Verse 8," intoned the actor, enunciating every syllable. "'He that hath no rule over his own spirit is like a city that is broken down, and without walls.'"

Burton's oratory skills were legendary, and his powerful voice had such a hypnotic effect that even blasé crewmembers watched spellbound. "I will not and cannot continue to conduct services in praise and worship of this angry, petulant old man in whom you believe!" he told the shocked churchgoers. His face darkened, and his lips quivered. It was the story's flashpoint – the moment when he denounces God.

"You've turned your backs on the God of love and compassion and invented for yourself this cruel, senile delinquent," hollered Burton. "Close your windows! Close your doors! Close your hearts against the truth about God!" Watching from the side of the set, Huston smiled his approval and ordered another take.

Elizabeth Taylor arrived at Churubusco at 11 a.m. to watch the filming and sat quietly in a corner of the soundstage with publicist Greg Morrison. She was wearing vaquero stretch pants, sandals, a white blouse, and blue leather sail jacket.

At midday, Taylor's ex-husband, Michael Wilding, showed up in a grey suit and matching fedora and waited with them for Burton to finish the scene.

The crew broke for lunch at 1 p.m. Burton changed his clothes, grabbed a sports jacket and walked with Taylor, Wilding and Morrison out a side door to the parking lot where a seven-seat Ford limousine was waiting to take them to Churubusco Country Club.

Before the group reached the limousine, they were intercepted by a gaggle of TV news reporters clutching microphones and barking questions: “Miss Taylor when are you going to marry Burton?” “Hey Richard, do you love Liz?” “Mr. Wilding, is it true you are still in love with your ex-wife?” “Liz, are you and Dick going to have any children?”

As the heavy sedan sped away, the reporters gave chase in a posse of convertibles and motorcycles. The cars followed each other at high speed down the Rio Churubusco Highway. One photographer hung his camera out the passenger seat window and focused the lens. The car’s driver overtook the limousine, calling out to the chauffeur: “Oye! Oye!”

The limousine slowed down, and the other cars sped up to take pictures. In the back seat, Burton was seething with anger. “For god’s sake,” he yelled at the driver, “go faster!” Taylor was scared. “Please, Richard, don’t provoke them!” Wilding and Morrison stared uneasily out the window.

At the entrance to Churubusco Country Club, the limousine accelerated through the main gate and raced along the tree-lined road, scattering leaves in its wake. The driver looked in the rear-view mirror and saw the press gang closing in on him. He turned down a driveway and brought the limousine to a screeching halt on the gravel in front of the clubhouse. Taylor, Burton, Wilding and Morrison slammed the car doors behind them and hurried up the steps of the building.

Inside the clubhouse, a *maître’d* escorted the quartet to a private dining room. Large bay windows looked out across a duck-filled lake on the eighteenth hole of the Churubusco Golf Course. The group sat down at a sunlit table and a waiter in a white jacket brought them four menus.

Wilding took off his hat. “I didn’t know the Mexican press could be so damned...”

“Annoying?” prompted Burton.

“Persistent?” suggested Morrison

"No," said Wilding.

"Oh, Michael," groaned Taylor. "Don't be so polite. Say what you mean."

"Alright," he smiled. "They're confoundedly obnoxious!"

The next morning, four trucks loaded with movie cameras, sound equipment and portable lights left Churubusco Studios and traveled twenty-six miles north to the colonial town of Tepotzotlán. Huston had chosen a provocative backdrop for the first scene in the movie: the Church of San Francisco Javier. The limestone and alabaster cathedral with its two bell towers stood on the former site of a Jesuit convent, which was founded by Spanish monks.

Huston relished filming on such a splendid location. The brief sequence, no more than two pages in length, called for the expelled Reverend, who was doing penance as a tour guide, to drink a bottle of beer on the church steps and then hide the empty bottle in a small alcove.

Huston hoped the Mexican censors would miss the subtle irony of Shannon's protest in which he was metaphorically pissing on the Catholic Church. Perhaps sensing the director's seditious intentions, the parish priest refused him permission to film on church property, so the cast and crew were confined to the sidewalk.

Built in 1682, this authentic Mexican Baroque church was one of the finest examples of the Churrigueresque style of elaborate ornamental stucco decoration in Mexico. It was regrettable that moviegoers were denied the opportunity to see the treasures that lay inside the basilica: sumptuously gilded altars, polished marble statues of the Immaculate Conception and John the Baptist, and hand-painted friezes with the figures of Archangels on the ceilings, which were enhanced with silver ornamentation.

For Huston, who waited outside in his white safari suit, hoping for admittance, the front double doors would be kept firmly locked. On the stone pathway, six grips had set up huge arc lights called "brutes" and placed metal sun reflectors in front of the stone wall and front steps leading up to the church, in readiness for the shot.

Richard Burton, Elizabeth Taylor, Sue Lyon, and Grayson Hall arrived at the church in two Cadillac sedans. Taylor was wearing blue jeans, a wool sweater and brown leather jacket. Because of the high elevation the crew had brought along two portable oxygen tanks in case anyone had difficulty breathing.

Since Burton's character was defrocked in the script, he had swapped his church robes for non-clerical attire: white band collar shirt, khaki pants and suede desert boots. Burton sat down in a folding canvas chair with a bottle of Carta Blanca beer while the film's hairstylist, Agnes Flanagan – a small, white-haired woman, who had worked on *The Misfits* – groomed him for the forthcoming scene.

As Flanagan styled Burton's hair, photographers began snapping pictures from behind trees and fences. For some unexplained reason, possibly to antagonize the press, Taylor grabbed a hairbrush and combed the actor's fringe which caused him to fidget in his seat. Flanagan patiently rearranged his hair to match the script and Taylor changed it back again.

Irritated by this tomfoolery, Burton poured the beer all over his head. Taylor shrieked "Richard!" and Burton shot her a disapproving glance. "You are a wonderful actress," he chastised, "but a lousy hairdresser." Flanagan handed him a towel to dry his hair. "Maybe we should leave it wet," she remarked good-humoredly.

Twenty minutes later, after drinking two more beers, Burton was ready to face the cameras. Huston called "Action!"

The wide-angle lens of Figueroa's camera panned down the two-story seventeenth century church tower with its stone *estipites* – delicately sculpted pilasters and niches containing relief carvings of statues and medallions.

As the scene began, Burton was reclining against the church wall – a copy of the *Excélsior* newspaper shielding his face from the sun. Lyon walked up to him wearing a long-sleeved cotton blouse knotted around her midriff, Capri-style pants, and sandals. She was holding a bright yellow wildflower. "What do you call it again?" Lyon asked him. "Copa de Oro," he answered. "Cup of gold," she translated. "Could you drink from it really?"

The sun disappeared behind a cloud and Huston, watching the sky, called out: "Cut!" The scene would have to be done again. To amuse himself while they waited for the light to return, Burton borrowed Taylor's new Kodak Instamatic camera.

"May I take some snapshots of Sue and the others?" he asked.

Taylor gave him a funny look. "Of course, you can. Why do you ask me?"

Burton blushed. "Because I'm afraid of you," he confessed.

oooooooo

On September 27, Ava Gardner arrived at Churubusco Studios for costume tests. It was her second visit to the studio since filming *The Sun Also Rises* with Tyrone Power.

Twenty newsmen were waiting for Gardner when she stepped out of a silver-colored Mercedes Benz sedan with Sandy Whitelaw. Flashbulbs exploded around the couple with the intensity of firecrackers.

Despite her personal troubles, Gardner exuded sex appeal. She wore blue jeans and moccasins with an alpaca sweater pushed up to the elbows. Her green eyes were framed in black horn-rimmed glasses and a Newport cigarette protruded from her lips.

"The last time I was here," Gardner told reporters, "I was in the middle of getting a divorce." The rejuvenated actress ogled a handsome young photographer, who was screwing a flashbulb into his Crown Graphic press camera. "This time," she smiled, "I hope to get married." Her comments triggered a barrage of personal questions. Was the lucky groom an actor, a bullfighter, or a singer? "I don't know yet," she shrugged. "I haven't found the right one!" More flashbulbs popped as Whitelaw and the actress strode inside the building.

For one hour, Gardner sat in the women's dressing room trying on different outfits that had been selected by the film's costume designer Dorothy Jeakins. The two women had never met each other until that day, so it was an anxious moment for both of them.

Tall and angular, her black hair tied up in a bun, Jeakins, forty-nine, was widely respected for creating realistic costumes that evoked a sense of time and place in history. Jeakins received the Oscar for Best Costume Design on the baroque epics *Joan of Arc* and *Samson and Delilah* – the first and second of three wins and twelve nominations. But gaining acceptance had been difficult because of male chauvinism.

Jeakins confided to Gardner that she had expected a much tougher assignment from Huston, who was known for doing things the hard way.

Those were the days when a custom-made dress might cost as much as $5,000. Movie studios expected their stars to be outfitted in the most glamorous up-to-date fashions.

For this reason, Jeakins was both surprised and relieved when Huston asked her to keep things a lot simpler for *The Night of the Iguana*. The character of Maxine, the slovenly innkeeper, was a far cry from Gardner's earlier roles as exotic vamps, torch singers and playgirls who modeled white fox furs, satin evening gowns, and silk negligees.

Because Gardner was reluctant to wear tight-fitting costumes, Ray Stark suggested "the possibility of shorts with a long over-blouse and a provocative kind of blouse with a skirt," like Bette Davis wore in the play. For a time, he even considered putting Gardner in a Hawaiian muumuu, which she thought was a great idea. But these shapeless outfits made her look too matronly.

Since fancy clothes were not required for the film, Gardner asked Jeakins to find garments that flattered her middle-aged figure but still gave the illusion of sexiness. They settled on a simple combination of a beige knitted poncho top and black stretch pants or leggings. "Shit, I lost fifteen pounds, and nobody will see the difference," moaned Gardner when she looked in the mirror. "Don't worry, Ava," soothed Huston when he saw the results. "You're supposed to look a little beat-up in this one – so that's how we dressed you. But you'll be the hit of the picture, I promise you."

That night, Huston took Gardner to Plaza Garibaldi – a twenty-minute taxi ride from her hotel. In the center of the plaza was a circular *quiosco* or bandstand. Local visitors and tourists milled about under brightly colored lights that were strung like Christmas ornaments in the trees.

The taxi pulled up at the curb and Huston paid the fare. He was wearing white safari pants, a blue shirt, bush jacket, and a Stetson hat and leather boots. Gardner was dressed flirtatiously in vaquero-style black pants, a long-sleeved white shirt with a black *chaleco* or waistcoat, a matching black jacket with a round collar and brown boots. Sitting on her head at a jaunty angle was a Spanish *cordobé* – a flat wide-brimmed hat.

Huston and Gardner walked to Salon Tenampa – a popular cantina on the north side of the plaza. Each night, various mariachi groups delighted customers with a mixture of ranchera, bravia and bolero songs.

In the main salon, Huston and Gardner selected a corner table. The director lit a large cigar and ordered a bottle of Don Julio Tequila and two glasses. They sat drinking the liquor while six mariachis strummed guitars and played violins. "You know, John, I'm finally starting to enjoy myself," said Gardner. "That's why I brought you here," he replied, "so you can have some fun."

As the tequila took effect, Gardner became immersed in the different songs. On the other side of the room, a smiling Mexican in a cowboy shirt, skintight chinos and snakeskin boots stood in the doorway. Their eyes met, and she returned his gaze. The man approached Gardner and asked her for a dance. She held out her hand and he pulled her towards him, her hips moving to the rhythm of the music.

Huston watched Gardner and the man dancing with voyeuristic pleasure. After several minutes, the man whispered something in her ear and she smiled at him in tacit agreement. Gardner glanced in Huston's direction. She blew him a short kiss and disappeared with her admirer into the night.

BIG SHOTS: Producer Ray Stark and director John Huston discuss making a movie.

PRESS STAMPEDE: Emilio Fernandez with Elizabeth Taylor at Mexico City Airport.

CHURCH SERMON: Richard Burton as Reverend Lawrence Shannon.

BUMPY RIDE: Sue Lyon with Richard Burton on the bus at Rio Pitillal.

DIRTY LAUNDRY: John Huston and Richard Burton with villagers washing clothes in the river.

SEXY SWIM: Richard Burton and Sue Lyon getting wet.

COOLING OFF: Richard Burton and Sue Lyon at Playa Conchas Chinas.

WARM WELCOME:
Ava Gardner as Maxine Faulk on the steps of the Hotel Costa Verde.

MÉNAGE À TROIS: Richard Burton, Ava Gardner and her Mexican beach boys.

HAPPY HOUR: Richard Burton and Ava Gardner having fun.

CIGARETTE BREAK: John Huston enjoys a Cuban cigar.

ON LOCATION:
Cinematographer Gabriel Figueroa, Tennessee Williams and Ray Stark in front of the bus.

KINDRED SPIRITS: Deborah Kerr and Richard Burton relax on the hotel verandah.

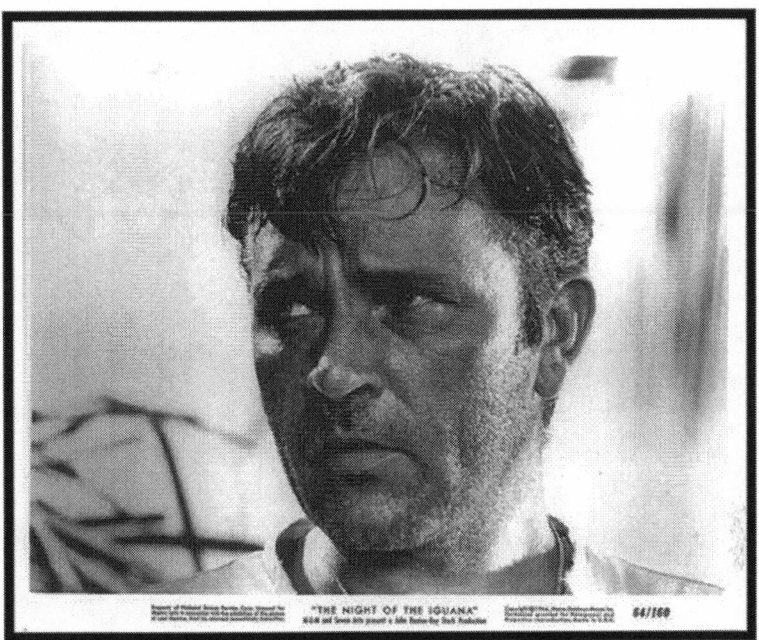

COLD STARE: Richard Burton gets in the acting mood.

MEXICAN SIESTA: Deborah Kerr, Richard Burton and Cyril Delevanti as Nonno.

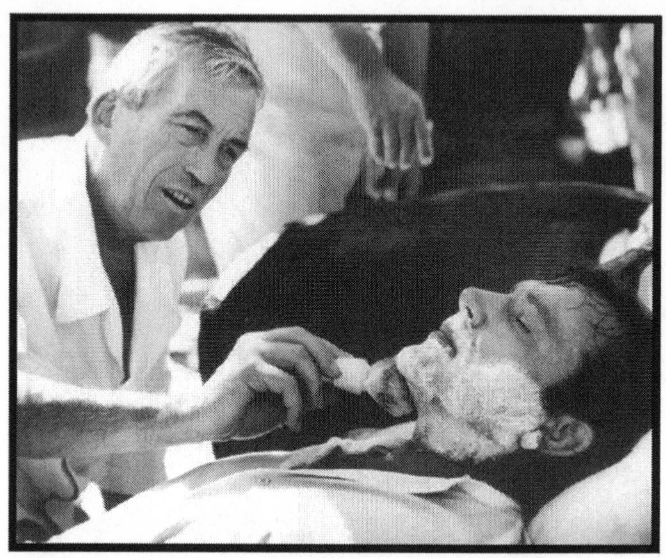

CLOSE SHAVE: John Huston and Richard Burton rehearse a scene.

WOUNDED PRIDE: Richard Burton as Shannon receives first aid from Deborah Kerr as Hannah Jelkes.

TEENAGE LUST: Sue Lyon as the naughty schoolgirl Charlotte Goodall.

STAR POWER: John Huston, Elizabeth Taylor and Richard Burton between scenes.

STEAMED UP: Ava Gardner, Roberto Leyva and Fidelmar Duran in the surf.

PLAYMATES: Elizabeth Taylor with daughter Liza Todd in the sand.

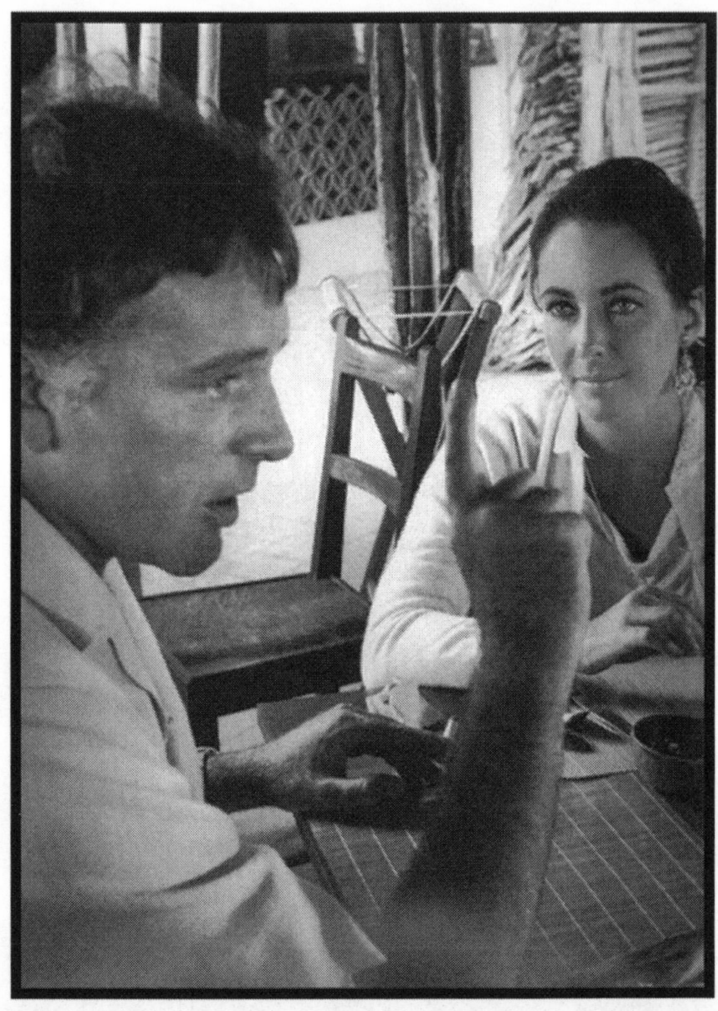

LOOK OF LOVE: Elizabeth Taylor and Richard Burton at El Dorado restaurant.

CANTINA DANCE: Sue Lyon practices her moves with Fidelmar Duran and Roberto Leyva

PLATONIC LOVE: Richard Burton and Deborah Kerr say goodbye.

CHECK OUT: Angry bus passengers leave the Hotel Costa Verde.

PART THREE:

SACRED MONSTERS

"I have a woman's body and a child's emotions."

– Elizabeth Taylor

ON SEPTEMBER 29, 1963, six million readers opened the Sunday edition of *The New York Times*. In the drama section of the newspaper was a full-page advertisement, which had been placed by Edward Feldman – the vice president in charge of advertising and publicity for Seven Arts. The graphics were bold and daring, but it was the eye-catching message that grabbed people's attention:

> TOMORROW IS THE DAY OF
> "THE NIGHT OF THE IGUANA"
>
> Tomorrow is the day in Mismaloya, Mexico, when director John Huston and producer Ray Stark begin filming for Metro-Goldwyn-Mayer and Seven Arts Productions the screen adaptation of Tennessee Williams' prize-winning play. Heading a distinguished international cast will be Richard Burton as Shannon, Ava Gardner as Maxine, Deborah Kerr as Hannah and Sue Lyon as Charlotte. Screenplay by John Huston and Anthony Veiller. This motion picture will be released by MGM throughout the world in late 1964.

That same afternoon, more than 2,000 miles away, a chartered Mexicana Airlines flight arrived at Puerto Vallarta Airport from Mexico City. The sleek, four-propeller DC-6 airplane touched down shortly after 2 p.m. and taxied to a halt outside the airport terminal.

Portable metal steps were wheeled into place at the front cabin doors and the first passengers exited onto the tarmac. It was a hot steamy afternoon, and waves of heat shimmered above the asphalt.

Waiting behind the guardrail were hundreds of spectators, waving Mexican flags and hand-printed signs with the words: BIENVENIDOS – WELCOME! Standing on the tarmac, vigorously playing music for the arriving guests was the ten-piece mariachi band Los Pipianes. The musicians were dressed in richly embroidered red charro suits with gold-belt buckles and wide-brimmed felt sombreros.

The first passengers to leave the plane were Ray Stark and John Huston with his secretary Gladys Hill, each carrying a variety of leather satchels and briefcases.

At the bottom of the steps, Stark and Huston grinned as photographers holding Kodak Brownie Hawkeye cameras clicked away. *Novedades* showbiz reporters Jaime Valdes and Raúl Velasco asked Huston to comment on the cultural impact of his film, which was destined to change the future of the colony.

"I believe that Puerto Vallarta will become the new Acapulco, attracting tourism from around the world," predicted Huston with an optimistic wave of his cigar.

Following them was Seven Arts publicist Greg Morrison and press agent Ernie Anderson, who were holding attaché cases. A fastidious dresser, Anderson was attired in a bright blue shirt, blue pants and horn-rimmed glasses with tinted blue lenses. Standing behind him was the film unit's still photographer, Josh Weiner – a dark-haired, reedy man lugging two bulky aluminum camera cases.

Sue Lyon descended the metal steps, accompanied by producer James Harris and her twenty-eight-year-old private tutor Eva Martin with an armful of schoolbooks.

Oscar Rosales Rodriguez, publisher of the English-speaking newspaper *El Costero*, approached Lyon, who dazzled in a sherbet-colored pantsuit and white sandals with stiletto heels. "What do you think of Mexico?" he inquired. "I'm delighted to be here in this beautiful country," she answered. "Everybody has been very friendly to me."

There were enthusiastic cheers from the crowd as Los Pipianes performed the state song *Guadalajara* – strumming guitars and singing in harmony.

Then, Grayson Hall appeared in the plane's doorway. She was followed by Mary Boylan, Eloise Hardt, Thelda Victor and Betty Proctor, who had been chosen to play the Texas schoolteachers, smiling from under an assortment of sunhats and headscarves.

In contrast to the women's cheerfulness was the somber expression of James Ward, wearing a cotton jacket, Levis and sneakers, his eyes heavy from lack of sleep, as he walked from the runway to the terminal.

The next group that exited the plane was the American film crew, many of whom were veterans of Huston's moviemaking battalion. At the front of the line was the first assistant director, Tom Shaw, whose gruff manner and military crew cut gave him the intimidating appearance of an army drill sergeant.

It was Shaw's responsibility to arrange the daily shooting schedule, organize the cast and crew, and liaise with the production office. His curt efficiency was welcomed by cost-conscious directors like Huston.

Second assistant director Terry Morse Jr., was born with moviemaking in his blood. His father edited sixty films, many of them produced by Warner Brothers where Huston had been employed as a screenwriter before he was promoted to fulltime director.

Script supervisor Angela Allen's professional relationship with Huston dated from 1951 when, at the age of twenty-two, she became the youngest continuity girl in England. She marked his shooting scripts with daily alterations and checked the continuity of actors' costumes, hair and makeup.

Jack Obringer supervised Ava Gardner's eyeliner and lip-gloss, while Eric Allwright applied heavy foundation and concealing makeup to Richard Burton's pockmarked face, and controlled Deborah Kerr's blusher.

Changing the music's tempo, Los Pipianes played *Jarabe Tapatio* – an energetic country dance from Jalisco – as the final group of passengers left the aircraft at Puerto Vallarta Airport.

The man of the hour, Burton wore a blue wool blazer, linen trousers, a silk necktie and Persol dark sunglasses. At his side was Elizabeth Taylor, dressed in a high neck cap sleeve lilac dress. Holding her hand was Liza Todd in a lemon-toned pinafore miniskirt.

Following close behind was Burton's agent Hugh French, Michael Wilding, and Swedish actress Karen von Unge, with whom Wilding had become romantically involved after divorcing his third wife Susan Neill.

The last two people to step off the plane were Jim Benton and George Davis carrying Taylor's two Yorkshire terriers, which had to be groomed and fed twice a day. The weary troupe hoped to avoid an altercation with waiting journalists. After the bedlam in Mexico City nobody knew what to expect, though everyone had been warned about the possibility of an angry press.

On September 30, production manager Abe Steinberg wrote a memorandum to Huston advising him: "All requests from any local or visiting press for interviews and photographs, either on the set or off the set, must be cleared through Greg Morrison."

But the press hardly needed the permission of Morrison or anyone else to be in Puerto Vallarta, which was a Wild West town in those days.

Publications from all over the world had dispatched representatives to cover the making of the film, though many journalists were still in New York, Chicago and Los Angeles, waiting for connecting flights.

The American press alone comprised more than 400 Hollywood correspondents, whose livelihood depended on their skillful reporting. Heading the list were the reigning queens of celebrity gossip: Hedda Hopper and Louella Parsons – catty archrivals for the nation's 100-million newspaper readers. Hopper wrote six daily columns for the *Los Angeles Times* and a Sunday column for the *Chicago Tribune* syndicate. Parsons had a regular column for more than thirty years in the *Los Angeles Examiner*; it also appeared in 600 worldwide newspapers.

In third place was Sheilah Graham, whose weekly showbiz column "Hollywood Today" had more than twenty million readers. The fearsome threesome, dubbed "the unholy trio," vied with Erskine Johnson – a syndicated columnist for the Newspaper Enterprise Association, with 786 global newspapers. Then came the wire service reporters that filed stories on a daily basis: Aline Mosby of the United Press, Bob Thomas of the Associated Press, Harrison Carroll and Jimmy Starr, who were columnists for the Los Angeles *Herald Express*, and Sidney Skolsky, Florabel Muir, and Lowell Redelings of the *Hollywood Citizens News*.

But even these hardened reporters, who came from traditional news desks, were unprepared for the threat posed to their authority by an unchecked style of journalism rapidly sweeping Europe. The commando tactics of this new breed of newsmen and newswomen, who ambushed their subjects, was typified by their unflattering nickname *paparazzi* – meaning annoying insects.

Nothing matched the fury surrounding the making of *Cleopatra*. It was on the Isle of Ischia that a paparazzo named Marcello Geppetti took the sizzling photograph of Burton and Taylor wearing bathing suits, their bodies entwined, kissing on the upper deck of a motor yacht.

The October 1963 issue of *Photoplay* magazine denounced the couple in big, bold letters: LIZ & BURTON – SHAMELESS LOVERS. The story's words were as sharp as daggers: "In Hollywood's history, there has never been a love affair to equal that of Liz Taylor and Richard Burton. Indiscretion has been their motto; taste has been thrown to the winds."

Wherever the pair went they were hounded by braying reporters. Leading the pack was British photographer William Lovelace – one of the elite group of Fleet Street newsmen that dominated Sixties photojournalism.

In the preceding months, Lovelace had tailed Burton and Taylor from London to Paris. He followed them from Toronto to Mexico City and, finally, to Puerto Vallarta, while taking pictures for London's *Daily Express*. Now, Lovelace was standing at the airport, dressed as a tourist, aiming his Rolleiflex camera at the world's most famous pair of lovers. He silently moved forward in the crowd and began clicking his shutter lens.

As Burton and Taylor made their way through customs, the couple's monogrammed Louis Vuitton suitcases and wardrobe trunks, totaling seventy-four pieces, was retrieved from the cargo hold of the plane. One trunk contained Taylor's colorful array of sundresses and bikinis, including forty-one outfits designed in Paris; another was filled with Burton's portable library of books, from historical biographies about Henry VIII and Winston Churchill to the works of Dylan Thomas. The huge consignment was loaded onto a truck and taken to the city.

The Lion's Club of Puerto Vallarta arranged vehicular transportation for the cast and crew. Five Chrysler taxis carried Stark, Huston, Morrison, Lyon, and Ward. Two rented sedans were allocated for Burton, Taylor, French and Wilding, four borrowed Jeeps for Hall, Boylan, Hardt and Proctor, and one Dodge passenger bus for Shaw, Morse, Allen, and the other technicians.

Weighed down by this precious human cargo, the motorized fleet set out in a long, winding procession. They trundled alongside fields of corn, banana trees and coconut palms. Grazing cows lifted their heads at the rasping sound of shifting gears, while farmers riding horses turned to catch sight of the rumbling engines and spinning wheels of the approaching convoy. "Driving from the airport to the hotel," recalled Thelda Victor, "we could see thatched-roof grass huts clinging to the steep slopes surrounding the town."

The first stop was the Hotel Playa de Oro, midway between the airport and downtown, where Lyon, Ward, Hall, and Boylan had reserved separate accommodations. The actors were warmly greeted by hotel staff, and two porters carried their bundles of Bergdorf Goodman, I. Magnin, and Saks Fifth Avenue luggage to the lobby.

Then the parade continued along the beachfront, stopping at the Hotel Rosita, where it deposited more passengers, and, finally, to the Hotel Paraiso. The crew filed off the bus like returning servicemen, hauling leather valises and canvas duffle bags, and gathered at the registration desk, where they were given the keys to their rooms.

Throughout the village, there was a feeling of jubilation. Thousands of excited onlookers filled the streets, hoping to see the black sedan that was carrying Burton and Taylor. Rows of *papel picado* or perforated green, white and red paper decorations fluttered from strings that had been stretched along Paseo Revolucion in front of the malecón. Balloon sellers, ice-cream vendors, folkloric dancers, clowns and jugglers entertained the crowds.

The surreal moment almost rivaled Cleopatra's entrance into Rome, through the Arch of Titus, on a two-ton, three-story-high, black onyx sphinx drawn by three hundred Nubian slaves and watched by 6,000 cheering extras. For the Mexicans it was a dream come true: Cleopatra and Mark Antony in person!

The people of Puerto Vallarta were no less effusive than the Romans in their greeting of "Liz! Liz!" Except instead of Cleopatra holding the hand of Caesarian, her son by Julius Caesar, Taylor was accompanied by her daughter Liza from the star's marriage to Mike Todd.

Men, women and children, standing four and five deep, lined the main avenue to catch a glimpse of Burton and Taylor waving from their car as it glided by hotels, shops and restaurants. Merchants stopped what they were doing, and customers stood and stared.

The enormous reception was unsurpassed until the goodwill visits seven years later of US president Richard Nixon and Mexican president Gustavo Diaz Ordaz, when the two leaders traveled the same route in matching open limousines amid a tickertape parade.

Because the main avenue went south, incoming traffic was required to make a left-hand turn before the bridge to order to reach the upper residential streets. On the corner of the malecón, where the road intercepted the town square, Burton and Taylor's sedan veered left on Calle Independencia. At the busy intersection, police had to move back the crowds to allow the vehicle to pass by. As the car sat idling, one little girl handed Taylor a posy of wildflowers through the open window, and the actress squealed with delight.

The sedan drove along Calle Juarez, passing the Cathedral of Our Lady of Guadalupe, its church bells tolling incessantly. "We knew Taylor and Burton's torrid romance was the subject of tabloid gossip," remembered city reporter Catalina Montes. "Everybody in Vallarta talked about the famous couple and they were the center of every conversation."

For most people, curiosity overcame criticism, though not everyone was awed. Some older folks looked on disapprovingly and four catholic nuns turned their heads away.

The car's driver made a right-hand turn on Calle Aldama and headed up El Cerro, the hill, to Calle Miramar. The vehicle continued right for five blocks, passing two-story colonial buildings painted in varying shades of pink, green and blue. Inquisitive heads peered out from behind mosaic-tiled doorways and windowsills. Curious eyes followed the sedan as it cruised towards the junction of Calle Zaragoza. There, at the end of the narrow road, hugging the left side of the hill was the car's final destination: Casa Kimberly.

ELIZABETH TAYLOR LIKED BIG HOUSES. In Rome, during the making of *Cleopatra*, she rented Villa Pappa – a pink marble estate with fourteen rooms, two swimming pools and cypress trees on Via Appia Antica. It was there that the regal actress, still wearing her Cleopatra eyeliner, engaged in hasty lunchtime trysts and boozy romantic evenings with Richard Burton. The opulence of these surroundings did not deter the paparazzi; to the contrary, at night they were attracted like moths to the glowing porch lights. Photographers climbed walls and trees, hoping to get incriminating evidence of the two lovers.

Taylor's presence had the same mesmerizing effect in Puerto Vallarta. As night fell, large groups of reporters gathered on the cobblestones outside Casa Kimberly.

The four-story, white stucco Mediterranean-style villa was built by Guillermo Wulff for his client William Wilson – the founder of Wilson's Furniture. The six-bedroom house, named after his teenage daughter, was symbolic of the conspicuous wealth that typified much of Gringo Gulch – the exclusive neighborhood where prosperous Americans built lavish houses for their amusement and lived in them for only two or three months of the year.

When Michael Wilding first inquired about renting Wilson's home, local real estate agent Ray Marshall asked him who wanted it. "Richard Burton," answered Wilding, hoping to receive a more favorable rate if he refrained from mentioning Taylor's name.

"Mr. Wilding," said Marshall with silky finesse. "The price is 2,000 dollars a month, including butler and maid service." Wilding was slightly taken aback. "That's rather expensive," he said.

"It's the biggest house in town," the real estate agent told him, adding "you won't find another like it." After mulling over the price, Wilding signed a rental contract for three months with an option to renew on a month-to-month basis.

The spacious accommodations were ideally suited for two powerhouse stars in need of privacy. The enormous villa was hidden from the street by a massive stone wall and wrought-iron gate. Papayas, banana trees, and coconut palms shielded the large courtyard, which was encased by a red tile roof and heavy wooden beams. A wide staircase led upwards to the first floor, containing four separate guestrooms with their own private terraces and bathrooms for use by Wilding, Hugh French, Burton's valet Bob Wilson, and bodyguard Bobby La Salle, whose job was to keep Burton out of trouble, sober him up when he drank too much, and massage his back.

Each room had white tiled floors and was furnished with hardwood closets, beds, and amours. Wooden shutters could be opened to let in the warm sunlight or closed to keep out the heavy rainstorms. Mosquito nettings hung over the beds. On the next level was the living and dining room, complete with a full-service kitchen. There was also an interior courtyard with servant's quarters, suitable for a live-in couple or extra guests. On this trip the room was occupied by the majordomo Richard Hanley and his partner John Lee.

Burton, Taylor and Liza Todd took the large penthouse on the top floor – a full-size suite with a master bedroom, heart-shaped bathtub and pink-tiled shower. On hot afternoons, a sea breeze cooled the thick adobe walls, which were adorned with handcrafted tapestries and paintings by local artists. A wraparound balcony and private bar, decorated with the figures of Catholic saints, offered panoramic views of the mountains, river and bay.

That evening, two uniformed butlers lit the polished candelabras on the oak dining table and opened a chilled bottle of Perrier-Jouët champagne for Burton and Taylor. Three maids in starched cotton aprons served a dinner of French onion soup, Provencal chicken with fried rice, and coconut cream pie for dessert.

As the chatter of the couple's voices wafted from the third-floor balcony, a reporter with a camera slung around his neck tightened his shoelaces on the street below and shinnied up the side of the building. When Burton's secretary Jim Benton went to the bathroom he noticed the reporter tiptoeing across the balcony and alerted LaSalle, who promptly had the man evicted.

Further up the street, under the cover of darkness, a tall lanky stranger walked to the steps of a majestic two-story house, unlocked the front double doors with a key and went inside. The ever-present cigar was a clue to the identity of this person, whose unseen face was that of the film's director.

To be close to Burton and Taylor, his two orbiting superstars, John Huston had taken bigger accommodations at Casa Tabachin. Named after the prolific trees with their bright orange flowers, the four-bedroom Mexican colonial-style mansion was built by Fernando Romero, who arrived in Puerto Vallarta in 1951 – the same year as the city's centennial.

There was an added incentive for Huston's move to larger premises: the arrival of his English-Indian mistress Zoë Sallis, who now stood in the doorway of the home with their sixteen-month old son, Daniel, in her arms.

Huston stroked Sallis' long black hair and she gazed up at him with unquestioning love in her wide brown eyes. He removed the cigar from his mouth and placed his lips firmly against hers. They kissed for a long time in silence – just the two of them standing in the foyer. Then Huston took the baby and lifted it high above his head and the boy made a happy gurgling sound.

Born in Rome in the spring of 1962, Huston's third descendant was the product of a passionate love affair between the gallivanting movie director and the aspiring teenage actress.

Huston had been separated from his fourth wife Ricki Soma for three years. Soma had given up her career as a prima ballerina to become the mother of his two children Tony and Anjelica. But the marriage had soured, and they now led incompatible lives. She complained that Huston was self-absorbed, preoccupied with his work and thoughtless of others. He was never a faithful husband and often an absent father.

Huston's relationship with Sallis had to be kept secret, because he and Soma were still legally married. Perhaps that is the reason why Huston enjoyed a good rapport with Burton and Taylor; he empathized with them, especially Burton, who had been admonished by the world's press for deserting his wife and family.

Huston and Sallis were also living in sin, but with one major difference: they had conceived a child out of wedlock. Huston risked shame and persecution for this indecent act. But divorce was not a viable solution for him. His wife was devoutly catholic, and he did not want to jeopardize the welfare of his children. So, Huston decided to tough it out. He invited Sallis to live with him in Mexico, where their indiscretion would have less of an impact.

Ensconced in their new home with a cook, chauffeur and maid, Sallis could care for Danny, who had curly dark hair and the same mischievous expression as his father. Each morning before Huston went to work, and every night when he returned, Sallis kissed him on the cheek, and Danny waved at the friendly white-suited phantom from his playpen.

In Mexico City, Sandy Whitelaw had given up trying to keep pace with Ava Gardner. She had proved too elusive, giving him the slip in crowded bars and disappearing down dark alleys.

"We would go into restaurants, and she would storm out over something," he remembered. "Or she would tell a taxi driver to stop and she'd jump out of the cab." Obviously, this was an attempt to lose him. Whitelaw knew better than to try and follow the actress into her netherworld of dingy clubs and midnight liaisons. So, he let her go.

Gardner's wanderings temporarily ceased when her favorite Hollywood hairstylist Sydney Guilaroff arrived in Mexico City from Los Angeles. For two months, Gardner had begged Ray Stark to let Guilaroff style her hair, even though his $1,500 weekly salary plus $600 in living expenses clearly exceeded the film's budget. "I told her that we absolutely couldn't afford him under any conditions," said Stark. Finally, he relented and Guilaroff – tall and patrician, impeccably tailored in his dark blue suit and matching neck tie – stepped off the plane.

As M-G-M's chief hairstylist, Guilaroff worked his special magic on their entire galaxy of stars, along with many actors, who requested his services at other studios. For Elizabeth Taylor's most significant role as *Cleopatra*, Guilaroff combed the British Museum for authentic drawings of the Egyptian ruler, who was descended from the ancient Greek dynasty Ptolemy. He was inspired to create two different styles for Taylor, one an elaborate headdress, which depicted her as the reincarnation of the goddess Isis, the other a softer more feminine look from the Greco-Roman period. Both these hairstyles were international fashion trendsetters.

When Guilaroff, age fifty-six, arrived at Gardner's hotel, she was waiting for him in the lobby. He kissed her on the cheek, and she hugged him, resting her head on his neck, which smelled of Imperiale Eau de Cologne. "Oh, Sydney, I am so happy to see you," Gardner sighed, her eyes brimming with tears. "I've missed you too, darling," he smiled. While they chatted over drinks at the hotel bar, a porter carried the artist's luggage, including two hair and makeup cases, up to his room.

Although Stark viewed Gardner's request for Guilaroff as an unnecessary expense, it proved to be a wise choice, as their friendship stretched back twenty years. Not only was he a great stylist, Guilaroff was also a trusted confidant. When actresses needed grooming tips or had marital problems, they sought his advice; he always had a practical solution. If anyone could talk reason to Gardner and make her cooperate with the press, it was Guilaroff.

Gardner was scheduled to arrive in Puerto Vallarta on Sunday, September 29 at 6 p.m. on a chartered Mexicana airplane, but the flight was delayed in Guadalajara because of mechanical problems. Gardner and Guilaroff wiled away the time in a hotel, where they registered as husband and wife to avoid being recognized. Even though the hairstylist and the actress were of different sexual orientation, there was a strong mutual attraction.

Like Taylor, who relished the company of gay men, Gardner was drawn to Guilaroff's wit and intelligence. It was on that lonely night, stranded in a Mexican town between flights, that their brief affair was consummated. They were assisted in their efforts by numerous glasses of Hennessey brandy.

But the romantic interlude was as fleeting as the airport stopover. "Who are we kidding?" moaned Gardner when they awoke in bed the next day. "A three times married divorcée and a confirmed bachelor. It will never work." Guilaroff was more hopeful. "There are lots of people like us. We can try," he said. "No, darling, I will cheat on you," she admitted, "and you'll be jealous."

On Monday morning at 11 a.m. the repaired Mexicana DC-6 finally reached Puerto Vallarta. It was a nerve-wracking flight; not only because of the plane's temperamental engine, but also due to turbulence that the pilot encountered flying over the precipitous Sierra Madres. Holding Gardner's hand, as she made her wobbly descent down the portable metal steps, was Guilaroff – smiling in spite of his ordeal.

Accompanying them was the actress's brother-in-law Larry Tarr, who had flown in from Los Angeles, along with her Spanish secretary Carmen Vargas. Gardner's longtime maid and traveling companion Mearene Jordan, known affectionately as Reenie, was holding two Welsh corgis, Rags and Cara, which Gardner had brought along for good luck.

Sharing the jarring plane ride was costume designer Dorothy Jeakins, who was pale from airsickness. The Mexican contingent of film technicians, who traveled on the same flight, proceeded with blessed relief into the airport.

Gardner did not hang around the airport to give interviews; she darted out a side entrance and into a waiting car which whisked the impatient actress and her staff to Casa de la Luna – a private villa on the hillside above the malecón.

Built by Guillermo Wulff, the white adobe manse, which comfortably slept four people, was located on Calle Mina. Gardner would later remember the house, which was her temporary digs for the next three months, as "a funny little place with a high wall, but one not high enough to deter the Mexican beach boys, young kids who climbed over every night looking for a place to sleep." Her hairstylist, Guilaroff, took a room at the Hotel Oceano, which allowed him more freedom for his own escapades.

Gardner felt like a queen without a castle. After the luxury of living in Madrid, the erratic plumbing and intermittent electricity service of Puerto Vallarta quickly got on her nerves.

Even a modern air conditioner, which had been provided for the actress's comfort, did not ease her stress. "Look where they installed it!" she complained. "In the wall between the kitchen and the living room! It blows cold air in the kitchen and hot air in the living room."

The saving grace was a swimming pool where she could go skinny-dipping in the warm evenings.

Reconciled to her fate, Gardner rummaged about in her luggage and found a bottle of Smirnoff vodka. Then she pulled out a portable General Electric stereo record player and some LP records of Chilean bolero singer Lucho Gatica. She put one of the vinyl discs on the turntable, sat down in a chair and lit a Winston filtered cigarette. While Gatica's voice crooned from the speakers, Gardner's maid fetched a cocktail shaker and a tray of ice cubes from the refrigerator. When she returned with an extra dry martini, Gardner purred: "That's my girl!"

EVERY DAY, PLAYA LOS MUERTOS was crowded with vacationers. On Monday, September 29, when Richard Burton, Elizabeth Taylor, Hugh French and Michael Wilding dined at El Dorado restaurant, things were noticeably different. Security guards had been posted on the beach, so the couple's mealtime would not be disturbed. All the same, people in hats and sunglasses kept gawking at the actors through the bamboo railings like they were animals in a zoo. Taylor resorted to making silly faces, which the spectators found amusing.

Afterwards, Burton and Wilding took a dip in the ocean. It was the first time Burton had worn a swimsuit. Earlier, Ray Stark had commented on the actor's flabbiness, suggesting that he slim down. Now it was French's turn. "You need to watch your weight," he told Burton. "No more alcohol for you!" Burton ignored him and proceeded to order another drink.

The group went and sat under a *palapa* – a palm-fronded umbrella – where Taylor took a tube of zinc oxide from her purse and rubbed some ointment on Burton's nose.

While they dozed in the sun, the actors were unaware they were being closely watched by two Europeans sitting on beach towels some thirty feet from them. One man was dressed in cotton shorts and sandals; the other wore a nylon bikini and was holding a shoulder bag.

When Taylor's daughter Liza ran over to Burton, he picked up the child and kissed her on the cheek.

The man in the bikini reached into the shoulder bag and pulled out a Canon camera with a zoom lens. He pointed the camera at Burton and Taylor and started clicking away.

French jumped to his feet. "Hey, stop that!" he yelled.

"Take it easy mister," the first man called out, "we are tourists!"

"I don't care if you're the bloody president," French seethed. "No photographs!" The sun gradually disappeared behind a bank of darkening clouds, and the rumble of thunder could be heard in the distance.

Later, back at the house, French informed Burton: "You know, *McCall's* magazine offered me $25,000 for photographs of you with Elizabeth and Liza. Maybe we should have taken the money. Now every cameraman is going to be chasing us." Taylor shot a disapproving glance at Burton. He took a swig of vodka and sneered: "They can all go to hell."

Suddenly, there was a deafening thunderclap. The skies above Puerto Vallarta opened and the mountainside was drenched with rain. Water cascaded off rooftops, and streets and gutters overflowed. It was the latest downpour to hit the village in a week.

On September 25, the eighth tropical storm of the season, which meteorologists named Hazel, struck the western state of Sinaloa, leaving thousands of families homeless. Mazatlan was hardest hit – boats sank, and highways and bridges along the coast were washed out by floods. The only passable route was the road from Tepic, one hundred miles from Puerto Vallarta, or over the mountains to Guadalajara – a hazardous eight-hour journey across sharp ravines and swollen rivers.

Although principal photography for *The Night of the Iguana* was scheduled to commence on the first day of October, it was postponed because of the wet conditions.

In the streets, young children played under broken drainpipes that gushed like huge spigots, while teenagers rode the fast-moving water in old rubber tires. For two days, there was no filming; indeed, there was precious little to do but sit and wait.

The city's 5,000 inhabitants were confined to their homes like prisoners in a minimum-security jail. Burton and Taylor remained with her daughter Liza Todd in Casa Kimberly.

Ava Gardner sat in bed at Casa de la Luna, reading the movie script with her two corgis. Eva Martin tutored Sue Lyon in English, French and History in their casita at Hotel Playa de Oro. The paparazzi grew tired of waiting under dripping awnings and retreated to their hotel rooms.

In the morning, Huston stood on the terrace of Casa Tabachin, watching the swirling current of the River Cuale as it raced towards the ocean. He was wearing a striped African caftan and smoked a Panatela cigar. Zoë Sallis came up to him in a sexy negligee, holding Danny in her arms. "Someone is here to see you," she said. A Mexican boy appeared with a note which he handed to the director.

"Honey, I have to go to the hotel," said Huston, "something important has come up."

"What is it?" she asked.

"Emilio is having a poker game!" he grinned. "Tell the boy to wait."

Huston went to the bedroom. He changed into a short sleeve white shirt, long cotton pants and sandals, and kissed Sallis and their son goodbye. Then he grabbed an umbrella and followed the boy out the front door.

At the Hotel Oceano, the American and British crew milled around the bar telling stories.

To pass the time, Huston sat on the verandah, playing New Orleans-style poker with Tom Shaw, Emilio Fernández and Mexican still photographer Gabriel Torres. Appropriately, Huston was the dealer; he shuffled the cards, cut the deck and dealt five cards to each player.

Everyone was anxiously waiting for a change in the weather, but Huston was totally calm – his mind focused on the game. He was so immersed in the cards he didn't even pay attention to a young female observer who sat down at his table – showing off her ample cleavage and bronzed thighs.

Huston paid her scant attention, only glancing up from his cigar once or twice and grinning with a hollow smile that lit up his face momentarily and then vanished. Pretty soon, the girl got the message and she vanished too.

The Mexicans thought Huston must have been a warlock because the woman's disappearance signaled an improvement in the weather. The skies cleared, the sun came out and the muddy puddles evaporated.

Because there were no telephones, production manager Clarence Eurist sent groups of runners through the village with written messages for Burton, Sue Lyon, Grayson Hall and James Ward: "Everybody on set!"

British tabloid photographer Bill Lovelace got up from his seat under a potted palm in the hotel bar, where he had been dozing with a hat over his face. Lovelace reached into his travel bag, pulled out a camera and loaded it with a fresh roll of Kodak film. Then he headed to the stairs.

The filmmaking unit sprung to life with the same energy and excitement as a three-ring circus putting down metal stakes and raising a big top.

Wednesday, October 2, was like no other day in the history of Puerto Vallarta.

"The quiet of the town was suddenly flooded, in broad daylight, with trucks, electric lights and movie stars," recounted Carlos Mungia Fregoso, whose family operated the city's first bakery. "Technicians, workers, residents of the American colony hired as extras, and bystanders moved like ants among cameras, reflectors, and a web of cables that covered the cobblestones."

Waiting patiently at the curb, giving no indication of her propensity for causing trouble was the film's other "star:" a 1950's traveling bus, which figured prominently in several scenes where Burton takes his bewildered passengers on a joyride. While in Mexico City, Huston and Eurist had found a weather-beaten bus, which they rented for the filming.

The thirty-six-passenger vehicle, which was still in active service in Tepotzotlán, had been manufactured by the International Harvest Company of Chicago, Illinois. Two weeks before it was needed, the bus was driven to Mazatlan, tied to a barge and then sailed down the coast to Puerto Vallarta.

Also, on the barge were a five-ton generator truck, plus the camera equipment and lights. The task was as risky as steering the old steamboat over the rapids in *The African Queen*.

Because of ongoing weather problems, it was anybody's guess when the bus would arrive – if at all. "We had to wait out two hurricanes and choppy water, but the old girl finally made it," said Eurist. "I think that day was the happiest day in our lives."

Dubbed "Iguana" by the film crew, the rusting bus had to be extensively overhauled to make it suitable for filming in the tropics. The original engine had manual transmission and column steering with three speeds forward and one reverse – adequate for city streets but not for bumpy off-road driving.

Two new motors, eight new tires, two new clutches and two new brakes were installed after she reached Puerto Vallarta.

Eurist had the outside of the bus repainted white with a red trim and lettered with the sign: "BLAKE'S TOURS – We tour the Southwest and Mexico."

Standing on the hot sidewalk, fanning themselves like a flock of wilted hens, were the twelve American schoolteachers. Great care was taken to give the appearance that each of the women had scrimped and saved for their vacation. "The tourists in the bus should look like they came from a markdown sale at Ohrbach's," said Dorothy Jeakins, who designed the women's costumes.

Sue Lyon was dressed in a long-sleeved cotton blouse knotted around her midriff, Capri-style pants, and sandals. Grayson Hall wore a white blouse, knee-length skirt and flat shoes, befitting a faculty member from a Baptist Female College. Mary Boylan was attired in a Sunday church dress, brown pillbox hat, and cat's-eye glasses.

Not all the teachers were played by actors; some had administrative or educational backgrounds. Thelda Victor was employed as a secretary at Four Star Productions in Hollywood. Betty Proctor was a retired high school teacher from Indiana.

Huston's friend Eloise Hardt, who was familiar to television viewers as Dennis O'Keefe's girlfriend in the CBS sitcom *The Dennis O'Keefe Show*, had an unbilled role as a bus passenger. His assistant Gladys Hill also made a fleeting appearance in the film. The remaining five teachers, who had been chosen by Alexander Whitelaw, were fulltime Puerto Vallarta residents.

Liz Rubey was a tall, angular blonde Texas divorcée, who started the local chapter of Alcoholics Anonymous. Bernice Starr, a curly-haired brunette, worked for the Los Angeles City School System before moving to Vallarta, where she became a founding member of the America-Mexico Foundation.

Dorothy Vance was a former teacher of modern languages from Columbus, Ohio. Barbara Joyce had once been a New York stage actress, while Billie Matticks, who played Miss Throxton, teacher of business administration, was spotted buying food in a grocery store.

Chatting with the women between scenes was Burton in a white band collar shirt, khaki pants and suede desert boots. His costar James Ward wore a cotton work shirt, grey denims and short boots.

The humidity was extreme, but Huston was oblivious to anyone else's discomfort. He strolled about in his white linen suit and moccasins without the benefit of sunglasses or a hat, while drawing breath from a smoldering cigar.

The writer Helen Lawrenson was on assignment for *Show* magazine. She witnessed the scene of the teachers getting on and off the bus being rehearsed multiple times – until the makeup was running off their faces.

Huston, whom she described as "inhumanly pleasant," seemed to take sadistic pleasure in other people's distress. The shirtless production workers, who hauled the heavy camera equipment and metal reflectors, were lathered in perspiration.

Between takes, Lawrenson sat inside the bus, which resembled a blast furnace, chatting with Ray Stark and Gabriel Figueroa. When Lawrenson almost had a fainting spell, she retreated to the Salon Bohemia and ordered a cold beer.

In the afternoon, Figueroa filmed the bus driving through town. The dispirited tourists, who are suffering from dysentery in the script, sang a brief chorus of *Happy Days are Here Again*, a Depression-era song with its optimistic refrain: "The skies above are clear again." The tune was used by Huston as an ironic counterpoint to the women's misery.

Early the next morning, Burton, Lyon, Ward, Hall and the other schoolteachers traveled to the film's next location: a sandbank in the middle of Rio Pitillal – five miles north of the city.

Today, Avenida Francisco Medina Ascensio is a paved six-lane highway. Fifty years ago, it was a two-lane gravel road connecting Puerto Vallarta to the neighboring townships of El Pitillal, Las Juntas and Ixtapa. The undeveloped area was largely comprised of salty marshland.

It was there, on a narrow cement bridge spanning the mouth of the river, that Huston filmed a short travelogue. The tourists on the bus observe what Shannon calls: "A moment of beauty, a fleeting glimpse into the lost world of innocence."

The shots of villagers swimming and making laundry was a clever juxtaposition between past and present. It was also a glimpse into Vallarta itself, depicting the river as a communal life source – a place of nourishment and renewal.

The choice of location was well-timed since El Pitillal was about to receive electricity service, bringing its residents from the Stone Age into the modern era.

Returning from their sightseeing trip, Miss Fellowes leads Shannon and the teachers in a sing-along of *Three Little Fishies* in the "itty bitty pool." The amusing tune was written by Horace Kirby "Saxie" Dowell – one of the most famous composers of comic songs from the Big Band era. Seven Arts paid $3,500 for the performance rights to Dowell's song.

Several of the other proposed songs – *It's a Most Unusual Day*, *If You Feel Like Singing*, and *Skip to My Lou* – were already owned by M-G-M, which meant there was no additional cost.

But Huston insisted on using the most expensive song from the available selection – if for no other reason than to assert his authority.

At the day's end of filming, the cast and crew celebrated Ray Stark's forty-ninth birthday at Hotel Playa de Oro, where the actors were staying on the northern end of the beach. Waiters sang the traditional Mexican birthday song *Las Mañanitas*, and Stark blew out the candles on a chocolate cake with peppermint icing. The bottles of tequila flowed like wine.

Burton, as was his custom, had been imbibing since early morning. He was in a talkative mood, according to Thelda Victor, and "never shut his mouth all afternoon and evening long." Taylor just ignored him, slathering her arms and legs with suntan lotion.

Having drunk her fill of margaritas, Hall decided to go for a swim and plunged into the ocean. But she didn't count on the force of the current, which quickly dragged her out to sea. Moments later she started calling for help. "Looks like Grayson's having an enjoyable time," said Ward, pointing in her direction. "What?" Burton questioned him. "Can't you see the woman's in trouble!"

Burton stripped down to his undershorts and ran into the ocean. He swam out to where Hall was treading water and gulping for air. Ward rushed after Burton, and the two of them brought Hall back to safety.

After putting the exhausted actress to bed, Burton commented: "I'm pretty fond of that Jewish girl." He rejoined the party, but Taylor was peeved at him. "Well, here comes Prince Valiant," she snickered. "Have you rescued any more damsels in distress?" Then she got up and walked past him, provocatively wiggling her derriere. "I think I'll go for a swim!" said Taylor loudly. "Look at her," Burton blurted out. "She walks and looks just like a French tart."

By 5 p.m., when Huston and Tom Shaw showed up, Burton was completely sloshed. He had downed twenty-two glasses of tequila – enough liquor to put a young bull to sleep. "Come on," said Taylor, helping him to his feet. "The bar's closed."

The next day when Burton awoke at Casa Kimberly, he couldn't remember how he got home. "Oh, we got you home all right," said Taylor acerbically. She was sitting on the edge of the bed. Standing next to her was Michael Wilding, holding a bottle of aspirin.

"What are you doing here?" inquired Burton. "I'm staying in the guest room," answered Wilding. "Who do you think I am, Florence Nightingale?" Burton sat up and rubbed his sore head. "Right now," he groaned, "I don't know what to think."

THE MAGNETIC PULL OF the equator, combined with the high intake of liquor that was consumed during the making of *The Night of the Iguana*, had a powerful effect on many of the cast and crew – altering their regular moods.

One night, James Ward was visited in his hotel room by two women. The first was Julie Payne – the twenty-three-year-old daughter of Western actor John Payne and his wife, the Oscar-nominated actress Anne Shirley. Their offspring, a slender brunette, was head over heels in love with Ward, even though he was married to another woman.

The buzz was that Miss Payne was going to marry him; at least that's what she told everybody. When news of her intentions reached the ears of Ward's first wife, Michelle Triola, she decided to make the long trip to Mexico, although their two-year marriage was over.

Journalist Dorothy Kilgallen broke the news of the Ward-Triola-Payne love triangle in her "Voice of Broadway" column, which was syndicated in 146 newspapers. According to Kilgallen, a lovesick Triola forced her way into Ward's hotel room, where he was entertaining Payne over drinks.

Mrs. Ward begged and pleaded with her estranged husband to come back – even warbling a few bars of Neil Sedaka's 1962 hit song *Breaking Up Is Hard To Do*. "She was bucking for a reconciliation," announced Kilgallen, "but Ward wasn't in the mood." Clearly, his affections were for Payne, who literally stood between them on the hotel floor.

The ensuing argument, which had Ward and Triola going round after round like two sparring boxers, woke up sleeping guests. The manager was called to calm things down, but his efforts were to no avail.

Unable to save her marriage, Triola fled the hotel in tears and returned to Los Angeles on the next plane. Overwhelmed by his domestic problems, Ward sat in a chair, studying the script with a half-filled bottle of tequila.

The scene of Ward driving the bus through the jungle was filmed two miles south of the town on a cliff that jutted out two hundred feet above the sea. Cast and crew were transported to the location in a group of trucks and Jeeps. Today, that same road, Carretera Barra de Navidad, is part of the Mexico Highway 200 that connects Puerto Vallarta to Manzanillo.

Huston had Figueroa set up his camera in a small clearing that had been hacked out of the jungle by five men with machetes. The action called for the bus to hit a bump in the road and the front right tire to explode – the result of a specially rigged electrical charge by property man Sam Gordon. But things didn't go exactly as planned.

Ward was negotiating a sharp curve when he got too close to the edge of the road. Maybe he was still frazzled from his wife's visit or had Miss Payne on his mind. All he remembered later was steering the bus.

When the tire burst, the soft shoulder of the road gave way and the front of the bus went over a steep embankment. Ward slammed on the brakes, almost causing an accident. The shocked expression on everyone's faces in the bus was real. Burton and the teachers scrambled off the bus as the front section teetered dangerously above a sharp precipice.

Huston, who was watching from the side of the road, glared at Ward. "I thought you knew how to drive a bus!" he growled. "I thought so too," blurted the actor. "But this road's about to collapse – like my marriage."

Huston cautiously peered over the edge of the cliff to see rocks and sand falling into the ocean below. It was a scary moment. The Mexican crew made the sign of the cross and exclaimed "Los Favorecidos," which means the lucky ones. Burton walked up to the script supervisor Angela Allen, and patted her on the behind. "I just wanted to make sure we were still alive," he said. "Richard," she smirked, "you are incorrigible." "No," he retorted. "I'm Welsh!"

Ernesto Ramirez was in charge of serving lunch to the cast and crew. Each day at one o'clock, Ramirez and his assistant could be seen riding over the ridge on a small caravan of donkeys with clanging casseroles lashed to the animals' backs.

Always on the lookout for tasty cuisine, Elizabeth Taylor was the first to inquire about the daily selection. One donkey carried four varieties of *tacos de canasta* – shredded beef with red chilies, black beans in melted cheese, chorizo with mashed potatoes, and chicken or pork in tomatillo salsa. The tacos were kept warm in insulated *tenates* – portable round containers woven of green palm fronds.

A second donkey had pots of barbecued *costillas* or short ribs, and sometimes there was *chicharron* – a delicious pork crackling accompanied with red and green chili sauce. On alternating days, there were steamed *tamales* – succulent portions of fish, chicken or pork, cooked in a mixture of cornflower and lard and wrapped in banana leaves.

A third donkey carried several varieties of *aguas frescas* – nonalcoholic beverages that were dispensed from sphere-shaped *jicaras* or gourds. The choice of flavors included Flor de Jamaica (a thirst-quenching red drink made from dried hibiscus flowers boiled in water), Horchata (a sweetened milky liquid gleaned from rice), and Tamarindo (a tangy brown juice extracted from tamarind seeds).

The subsequent scene, when Ward repairs the blowout while the teachers go down to the beach, was filmed at Playa Conchas Chinas – Beach of the Curly Shells.

The small cove derived its unusual name from the myriad seashells in the shape of cones, tubes, and spirals, which were the exoskeletons of thousands of mollusks, small crabs, urchins and other marine life. The crew set up at the base of a short access road, named Easy Street, which wound its way from the highway to the beach. The area has since been overbuilt with million-dollar homes and condominiums.

The shot of Burton stripping down to his underwear and taking a running dive into the ocean was filmed among the rocky shoals in front of the Hotel Playa Conchas Chinas, which was erected in 1980. But when Huston was making his movie on the deserted beach there were no obstructions. In the scene, Sue Lyon, who is watching Burton from the road, changes into a two-piece pink bikini with white polka dots and joins him in the water. To make Burton appear younger, if not slimmer, his hairy chest was shaved.

Throughout the day's filming, Taylor jealously eyed Burton from the sand. She was wearing gold and turquoise beaded thongs and a handcrafted green and white cotton shift over a two-piece bikini. At her request, all photographs of Burton and Lyon together were vetoed, which angered the press but reassured Taylor that her future husband would not be seen flirting with another actress.

"I don't see how anyone could connect us when he spends all his time with Elizabeth," Lyon told waiting reporters, "and I spend all of my time with Mario," the name of her boyfriend, who would soon be arriving from Hollywood.

Shannon and Charlotte's erotically-charged swim was photographed by Gabriel Figueroa, wearing a Panama hat and shorts. He was using two cameras, one of which was bolted to a wooden pontoon offshore. When the actors were in their correct positions, Huston, who was standing in the shallows, called out "Action!" Off shore, Burton and Lyon were lying on their backs – trying not to swallow water as they delivered their lines.

"Take my hand, Larry," said Lyon.

“What for?” asked Burton.

“So that we don’t drift apart.”

Grayson Hall as Judith Fellowes stood fully clothed on the beach. “Stay away from that man!” she shrieked over the noise of the surf. “You only got to come on this trip because of me!” When Burton and Lyon emerged from the water, the outlines of their genitalia were clearly visible through the clinging fabric of their wet swimsuits. “Dreadful girl!” accused Hall. “You deliberately defied me! She slapped Lyon hard across the face, then vented her anger at Burton, hissing: “Oh, you beast!”

Figueroa monitored the scene through his viewfinder. When it was over, the cinematographer asked Huston if he thought the transparent nudity would be a problem. Huston responded by saying that he thought it was entirely appropriate. “Gaby,” he smiled, “you are a genius.” The provocative image would become seared in the consciousness of moviegoers, who talked about the scene for years afterwards.

That evening, Lyon was completing her school homework at the kitchen table of the casita at Hotel Playa de Oro. She was attired in a check blouse and hot pants. Eva Martin, her tutor, answered a knock at the front door and was confronted by a tall, skinny man of twenty-five, who looked like an assailant in a tee-shirt and blue jeans. He had a messy thatch of black hair and piercing dark brown eyes. Lyon shrieked “Mario!” He ran into the room, snatched the actress up from the table and smothered her in kisses. Standing at six-foot four-inches, he towered over her five-foot two-inch frame.

The man carried Lyon to the bedroom where they fell onto the bed, laughing. He pulled off his tee-shirt, revealing a hairy chest, and she unbuttoned her blouse. While the couple lay on the pillows, making love, Martin went outside and smoked opium, inhaling the vapors from the small ceramic bowl of a long-stemmed bamboo pipe, while sitting on the verandah.

Afterwards, Lyon and her boyfriend took a walk along the beach. "I'm sorry I couldn't get here sooner, I've been busy working in Hollywood," he explained. Lyon looked up at him with stars in her eyes. "That's great, Mario. It was always your dream to become an actor."

"Yes," he said. "Except that Warner Brothers, where I signed my contract, wants me to use my real name, which is Hampton Fancher."

"That's such a square name," exclaimed Lyon. "Mario Montejo is much better."

"I know," he admitted, "but I'm not a dancer anymore."

"That's not true," said Lyon, grabbing his hand. "Please dance for me, Mario."

"Alright," he smiled. They stopped walking and he performed a few graceful dance movements on the sand. "Look at me," he beckoned, "I still have the fire in my soul." He arched his body, snapping his fingers and stomping his feet to an imaginary guitar rhythm that was playing in his head.

Fancher was sixteen when he took a freighter from Texas to Spain, where he studied flamenco dancing. He changed his name, dyed his hair black and spoke with a Castilian accent. When he returned to the USA he found work in television as an actor. But his heart was still in Spain. Now, standing on the beach in Puerto Vallarta, those feelings of loneliness welled up in him. He ceased dancing and his arms went limp.

"Sue," he hesitated, "there's something else."

"What is it?" she asked with childlike concern.

Fancher held her close to him. "You know that I'm still married."

Lyon seemed confused. "Yes," she said, "so what?"

"Well," he paused, not wanting to break their reverie, "my wife is here."

Lyon stared at him. Fancher's first wife, Joann McNabb, a psychiatric nurse, with whom he had a daughter, had come with him to Mexico to get a divorce.

Lyon's joyful expression changed to a look of betrayal and she burst into tears. "I thought you loved me!" she wailed.

"I do!" cried Fancher.

Inconsolable, Lyon ran back to the hotel leaving him alone in the darkness. For the next two days she was in a sullen mood, unable to comprehend her boyfriend's actions. Producer James Harris, who had rented a house in Puerto Vallarta, so he could be close to Lyon, became concerned that Fancher's proximity to the actress might affect her performance – or perhaps he was jealous of their sexual attraction.

Columnist Hedda Hopper suggested that Harris was in love with Lyon, which he denied, though his devotion to her suggested more than paternal interest. In any case, Huston hoped the emotional stress would improve the quality of Lyon's acting by providing an outlet for her anger. It remained to be seen if his hypothesis was correct.

Filming of *The Night of the Iguana* continued the streets of Puerto Vallarta. The interior shots of the teachers in their hotel rooms were filmed at Hotel Paraiso – the city's first four-story building – on the corner of Morelos and Iturbide streets.

The thirty-five-room hotel was modest but comfortable with twin beds, mosquito netting, and shared bathrooms. "It was best to have a room on the top floor – the Paraiso had one toilet for each floor," said Huston, "and they all ran over." There was a small bar and dinner garden on the ground floor with a view of the ocean. Unfortunately, in the rush to make up for lost time caused by the recent storms, none of the outdoor scenery was photographed. Filming was confined to inside the hotel.

In the unfolding scenes, Charlotte goes to Shannon's room on the second floor and waits for him to return so she can seduce him. But their lovemaking is interrupted by Miss Fellowes banging on the door and yelling: "You hear me Shannon! You've got that child in there! Open up right now!"

Since the script was first written, considerable debate had ensued over how much of Fellowes' sexuality should be revealed. Huston felt that the character, as written, was one-dimensional, and wanted her to be portrayed as "a person of strong-mindedness, strong-willed and thoroughly unaware of her Lesbian tendencies."

Between scenes, Lyon waited in the restaurant, her straight blonde hair in curlers, smoking a Kool menthol cigarette. A repentant Fancher came over and kissed her on the cheek. "Don't worry," he smiled. "Everything will be okay." Assistant director Tom Shaw walked over to Fancher and told him to leave the room. "Why?" asked Lyon. "Because those are the rules," explained Shaw. "We don't allow visitors on the set." Lyon started crying and dabbed her eyes with a Kleenex.

"I know you are only seventeen," said Huston, who was sipping a bottle of Coca-Cola laced with whiskey. "It's natural for you to experience these growing pains. But you need to be strong willed. The character you are playing is a vixen."

"Yes, Mr. Huston." she sniffed. "I'll try to remember."

Adjacent to the Hotel Paraiso was the Puerto Vallarta Telegraph Office, which was shown briefly in the film. Today, the remodeled building is part of the Presidencia Municipal – or City Hall. It was on the sidewalk outside the hotel that Shannon tosses the crumpled paper doves in the street and starts up the bus for his frenzied dash to Mismaloya.

In the film, Burton is supposed to take the distressed schoolteachers to the Hotel Ambos Mundos where they can rest and have a bath, but he accelerates the bus and zooms along the malecón.

Ignoring the teachers' frantic pleas to stop, he drives right past the Hotel Oceano – renamed the Ambos Mundos by Huston in tribute to his late friend Ernest Hemingway, who committed suicide in 1961. The adventurous writer had lived for seven years in a top-floor room of the original Ambos Mundos, which was located in Havana, Cuba.

FRANK MERLO, WHO WAS THE companion of Tennessee Williams for fourteen years, succumbed to lung cancer at New York's Memorial Hospital on September 21, 1963. He was forty-one. The loss of Merlo left a large void in Williams' life. "When he died, I went to pieces," said Williams. "I retreated into a shell." The only thing Williams had now was his work, and even that wasn't enough to sustain him. He had recurring dreams about suffocation and was taking a variety of drugs for anxiety and depression.

One week after attending Merlo's funeral, the anguished playwright and his current boyfriend, Fred Nicklaus, flew to Mexico. It had been three years since Williams last visited the country. How ironic that his constant roaming, a subtle form of procrastination, brought Williams to Puerto Vallarta, where he was pressed into service to rewrite the cinematic ending to *The Night of the Iguana*. But getting him to make the long trip had proved difficult.

Ray Stark bribed Williams with the offer of a sailing boat to get him to leave his air-conditioned New York apartment for the sweltering Mexican beaches. In the end, Williams surprised everyone by asking only for his expenses. Friends questioned his decision to come at all. The explanation was simple: Williams agreed to get involved as a favor to Huston, whom he genuinely admired. He dared not tell anyone about his reticence to write another screenplay, that his reluctance to write again was because he had lost his creative spark.

In Puerto Vallarta, Williams hesitated on the front steps of the Hotel Rio – the same hotel where Shannon's wayward bus careened on its way out of town. The round cherubic face was almost unrecognizable, his black hair had grown thick and curly, and he sported a luxuriant Van Dyke beard.

Williams held a bulging Oriental-brand suitcase covered in travel stickers, and a portable Royal manual typewriter in its battered case. Standing next to him was Nicklaus wearing tight fitting beach shorts, tee-shirt and slippers, while cradling a miniature Boston female bulldog with soulful eyes. The dog was whimpering, and Williams was strangely agitated.

Manuel, the hotel manager, who was watching from the window, came outside and spoke to them. "Can I help you, senor?" he inquired. "Yes," twitched Williams. "We just arrived here today from Mazatlan. A wild bull attacked my little dog at the airport." When the manager reached out his hand to pet the frightened animal it growled at him. "Gigi needs a bath," leered Nicklaus.

The hotel manager frowned. "Do you have a reservation with us?" he asked.

"I surely do," answered the bearded playwright. "My name is Tennessee Williams."

The manager was shocked. "I'm sorry. I was expecting someone else. You look different in your photographs."

"I always get told that!" Williams grinned. "Everyone says the beard makes me look more European!"

Nicklaus wiggled his head. "I'm Freddy, Mr. Williams' secretary." They shook hands. The bewildered manager picked up Williams' suitcase and escorted the two men and their dog to the front desk.

The hotel was an eye-pleasing combination of traditional Mexican architecture and contemporary design. Fifty rooms were connected by a three-story tower with trellised walkways of red and white bougainvillea, surmounted by an oasis of sago and queen palms.

Williams and Nicklaus took a large room with a king-size bed on the top floor of the hotel, overlooking the main road, which continued across the southbound Rio Cuale Bridge – dividing the village in two sections. Beyond the river was a tidal lagoon, where villagers splashed and swam in the water.

When Williams checked in, workmen were painting the hotel railing with red lead to protect the metal from the corrosive effects of salt.

On Friday, October 4, the day of Williams' arrival, Hurricane Flora, one of the deadliest tropical storms in history, killed 7,200 people in Haiti and Cuba. It was a natural disaster of epic proportions, radiating damage across much of Latin America. Many people thought it was a portent of things to come. The widespread death and destruction caused consternation among the people of Puerto Vallarta, which was far removed from the tragedy.

Williams closed the curtains of the hotel room and plopped himself on the bed. "I'm so tired," he sighed. "I need something to pick me up." Nicklaus smiled despairingly. Williams wasn't referring to a martini; he craved a more potent stimulant.

Four months earlier, his energy flagging, Williams had consulted Elizabeth Taylor's personal physician Dr. Carl Heinz Goldman in London.

Taylor and the playwright struck up a lasting friendship after she appeared in the film adaptations of *Cat on a Hot Tin Roof* and *Suddenly Last Summer*. Naturally, she was concerned about his health, and recommended that he talk to her doctor.

Williams was diagnosed with a pre-cirrhotic condition of the liver, which was enlarged by almost three inches. Dr. Goldman instructed the exhausted writer to reduce his intake of liquor and prescribed some green tablets, which temporarily restored his vigor.

Williams said the drug had the same effect as the amphetamine Benzedrine, but didn't give him heart palpitations.

While Williams rested, Nicklaus unzipped a brown leather toiletries bag and took out an amber-colored glass pill bottle. Nicklaus unscrewed the cap and handed one of the tiny lozenges to Williams. He gripped the tablet between his fingers and placed it on his tongue. Then he swallowed the powerful drug, lent back on the pillows and closed his eyes.

"When Frankie was alive we were going to move to Italy," remarked Williams, lying on his back, "but now I think I want to live in Mexico." A beatific smile spread across his face, and he intoned: "No se puede vivir sin amor."

"What did you say?" asked Nicklaus.

"One cannot live without love," he sighed.

Following Merlo's death, Williams entered the darkest period of his life, which would result in a nervous breakdown. The strict order of his daily routine, which Merlo had maintained, was slowly unraveling like a loosely coiled rope.

Nicklaus had neither the maturity nor the experience to help him. "I don't understand why we had to go to Mazatlan," he complained while unpacking their luggage. "All it did was to make you depressed."

Williams smiled wistfully at him. "You'll never understand what Frankie and I had together." Nicklaus shrugged and went to the bathroom.

Mazatlan held special significance for Williams, who, in spite of his widely-perceived cynicism, was a sentimentalist at heart. By returning there, Williams hoped to relive some of the magic he had experienced with Merlo – or maybe it was to bury those restless ghosts. But the memories his visit revived were mostly melancholy ones.

Nicklaus came out of the bathroom wearing yellow Speedos. He twirled around, showing off his trim body. "I want to go for a swim," he implored his smiling benefactor. Williams reached out and touched the poet's smooth legs. "First, we need to take a siesta," insisted Williams. "Okay," smirked Nicklaus, and climbed into the bed.

That weekend, John Huston took Williams to visit the completed set of the movie in Mismaloya. The sun had already risen from behind the mountains and was casting its warming rays on Playa Los Muertos when Williams ambled down the sandy path that wound between the Tropicana Hotel and El Dorado restaurant.

Williams was wearing a short sleeve blue cotton shirt, knee length shorts and sandals, with a planter's hat and sunglasses, which gave his bearded countenance a devilish appearance. Huston was waiting at the water's edge smoking a Cuban cigar. The two men exchanged greetings and then waded in to the knee-high surf.

A bare-chested Mexican youth helped Huston and Williams into a canoe and the men paddled out to a waiting speedboat. Moments later, the outboard motor sputtered to life and the small vessel cut across the breakers, the painted wooden bow bucking against the incoming tide. Williams sat in the stern, smiling from the exhilaration of the bouncy ride.

Arriving in Mismaloya, the speedboat slowed down and came to rest at a small wooden dock. Waiting to meet Huston and Williams was the set designer Stephen Grimes, who looked like Robinson Crusoe in a faded cotton shirt, frayed shorts and red beard.

The viridian jungle was serene – in contrast to the months of bustling activity that had preceded the men's visit.

Looking in the direction of the trees, Huston and Williams felt a surge of adrenalin. There, emerging from the hillside, like a recently excavated temple, was the Costa Verde Hotel. In the glow of late morning, the ancient structure shone with the brilliance of polished citrine – a gemstone prized for its luminosity.

Slowly, Williams walked up the hotel steps and looked around. "This is precisely what I meant," said the beaming playwright, referring to the quaint dwelling that he had stayed in above Playa Caleta when he a young man. "This is Acapulco twenty years ago."

Grimes' realistic-looking set belied the confusion that surrounded its creation. The main building was designed in a traditional cantera style. Three large symmetrical stone arches made from chunks of sandstone, pebbles and bricks were cemented together. The front verandah, which faced the ocean, was enclosed in a decorative railing constructed of interweaving lattice-style clay blocks.

Above the second arch was an elliptical window, resembling a giant eye, which provided ventilation and allowed the wide structure to breathe during the hot summer months.

The decorative aperture not only served a functional purpose but was deeply symbolic. Williams studied the opening with prolonged interest. Reminiscent of the mystical Eye of Providence or the all-seeing eye of God, its appearance was closely associated with Freemasonry – the ancient fraternity, whose classic symbols are the tools of the stonemason: a square and compass.

Like the majority of Mexicans, Guillermo Wulff was devoutly Catholic and believed in the power of divinity. His buildings, while filling a practical need, also served as houses of worship, radiating a strong aura of spirituality.

The hotel set and adjoining bungalows that Wulff constructed for *The Night of the Iguana* were no exception.

Although few people at the time other than Huston and Ray Stark understood the film's potential, Wulff's faith in Mismaloya as a tourist magnet was unequivocal. Therefore, his confidence must have been shaken when Seven Arts began cutting costs, requiring him to make unfair compromises that jeopardized the quality of the project.

It had been more than four months since the idealistic builder and the crafty producer first shook hands in the bar of the Oceano Hotel. Now, on the eve of location filming, Wulff was even poorer than the day he started. Held to a contract he didn't fully comprehend, Wulff became a victim of his own avarice.

In addition to supplying the building materials and labor, Wulff entered into a deal to provide three meals a day to the production staff and workers – a total of 500 people. This involved hiring twenty cooks and transporting one ton of tortillas, meat, beans and rice by boat six days a week to the movie location.

Although Seven Arts agreed to pay Wulff five pesos for each meal, the total cost amounted to 15 pesos a person or 5,000 pesos a day. The movie company refused to pay for the difference, creating a deficit for Wulff of 250,000 pesos – the equivalent of $15,000.

After the main hotel was finished, Stark told Wulff that the set looked empty and that he needed to have the grounds landscaped. The producer authorized an expenditure of 10,000 pesos or $500 on greenery. When Wulff presented Stark with the cash receipts, he denied ordering anything. It was the straw that broke the camel's back.

On the verge of insolvency, Wulff issued an ultimatum to Seven Arts: "Tomorrow, if you don't give me more money there won't be any water, no lights, no boats, nothing, unless you discuss this with me."

The next day, a plane with the Secretary of the Government and the Governor of Jalisco, arrived to try and convince Wulff not to stop the movie. "If you do that to this company," the officials informed him, "other companies will never come back to make movies in Mexico."

Faced with this unexpected political development, Wulff had no choice but to back down. In the process, he made an enemy of Stark and lost a friend in Huston. The builder's only ally was Richard Burton, who later gave him a check for $1,000 out of pity for his dilemma.

There was no mention of this volatile dispute when Williams toured the set with Huston and Grimes. The lush new plantings of coconut palms, queen palms, sago palms, and mango, papaya and banana trees, which had quickly taken root in the fertile soil, were indistinguishable from the old ones. The only evidence of any recent disturbance was the freshly raked mounds of earth and gravel behind winding cobblestone pathways and trellised garden walls. Otherwise, the hotel, as designed by Grimes, looked like it had been there for years.

Handmade tables and chairs called *equipales*, made from two kinds of varnished jungle wood, lashed together with vegetable fiber and covered in tanned leather, adorned the lobby. Brass-framed beds, carved pinewood dressers, porcelain oil lamps and woven rattan mats had been carefully arranged in each room to give the approximation of a working hotel. There were metal pots and pans in the kitchen, and a Chinese gong and bamboo liquor cart in the dining room.

Outside, a small wicker birdcage containing four yellow canaries hung in front of an open window. A folding chaise longue, striped canvas beach chairs, and two empty hammocks waited for arriving guests on the verandah.

As Williams marveled at the results of this strenuous labor, Huston unveiled his filmmaking plans. "This is going to be an interesting experiment," he revealed, "something I've always wanted to do."

Williams was intrigued. “And how will you accomplish that?” he asked. The question hung in the air like the plume of smoke from the director’s cigar.

Huston took a folded sheet of paper from his shirt pocket and unfurled it like a treasure map. There were diagrams and numbers written on the sheet, indicating a detailed filming schedule. “When you put *Iguana* on Broadway,” he explained to Williams, “your actors created their characters each night for two-and-a-half hours. Here, we’re keeping them in character for three months and they will actually be living in the setting you conceived.” Huston glanced at the paper. “Our actors will live here without distraction while we film the story in exact sequence. Yes,” he grinned, “it’s going to be an interesting experience.”

Back at the Hotel Rio, Williams was approached in the bar by some American reporters, who wanted interviews. As he sat drinking an extra dry vodka martini, several photographers snapped his picture. “I usually do my writing in Key West,” he told Bob Thomas of the Associated Press. “I’ve never been able to write very well in Mexico; it is too humid and enervating here. It is hot in Key West, too, but there you have the trade winds that make the climate continually interesting.”

Even though Williams had written the screen adaptations of *The Glass Menagerie, A Streetcar Named Desire, The Rose Tattoo* and *Baby Doll*, he said he no longer had the time or patience to write for the screen. “I would rather let someone else handle the movie treatment, particularly if it is someone whom I respect,” Williams told the newsmen. He lit a Philip Morris cigarette and inhaled the smoke through an ivory cigarette holder. “However, I do care what happens to my plays on the screen. That’s why I’m here now.”

FOR YEARS, AMERICAN TRAVEL WRITERS referred to Puerto Vallarta as "a sleepy village." There was just one problem with that fanciful description: Vallarta had never been sleepy. Apart from a daily cacophony of music, heard in practically every neighborhood, there were weekly fiestas, traditional folk dances, and monthly *charreadas* – the Mexican equivalent of rodeos that derived from the haciendas with their mounted cattle herders. There were high-stakes poker games on Friday nights, and spirited Jai alai or fronton competitions on Saturday afternoons. On Sundays, local businessmen spent a good portion of their earnings betting on the Peleas de Gallos or Cockfights.

But the city's biggest attractions were its sophisticated nightclubs, whose cosmopolitan influence helped pave the way for modern tourism. Los Jardines, which was awash in tropical décor, offered midnight floorshows. A second club, El Patio, decorated in leopard skins and stuffed deer heads, promised a live mariachi band every night. At Bagatelle, hip couples danced the mambo and cha-cha under dim purple lights.

Manuel Capetillo, who was applauded for his elegant passes in the bullring, often sang for appreciative customers at La Escondida, a late-night supper club, where the rich and famous mingled over cocktails. One of those recognizable names glimpsed sitting in the audience was Hollywood movie star Rock Hudson. His tall physique, brown eyes, and bashful smile caused female moviegoers to swoon when they watched him in *Magnificent Obsession*, *Giant*, and *Pillow Talk*.

Indeed, Hudson's popularity had achieved legendary status. He was voted the Number One box-office attraction five times by American motion picture exhibitors in 1957, 1959, 1960, 1961 and 1962. His latest film, *A Gathering of Eagles*, a supersonic drama about the US Strategic Command, was produced by Sy Bartlett, who had become enchanted with Mismaloya.

It was on a holiday to Puerto Vallarta in the spring of 1963 that Hudson met a smiling, dimpled fashion designer named Xavier de la Torre. Hoping to capitalize on Hudson's friendship, de la Torre rolled out the welcome mat for him at Villa Leonarda – a hacienda-style home, which the designer owned on Calle Guerrero. There, shielded from public view by three-foot-thick stucco walls, heavy trestle doors and large wooden shutters, the handsome movie idol was entertained by a constant stream of admirers – most of them randy males.

At nightfall, guests were treated to a succulent buffet, live music and one of the town's requisite pastimes: the sweet aroma of marijuana. Men shed their tee-shirts and jeans and jumped naked into the oval-shaped swimming pool. In the early morning hours, the remaining guests paired off and withdrew to the five bedrooms with their high ceilings and flowing muslin curtains overlooking the paved courtyard, statuary and gardens.

When Hudson returned to California, the glow quickly faded from his visit. Apart from handing out autographs, he also left his signature on unpaid checks for hotel drinks totaling $300. Nobody seemed to care. The magic of Hollywood had touched the small town.

Back in Los Angeles, the first person that Hudson told about the eventful trip was Elizabeth Taylor. Now, six months later, Taylor was standing on the third floor balcony of Casa Kimberly, watching a glorious crimson sunset. She was wearing a traditional Mexican *huipil* – a low-cut dress made of lightweight cotton and richly embroidered with flowers.

Richard Burton wore a lime green shirt, chinos and sandals. At the rooftop bar, he refilled his whisky glass with vodka and 7-Up, and made a second drink, Jack Daniel's and ginger ale, which he gave to Taylor. "What a beautiful view," she said, gazing out at the ocean. "It reminds me of Greece."

"Maybe we should buy a boat," suggested Burton.

"Whatever for?" asked Taylor.

"So we can go fishing," he replied.

At Taylor's suggestion, Michael Wilding contacted Louis Benoist, the owner of Almaden Wineries and proprietor of the Hotel Oceano, about leasing his 138-foot luxury yacht *Le Voyageur*, which was moored in the French port of Martinique. Benoist, however, refused to rent the two-mast schooner. He said he planned to sail the boat through the Panama Canal to Puerto Vallarta that summer.

Unconcerned, Taylor bought a gleaming white motor launch, trimmed in blue, and christened it *Taffy*, which means Welshman – one of her pet names for Burton. They used the boat to cross the bay and take visiting friends like fellow Welsh actor Stanley Baker sport fishing.

ON OCTOBER 9, 1963, Deborah Kerr arrived in Puerto Vallarta with her husband Peter Viertel on a Mexicana flight from Mexico City. Observing Aztec tradition, they were the fifth and sixth deities to be honored at the Teotleco festival. Kerr and Viertel had been traveling two days from New York and were tired but otherwise in a pleasant mood. Both were dressed in elegant pantsuits, which were more suitable for lunching on the French Riviera.

The couple had eight pieces of Asprey luggage, containing her summer slacks and blouses, and his sport shirts and shorts. They also carried with them two wooden Slazenger tennis rackets, and a metal canister of tennis balls.

Kerr's arrival didn't stir up the usual tumult of journalists and photographers because there was no warning of her arrival. She preferred to travel incognito; this was not an affectation but was part of her innate shyness. The actress hid her freckled face and auburn hair under a brightly-colored headscarf and her green eyes were covered by large-framed red sunglasses.

Although Kerr had already made three trips to Spain, this was her first visit to Mexico – a country she had heard much about from her best friend in Madrid, the Italian actress Lucia Bosé, who was married to Luis Miguel Dominguin, the world-famous bullfighter. Viertel, who was fluent in several languages, had been teaching Kerr to speak Spanish, which she hoped to practice in Mexico.

A dedicated diarist and picture taker, Kerr was determined to make the most of the new experience, bringing with her an Asahi Pentax camera and several notebooks. Her husband brought along the manuscript for his forthcoming novel, *Love Lies Bleeding*, based on the life of Dominguin's brother-in-law Antonio Ordóñez, which he was editing for publication.

Viertel also had with him a wooden surfboard to test the waves. An expert skier and swimmer, he was credited with having introduced surfing to France. Few people at the time were aware of Viertel's cultural influence when he and Kerr stepped off the plane at Puerto Vallarta Airport on that balmy weekday afternoon. Apprised of the gathering media storm, they had wisely selected accommodations on the north side of the river, where the paparazzi were less likely to find them. It was, Helen Lawrenson wrote, "a refreshing oasis of sanity compared with the tempestuous phililoo that raged elsewhere."

The well-chosen address, Casa del Cielo or House in the Sky, was situated at the top of Calle Iturbide – on the terraced section of hillside known as El Cerro. The exclusive residence was leased from Luis and Selma Gordon – founders of the First Committee of the American Colony. The Gordons organized many social events such as the annual Shawl Dance to benefit the indigenous residents of Puerto Vallarta.

The home's architect, Fernando Romero, whom his friends called Freddy, specialized in creating dramatic living spaces around stairwells, loggias and swimming pools. All his houses were imbued with a whimsical touch, which was both artistic and functional, for example, the addition of red, blue and yellow glass bottles, which he embedded in the walls for diffused lighting.

The view from the back patio of Kerr's rented house offered a dazzling panorama of the city skyline, which was the equivalent of anything in Athens or Naples.

The twinkling lights at dusk were almost as invigorating as the evening's aperitifs – a Schweppes club soda with lemon and ice for him and a Beefeater gin martini with two cocktail onions for her.

But when Kerr awoke the next morning, her body covered in unsightly pink welts, the harsh reality of life in the tropics set in. The actress's daily existence would require fast acclimation if she was to stave off infection from mosquitoes and other biting insects. Kerr observed that "the house has no screens, which seems curious to me in this climate," stating she intended to get some screens made to keep out the huge moths and flying beetles. "I don't fancy myself groping my way around in the dark and stepping on a scorpion. Despite these drawbacks our house is charming and comfortable with plenty of hot water and toilets that work (so far)."

After settling in, Kerr attended wardrobe fittings for her character Hannah Jelkes – the lovelorn spinster whose romantic past is anything but chaste. The actress didn't have far to go for the appointment as her costumes were being assembled in a small building at the bottom of the street. In midmorning, Kerr and Viertel set off down the road, no longer celebrities but two cheerful tourists, eager to explore the neighborhood. They wound their way down the terraced *andadors* – garden paths that connected neighboring houses and streets.

At the corner of Calle Hidalgo, the sun was momentarily obscured by the three-tiered bell tower of Our Lady of Guadalupe Church. The red brick steeple was designed by engineers Rafael Flores Miranda and Carlos de Alba. The final addition of eight sculpted angels holding aloft a giant crown topped by a golden sphere with a standing cross was added in 1965.

The parish priest Father Rafael Parra Castillo stood on the front steps of the church in a black cassock, a gold chain around his neck, welcoming parishioners. He shook hands with Kerr and Viertel as they passed through the stone doorway.

Inside, worshipers sat behind rows of communal railings cut from precious wood, their faces illuminated by the soft light of four crystal chandeliers.

Viertel and Kerr walked down the center aisle, their footsteps echoing off the interior walls with its sculpted tableaux, Stations of the Cross, depicting Christ's crucifixion, carved on the naves. Kerr knelt in front of the antique marble altar, next to the gilded pulpit and confessional. Directly above the retable, in a large wooden frame was the serene image of Our Lady of Guadalupe. Viertel stood in silence while his wife prayed under Guadalupe's watchful gaze.

Afterwards, the couple left the church and walked hand in hand to Luz's Dress Shop on Iturbide Street, where an unexpected surprise awaited them. Costume designer Dorothy Jeakins had invited Tennessee Williams to meet Kerr, who was going to be measured for her artist's smock by local dressmaker Luz Contreras.

Williams was both delighted and nervous at the prospect of seeing Kerr. The moment was made even more exciting because, like many shooting stars, their trajectories had already crossed. The last time Williams and Kerr had talked was outside the Ethel Barrymore Theatre on West 47th Street in New York City. Now, they were about to be reunited half a world away.

The jubilant reunion took place behind a storefront of fringed curtains and plaster-of-Paris mannequins wearing tight bodices, petticoats and bridal dresses. When Williams arrived, Kerr was standing in front of a full-length mirror with yards of fabric draped around her. Standing by her side was Jeakins with a handful of dress pins and measuring tape. Contreras' younger sister Yolanda was helping Jeakins to cut and sew the material. "It was terribly hot, and you didn't feel like taking all your clothes off and getting other clothes on," admitted Kerr.

Characteristically shy, Williams poked his head around the front door, his eyes adjusting to the light.

At first, Kerr didn't recognize Williams because he had grown a beard. But the thick eyeglasses and sweet voice were unmistakable. "I remember he came in and made some very complimentary remarks about Deborah," said Viertel. After fifteen minutes, Williams said his goodbyes and left. "He thought the outfit was great," said Kerr, clearly flattered by the attention. They planned to see each other again on the beach.

In the afternoon, Williams went swimming in the ocean at Hotel Playa de Oro. On the shore sat Burton and Taylor drinking two rum punches. The film's cast and crew, who regularly convened there, dubbed it "Hotel Iguana." Once in the water, Williams was so intent on his backstroke that he didn't notice the couple until later. "Oh, look!" Taylor giggled. "Tennessee is wearing a bathing cap. I'm amazed he doesn't have one on his beard!"

Ava Gardner and Sydney Guilaroff presently joined them. They were wearing Jantzen swimsuits and carried two beach towels. Taylor said "You know, Ava, you love to water-ski. You ought to go waterskiing. Maybe you'd enjoy it."

"Why don't *you* go waterskiing?" Gardner responded.

Taylor raised her blouse and turned to Gardner, revealing an ugly surgical scar that ran halfway down her back. "I can't water-ski," she said. "If I could I would."

"I'm sorry, Elizabeth," apologized Gardner. "It's a good idea. I think I'll try it." She got up and walked to a spot on the beach where several boatmen were talking with each other.

A few minutes later a speedboat whizzed by the shore, sounding its horn. The driver was pulling Gardner behind the boat on two wooden skis. Her right hand was clutching the boat's towline, and in her left hand was a half-filled highball glass. Taylor stood up, laughing, and waved to Gardner. "I don't believe it!" said Guilaroff with a look of astonishment.

The speedboat sped past Williams, who was still paddling in the water, and then it made a large circle, turned around and headed back to the beach.

That evening, there was a Mexican fiesta complete with spicy tacos, salt-rimmed margaritas and strolling mariachis. Williams joined the two couples for dinner in the hotel restaurant, which he described as "a small Trader Vic's," where they reminisced with each other. The combination of twilight and tequila created a warm glow.

After dessert, a six-piece band played a selection of tunes. Williams sent a message to the musicians, asking them if they knew a particular song. When they answered affirmatively, the tipsy playwright took Burton aside.

The two men excused themselves from the table and a short time later, Burton's voice could be heard over the public-address system. "Ladies and gentlemen," he announced, "tonight, for your special enjoyment, the Hotel Iguana is proud to present the one and only Miss Rose Tattoo!" There was polite clapping from the diners, several of whom turned their heads in the direction of the bandstand.

The lively percussive strains of a popular ballad, *South of the Border*, which had been made famous several years earlier by Frank Sinatra, resonated throughout the room. Miss Rose, a smiling bearded woman in a red wig, black cocktail dress and high heels sauntered onto the stage, evoking snickers from the audience. She took the microphone, and on the downbeat began singing in a falsetto voice:

South of the border, down Mexico way
That's where I fell in love, when the stars above came out to play
And now as I wander, my thoughts ever stray
South of the border, down Mexico way

Miss Rose sashayed over to James Ward's table and sang directly to him.

He was a picture in old Spanish lace
Just for a tender while, I kissed a smile upon his face
'cause it was fiesta, and we were so gay
South of the border, Mexico way

The audience, which included Grayson Hall, was convulsed with laughter. Miss Rose strolled to another table, picked up a white linen napkin and waved it in the air.

Then he smiled as he whispered "manana"
Never dreaming that we were parting
And I lied as I whispered "manana"
'cause our tomorrow never came

Then she grabbed the arm of a passing waiter and motioned him to the ground. The startled man knelt before Miss Rose like she was a Madonna and looked up at the odd face.

South of the border, I jumped back one day
There in a veil of white by the candle light he knelt to pray
The mission bells told me that I mustn't stay
South of the border, Mexico way

At the song's conclusion, the audience whistled and cheered. Miss Rose took a bow and exited the stage. Nowadays, female impersonators are a common sight in Puerto Vallarta, vamping and lip-syncing to popular songs. But in 1963, when Tennessee Williams appeared as Miss Rose, the sight of drag queens or *travestis*, as they are referred to in Mexico, was a rarity.

The next morning, Williams awoke in his hotel room with a hangover. While Nicklaus took Gigi for a walk, Williams studied a mimeographed copy of the screenplay with Huston's penciled notations. Privately the director conceded there were problems with the script. Chief among them was the relationship between Shannon and Charlotte. Determined to improve the script, Williams popped pills and consumed half a bottle of whisky and vodka, which he hoped would relight the extinguished spark of his creativity. The results, given his lack of sobriety, were wildly uneven.

The inspiration for one essential though problematic scene – a parallel between Shannon's martyrdom and Christ's suffering – was an accident. The original scene, as written, never made a lot of sense. "The situation was good," commented Huston of Charlotte's attempt to make love to Shannon "but the dialogue didn't work. Burton was in his hotel room and she comes in to see him surreptitiously. She wants him to make love to her and he resists. He's shaving and there's a whiskey bottle on a shelf."

Williams was busily typing when his arm knocked over a martini glass and it shattered on the floor. When Nicklaus bent down to pick up the fragments, Williams warned him not to step on the shards of glass. It was a moment of divine intervention.

"Yesterday I made myself popular by re-writing a scene for Burton and Sue Lyon which everyone liked," said Williams, referring to the moment when Charlotte startles Shannon and he bumps the whiskey bottle, which falls and breaks on the floor. While strongly rebuking her, he accidentally walks barefoot on the broken pieces of the decanter. She takes off her shoes and follows him in a kind of painful exhilaration.

"It just lifted the scene on to another sphere," commented Huston. His enthusiastic response boosted Williams' confidence, if only temporarily.

"Today I'm re-writing the ending which had been sentimentalized," he said, describing the film's conclusion, which Huston changed from the play.

"Williams saw the Reverend Shannon as a broken man, destroyed finally by Maxine," explained Lawrence Grobel. "But John saw the Ava Gardner character as providing Shannon with his salvation. It seemed more fitting and uplifting." Williams, however, intended the last scene to be straightforward and to the point. "I'm trying to replace the sentimentality with some more honest emotion."

Armed with the rewritten scene, Williams was in good spirits when he attended a script conference that night with Stark and Huston at Casa Tabachin. However, any goodwill between them and Williams evaporated as the session dragged on into the wee small hours without a suitable resolution. "I am not convinced that this ending is right," said Huston, leafing through the new pages. "But John," argued Williams, "it's the destiny of these characters for their lives to end in purgatory. There is no other way."

"Nonsense!" roared Huston. "I am not leaving this room until we have a better ending."

Williams took off his glasses and rubbed his eyes.

"Maybe Tennessee has a point," said Stark. "The characters still die in the end but they die with a smile, right?"

Williams sighed in exasperation. "Shannon is doomed, John, even you cannot redeem him."

Huston became so angry he almost swallowed his cigar. "This film is my redemption for all the years I spent in limbo. Everything I have is riding on its success. There won't be another chance."

"Don't you think you're taking this too personally, John?" asked Stark. "After all, the play was very successful the way Tennessee wrote it."

"There's no denying that," said Huston. "But our audience is much bigger than any theatre. Maxine is a wonderful character. She's smart and sexy. But at the end she turns into a monster and devours Shannon. It's ridiculous. Moviegoers won't accept it."

Stark turned to Williams. "You and I both know the movie business. The name of the game is entertainment. We have to please the public, for the sake of our jobs if nothing else."

Williams laughed sarcastically. "And what about the truth?"

Huston pointed his finger at him. "I'll tell you the truth. I think you see women as your rivals. Face up to it. You don't want a woman to have a place in the love life of a man. That's why you chose to do this with Maxine. You've been unjust to your own creation!" There was embarrassed silence. Then Williams snatched up the pages and left the room.

It was almost 5 a.m. when Williams arrived back at the Hotel Rio with the scene changes rolled up in his pocket. He was drunk and couldn't find the keys to his room. As he stood banging on the door, Gigi started barking. Nicklaus, who was half asleep, unlatched the door and Williams staggered inside the room. In his confusion he accidentally kicked Gigi. The dog squealed and ran out to the terrace.

Helen Lawrenson was sleeping in the room below Williams, when she was awakened by the sound of Gigi falling from the overhead railing and landing on her balcony with a terrified yelp. She took the dazed pet into the kitchen and gave it a bowl of water.

The next day, there was more drama when Gigi escaped from the hotel, sending Williams into a blind panic. After running up and down the beach, yelling his pet's name, Williams discovered Gigi being humped on the sand by a black Labrador. In tears, he carried her back to the hotel. Nicklaus bathed the soiled animal while Williams sat on the bed, drinking vodka. "Oh Frankie," he cried. "I am so tense, I need a sedative." Nicklaus bristled at the mention of Merlo's name. "My name is not Frankie. It's Freddy!" he insisted. "Yes, I know," slurred Williams. "I'm sorry, baby."

The following morning, Williams showered, dressed and packed his bags. Then the morose dramatist took a taxi to the airport with Nicklaus and Gigi in the backseat. What caused their abrupt departure? "Williams was unhappy about the film script changes that beefed up Sue Lyon's role and tenderized the part played by Ava Gardner," speculated Richard Oulahan in *Life* magazine.

Huston and Williams had never seen eye to eye on the script, despite their best attempts to modify it. Lawrence Grobel theorized that Williams' homosexuality was the cause of the rift. Nobody took into consideration that Williams was heartbroken over the loss of his former partner and was extremely vulnerable to criticism at that low point in his life.

When informed of Williams' hasty exit, Ray Stark became apoplectic. Clarence Eurist searched the empty hotel room but found nothing. He assumed that Williams must have taken the script revisions with him – only Williams hadn't. He left the typed pages on the kitchen table. Unaware of their importance, the hotel maid, who did not speak English, threw the sheets of paper in the trash. The missing pages were lost and so was the opportunity for greatness.

Stark sent an urgent message to screenwriter Anthony Veiller in Los Angeles, instructing him to take the next plane to Puerto Vallarta.

Veiller was reminded of his continued dependence on Huston. Although Stark provided a three-story house with a rooftop *palapa* and a Jeep, Veiller still resented being dragged away from his wife, Grace Rowley, which is why he insisted she accompany him. Even so, Veiller must have felt he was being taken advantage of, since it was Huston's habit to extract as many ideas as possible from his writing partners, while always taking half the credit.

PART FOUR:

HOLLYWOOD ON THE ROCKS

"John Huston is a simpleton."

– Richard Burton

IN *THE NIGHT OF THE IGUANA*, the bus that Richard Burton steals and drives to Mismaloya is symbolic of his character's mental condition – unstable and about to break down. The bus stalls going up a hill, the reverse gear has worn out, and the emergency brake no longer functions. Such were the variable mechanics of Mexican buses at that time. These clanking vehicles often bore the names of sweethearts or loved ones inscribed on the windshield.

Above the driver's instrument panel was a small ornamental figure of Guadalupe or Christ on the cross. There might be a bronzed baby shoe, several Saint Christopher medals, and other good luck charms hanging from the overhead mirror. These totemic objects conveyed the same unspoken message: Trust in God.

Similarly, actors in need of guidance trusted in the almighty John Huston. Mesmerized by his rhetoric, they underwent a spiritual conversion and became his faithful disciples. "Certainly, he is in absolute command on this particular location," affirmed Richard Burton. "His word is law, and I approve of that very strongly." That law was rigorously obeyed by the film's 130 personnel, who gathered on this remote strip of the Pacific coastline.

The crew had been shooting scenes in and around Puerto Vallarta for more than two weeks. Now, impatient to get on with the business at hand, they awaited Huston's next command.

As summer gradually changed to autumn, the date of departure to the film's second location arrived: Friday, October 18, 1963. One by one the film's cast gathered near El Dorado restaurant on Playa Los Muertos to make the fateful journey to Mismaloya – their shared dominion until the end of November.

Huston was typically the first person on the set and the last to leave it. That day was no exception. Looking spruce in a white linen suit and brown leather moccasins, Huston and his girlfriend Zoë Sallis sat on a tartan picnic blanket, playing with their son Danny, who was learning to walk.

The first cast member to arrive on the beach was Deborah Kerr in a pink-and-white check shirt, blue jeans and sandshoes. She was accompanied by Peter Viertel, wearing an apricot-colored polo shirt and beige slacks that toned with his short blonde hair. The couple strolled past the resort wear shops selling French bikinis, Bermuda shorts and Hawaiian flip-flops.

Snowy-haired actor Cyril Delevanti, his bony armature covered in a white cotton shirt, gray Angora sweater and fawn-colored slacks, joined the couple on the beach, where he smoked a Camel cigarette. Delevanti, age seventy-five, had flown from Los Angeles one week earlier in preparation for his role as the ancient poet. Conforming to Aztec beliefs, he was the oldest and last deity to arrive for the Teotleco festival.

More film players gradually came into view: Grayson Hall in an orange sundress and dark tortoiseshell sunglasses, James Ward in a sport shirt, plaid madras shorts and black wayfarer sunglasses, and Sue Lyon in a peach-colored cotton top, matching stretch pants and plastic thongs, her shoulder-length blonde mane pulled back behind an elastic headband. Holding Lyon's hand was her boyfriend Hampton Fancher in a white tee-shirt, chinos and sneakers.

All heads turned toward Ava Gardner, who was accompanied by a slim-waisted Mexican man. She was wearing a strawberry-colored blouse, striped Capri pants and Japanese sandals.

The last actors to show up were Burton with Elizabeth Taylor, both tanned and smiling like two Wimbledon tennis players. He wore a blue silk shirt and white pants, while she had on a pink headscarf and purple blouse and slacks with a turquoise beaded necklace.

Looming over the sand was the modernistic architecture of the Hotel Tropicana, which seemed strangely out of place between the traditional Mexican-style bars and restaurants. The radical-shaped structure was symbolic of the city's culture clash – one style competing against the other.

A gaggle of American and European tourists crowded the shore, taking photographs of the stars with their pocket cameras. Unlike the shouting fans of today, these privileged onlookers were too timid to ask for autographs – they merely stood there in hushed reverence.

In the same way that circuses have clowns to entertain the crowd, so carnivals provide an amusing sideshow. Like a scene from a Fellini movie, several muscular young men with pompadour hairdos and wearing imitation leopard and zebra-print bikinis, pranced and posed for a group of aging female admirers who sat under a *palapa* drinking Bloody Marys.

The pixilated women laughed and giggled like schoolgirls at the sight of gyrating hips, clenched buttocks and wriggling torsos. Taylor gently steered Burton away from this tawdry exhibition, but he turned back in bemused fascination. "Everyone seems to turn queer down here," he remarked. "I hope it's not catching."

Then, mimicking a philharmonic conductor about to lead his orchestra from the podium, Huston walked out into the sun. Bowing courteously, cigar firmly in mouth, he showed everyone the way by rolling up his trousers and wading barefoot into the ocean. Under cloudless skies, with elegant brown terns and white and gray gulls hovering overhead, the cast bravely followed Huston's example.

The powerful undertow was an intimidating experience for those present, many of whom were unused to the ocean's ebb and flow. Wading into the swell, Kerr nearly lost her balance but was caught by Viertel. Lyon sank up to her thighs, gasping at the water's coldness, and clung to Fancher, while Hall joined hands with Ward and boldly took their first steps into the foaming sea.

Smiling men in canoes and rowboats extended their arms and hauled the wet actors above the waves, lifting them into the bow and stern of the bobbing vessels. The fear of drowning was very real. Just the week before, a lifeless body had been pulled from the surf. The deceased was not a tourist as expected but a local who had met with a misadventure. "I am absolutely terrified I am going to fall into the sea," Kerr told Viertel, "or get my foot crushed or some other horror."

One after the other, the small flotilla set out in a westerly direction, paddling furiously against the incoming tide. Various motorboats lay at anchor in the deep water: the high-speed launch, *Taffy*, which had been Taylor's gift to Burton; a modern fishing boat, *Bonito*, renamed *Lolita* in honor of Lyon; and two commuter ferryboats, painted red and green, for the remaining cast and crew. For their first crossing, Kerr, Viertel and Delevanti boarded an elegant vessel with teakwood decks named *Santa Maria*. Gardner chose a fast speedboat, dubbed *Ava*. Her aquatic chauffeur, a Yaqui Indian named Ramón, kept the icebox stocked with beer, tequila, and gin.

All the boats flew the national flags of their respective countries: The United States, Canada, Mexico, even the Dominican Republic. The colorful spectacle resembled the starting line of an international yacht race. Huston raised his arm from the stern of a rolling cabin cruiser and fired a racing pistol into the air. The loud shot rang out across the bay and the boats set off, horns and sirens blaring, for the twenty-five-minute ride to Mismaloya.

Eight miles away, half a dozen pleasure crafts filled with cheering expatriates waited near Los Arcos for the winners to cross the finishing line.

Today, the luxury Barceló all-inclusive resort occupies the northern stretch of Playa Mismaloya, while to the south are lines of palm-thatched restaurants and beachside kiosks with waiters taking lunch orders. Things were not that way in 1963 – there were only a few grass huts on the beach.

Wooden dugouts were the sole mode of water transportation. *Pescadores* or fishermen paddled out from the shore with their nets to catch snapper, mackerel, and tuna, or went diving with wooden spears to depths of sixty and eighty feet in search of large grouper, sea turtles and octopus.

It was into this antediluvian time warp that Huston's fleet sailed that glorious day. "Oh, look!" cried Hall, on seeing three bottlenose dolphins racing ahead of her speeding boat, the bow awash in ocean spray.

In the far distance, creating the effect of a heavenly cathedral above the horizon, were brilliant shafts of light illuminating thick sheets of falling rain. "The jungle comes right down to sea level," marveled Delevanti at the thick vegetation along the coastline. "I've never seen that before."

The event was not only a social occasion, it was a historic one. Wondrously, this modern voyage coincided with the Aztec ceremony for Tepeilhuitl, Feast of the Mountains. In ancient times, these festivities were marked with offerings at shrines and sacrifices on mountaintops. Among those honored deities were the powerful mountain gods Popocatepetl, Ixtaccihuatl, and Matlalcueye, along with the rain gods Tlaloc and Tepictoton, who brought nourishment and fertility to the earth. There had been a time, long past, when such cults were worshiped even in Mismaloya. Mat-makers prayed to Nappatecuhtli and fisherman gave thanks to Opochtli. Turpentine makers bowed down to Zapotlantenan, and weavers, embroiderers and painters knelt before dough effigies of Xochiquetzal.

Now, in the presence of Hollywood, villagers who had never seen an ancient god came to see a modern one.

The first part of the Hollywood armada to reach the cove was Burton and Taylor aboard the *Taffy*. In second place was the *Ava*, followed, a few moments later, by the *Lolita*. Everyone transferred from the boats into canoes which rowed them ashore. Standing in seawater up to their ankles, the cast looked as if they had been shipwrecked on a desert island. “I think this calls for a drink,” said Burton, squeezing the water out of his pants leg. “That’s a splendid idea,” agreed Taylor. Then Gardner turned to Huston and implored: “Where’s the goddamned bar?”

Grinning from behind his cigar, Huston escorted the actors towards a gravel pathway leading from the beach to the jetty, where bare-chested men were unloading wooden crates from a supply boat. “They had a wharf and a small road that went all the way up to the set from the wharf,” recalled Robert “Bud” Acord, who was a groundskeeper on the set. “Down near the water, to the left after you got off the dock was the restaurant dining area covered with palapas, and to the right was the bar.”

Gardner dropped her wet shoes on the sand and sprinted ahead. Burton and Taylor followed her, whooping and whistling with delight. Perhaps sensing that his thirsty cast would be more pliable after a few drinks under their belts, Huston had spared no expense on giving them a first-class watering hole – the equal of any New York saloon or London tavern. Even a Hollywood special effects wizard could not have created a more perfect illusion.

There it stood, gleaming in the sunlight like Chasen’s – the white-and-green canopied-restaurant that was a fixture in Beverly Hills for almost sixty years. The new establishment was a wonderful achievement, honed entirely out of the sloping jungle.

A huge umbrella-shaped *palapa*, made from three types of local timber and covered with palm fronds, functioned as the roof. Spread out beneath the palms was two dozen sets of restaurant chairs and tables, covered with white linen tablecloths, water glasses and silverware.

Short trails connected the dining area to the kitchen and restrooms, which were fenced off with vertical screens of fresh-cut *carrizo* wood. The entire perimeter was adorned with tropical shrubbery – flowering red and yellow hibiscus, orange-and-red-plumed *pico de loro* or parrot's beak, and blooming red ginger. Nailed to a palm trunk, was a painted sign: THE IGUANA CAFÉ.

Under a second palapa was the eatery's centerpiece: a long-polished bar carved from *tampiciran*, native cedar, surrounded by rows of high-backed wooden chairs with padded seats. The furniture was arranged on a patio, encased in horizontal *chinillo* railings and lashed together with *quamecete* vines. "Sort of like an elegant, more upscale version of the Swiss Family Robinson," Burton quipped upon seeing it. The shelves of the bar were stocked with imported liquor: Johnnie Walker Red Label Whisky, Beefeater Dry Gin, Smirnoff Vodka, and Bacardi White Rum, along with various brandies and liqueurs: Grand Marnier, Kahlúa, Drambuie, Cointreau, Benedictine, and Pernod.

Gardner sat with Taylor and Burton, while Kerr and Viertel occupied the adjacent seats. "Bienvenidos amigos," said the bartender with a welcoming smile.

After a few minutes, Huston sidled up to the bar. "So, kids, how do you like it?" he inquired.

"You've really outdone yourself this time," said Kerr, sipping a tall glass of beer.

"It's wonderful," grinned Taylor, savoring the taste of a margarita.

"Well," said Huston. "Just so you don't too get tired running up and down the hill, I also had them build another bar next to the set."

Gardner raised her martini glass. "I hereby christen this joint Hollywood on the Rocks."

"I'll drink to that," said Burton, downing a Campari with vodka and soda.

On a typical Hollywood film made in the Sixties, the average daily expenditure was $30,000 – a trifling amount when compared with today's high production costs but a considerable expense for that time. An idle film crew standing around waiting for the director and actors typically cost $5,000 per hour, whether anything was filmed or not.

Huston didn't believe in burning a producer's money on such wasteful extravagance. He liked to get his actors in the mood before they walked onto the set. "So far as directing the actors and the crew is concerned," he explained, "I direct just as little as possible, and I get as much from others as I possibly can."

That involved letting the actors get into character by any method, whether it was drinking alcohol or taking other chemical stimulants. "He didn't give a shit," said assistant director Tom Shaw. "He never bothered them. He'd never say anything about that. He might be as drunk as they were." But if Huston was under the influence it never showed, even if his actors might have trouble remembering their lines.

"Otra mas?" asked the Iguana Café bartender, inquiring if the famous guests seated before him wanted another round of drinks.

"Sure," said Gardner. "Fill 'em up, baby."

For this choice group of actors, many of whom had intimate knowledge of each other, it was like a high school reunion. At the same time, Huston took advantage of their closeness to plug the film for a selected group of American journalists who had been invited to Mismaloya to witness the cast in a round-table-reading of the script.

"Ladies and gentlemen," announced Huston. "I give you the cast of *The Night of the Iguana*!"

While the stars posed with friendly smiles, Huston declared to the assembled journalists, "I plunked these people down together, and they have to live their parts twenty-four hours a day." There followed the rapid popping of flashbulbs and clicking of camera shutters.

Although everyone assumed that Burton and Taylor had first met on the set of *Cleopatra*, they had, in fact, known each other for ten years. Their paths first crossed at a cocktail party at the Bel-Air home of the British leading man Stewart Granger and his actress-wife Jean Simmons.

In those days, Hollywood, like Puerto Vallarta, was a fish bowl. "For one thing, Elizabeth and I were friends from the old Metro days," remarked Gardner, who was Taylor's former screen rival. "It's like we were two graduates from the same alma mater, pleased to find each other in the wilderness."

Deborah Kerr felt the same way. She had been a Metro star during Taylor and Gardner's tenure, and was friendly with both actresses. Huston and Gardner's lives were also intertwined.

Early in her career, Gardner costarred with Burt Lancaster in *The Killers*, which was scripted by Huston and Anthony Veiller. By the time Gardner made *The Sun Also Rises*, the new man on her arm was Peter Viertel, who collaborated with Huston on the screenplays for *We Were Strangers* and *The African Queen*. Then Viertel met and fell in love with Kerr.

Reporters marveled at the extraordinary coincidences that had brought these people together. "I was delighted to see Richard again," remembered Kerr, who had first made Burton's acquaintance some four years earlier. Now, they were imbibing at the same table. "Elizabeth was there too, with her devastating turquoise black-fringed eyes, Ava warm and friendly but very nervous, and Sue Lyon looking much more grown up than when I met her briefly in London when she was doing *Lolita*."

The coincidences didn't stop there. To add to the sense of mystery, Gardner's second husband, the swing era bandleader Artie Shaw, was currently married to actress Evelyn Keyes, who had been Huston's third wife. The insinuation, which the media seemed to be making, was that love and sex knew no boundaries. But Gardner wasn't having any of it. "For the moment, I'm thinking just how marvelous it is to be here," she told reporters. "It's quiet. Almost no one bothers you. You can sit on the beach in town and have privacy." And with that well-chosen remark, publicist Ernie Anderson thanked the press for coming and escorted them back to the boats.

THEN AS NOW, PUERTO VALLARTA boasted one of the most diverse tropical and subtropical forests in the world. It is the natural habitat of fifty endangered species of mammals, including the white-tailed deer, boar, gray fox, jaguar, ocelot, margay, white-nosed coati, nocturnal badger, nine-banded armadillo, ghost bat and marsh mouse, along with hundreds of varieties of birds and reptiles.

While John Huston entertained the press, which had been invited by producer Ray Stark to watch the first day of filming in Mismaloya, a chorus of military macaws with their distinctive red and blue markings, along with green parrots and orange-fronted parakeets, squawked from the treetops of the adjoining mountain plateau.

Below this aviary choir, fifty American and Mexican technicians stood around the veranda of the Costa Verde Hotel, reachable by a strenuous climb up 134 steps, which had been hacked out of the cliff.

Some of the men were balanced on stepladders – aiming heavy arc lights called "brutes" at the hotel doorway where Ava Gardner and her dancing beach boys would make their entrance.

Using an incident light meter with a flat disc receptor, cinematographer Gabriel Figueroa measured the key light or main light, setting it at forty-foot candles – the standard level of light intensity.

For this reading he pointed his meter at the source of the light, not the camera. He then instructed the two key grips Karl Reed and Antonio Mendoza to make changes to improve the illumination.

Figueroa wanted to get everything in deep focus, so the set would appear more three-dimensional on screen. Standing behind the Mitchell 35-millimeter movie camera, he took a black-and-white contrast viewing glass that hung on a cord around his neck and held it up to his left eye momentarily to gauge the level of brightness on the actors' faces. Burton and Gardner's stand-ins, Nicolas Zarate and Angela Rodriguez, who were the same height and coloring as the actors, substituted for them during these tests.

Because much of the set was covered in shadow from the overhanging jungle, Figueroa deployed some auxiliary lighting, called "fill lights," which filled the dark areas and lifted them out of the black. He then took a second light reading by switching from a flat disc incident light to an incident meter with a hemisphere which read all the light that struck the meter.

Watching from behind the jumble of electrical cables was Figueroa's twelve year-old-son Gabriel Figueroa Flores, who had joined his father on the inaccessible location. He looked up at yellow-winged caciques making suspended nests in the trees. Red and gold-headed woodpeckers were boring into the tree bark and golden silk spiders spinning webs between the branches.

Below, on the rocks were small alligator lizards with triangular heads and striped basilisk lizards with tiny helmets resembling reptilian soldiers. For Flores, who marveled at such incredible sights, spending time in the jungle came as a revelation. "It was," he remembered, "a poetic experience."

The crew, however, was oblivious to the wonders of nature. Their eyes were preoccupied by the movement of the sun, the position of the movie camera, or checking the script.

Throughout this lengthy process, Gardner rested in her dressing room. She was seated in a portable makeup chair in front of a table with a large mirror, her famous swan-like neck and shoulders covered in a beige-colored poncho shirt, which hung loosely over elasticized black leggings. From her short earlobes dangled a pair of crescent-shaped gold earrings. In her manicured hands were a glass of vodka and a Marlboro cigarette.

Standing behind Gardner, holding a tortoiseshell brush and comb, was the hairstylist Sydney Guilaroff. He was wearing a short sleeve manila shirt, navy-blue pants and black slip-ons. After many years shampooing famous clients in his air-conditioned beauty salon, the prospect of styling hair on a stone slab on the fringes of the jungle crawling with insects must have filled him with consternation. If so, he never uttered a word of complaint.

As Guilaroff gazed into the mirror, Gardner applied her own lipstick and added a little mascara to her eyelashes, then powdered down. But she was still puffy around the eyes, the result of heavy drinking. "For god sakes, Sydney," she moaned. "I look like a scrubwoman." Guilaroff brushed and teased her hair while smiling at her reflection with the deep abiding love that exists between two close friends. "I'm not responsible for the costumes," he said reproachfully, "only your hair."

Gardner sighed with resignation. She picked up a bottle of 4711 Eau de Cologne and sprayed it on her skin. "Louis B. Mayer would never have allowed me to look like this."

"Absolutely not," said Guilaroff, affecting a European accent. "Not at M-G-M!"

They both laughed. He grabbed her hair and pulled it back into a tight ponytail. "Ouch!" she cried. "I'm sorry, darling," he apologized.

After checking the camera equipment, the moment of truth arrived.

On a nod from Figueroa, the second assistant director Terry Morse went to Gardner's dressing room and rapped his knuckles on the door. "Ready on the set," he announced. Gardner finished her vodka and got up from the table. Guilaroff opened the door with the finesse of a butler and she regally swept past him. He loved the way she walked, taking long elegant strides, only this time Gardner was not wearing high heels or even slippers. She was totally barefoot!

Gardner walked out onto the hotel verandah and paced back and forth like a tiger in front of the crew. Then Figueroa asked her to stand in the doorway and Gardner obeyed him, because she knew that he literally held her beauty in his hands. "Let's look at you in the light," he said. Figueroa took a Weston light meter and held it up to her face to measure the brightness and intensity of the light. The reading from the light meter indicated what adjustments in the camera's aperture or shutter speed might be needed in order to get the best possible exposure.

Figueroa ordered some more lighting adjustments so that Gardner's delicately worn features would appear softer against the mottled stonework and pointed greenery. When he was satisfied with the results, Figueroa looked at Huston, who was waiting to commence filming.

Twenty feet away, Huston sat in a director's canvas chair with his name stenciled on the back. He smiled at Figueroa, who made a circle with his index finger and thumb, signaling "OK."

Sitting next to Huston in another chair was Emilio Fernández, with his name painted on the armrest. He tapped a fresh cigarette from a packet of Delicados and scratched an all-purpose striking match against the chair leg. The red phosphorus match head ignited with a blue spark and he lit the rolled paper between his thick lips with the bright orange flame.

The sound mixer Basil Fenton-Smith, who was sitting at his veneered sound mixing console on the other side of the set, heard the crackle of the match on his headphones.

He glanced over at Armando Bolanos, the sound man, and Octavio Morones, the boom operator, who controlled the overhead microphone that hovered like a giant fishing pole above the set.

The sensitive microphone could pick up the rustle of wind in the trees and the approach of footsteps on the ground. Fenton-Smith adjusted the volume on his meter by turning the round knobs on the Bakelite control panel.

The assistant director Tom Shaw, who was accustomed to exercising his authority hollered: "Silence!" Huston lifted up his head and called "Roll 'em!" Seconds later Figueroa's camera operator Manuel González flipped a switch on the Mitchell camera. When the director could see the whirring mechanism of the apparatus, which was housed in a soundproof blimp, he made the welcome long-awaited pronouncement: "Action!"

Slowly, Burton staggered up the hill. He was perspiring heavily through his long-sleeved collar band shirt and khaki pants and struggled to maintain his balance on the uneven trail in his suede desert boots. In his dirty hands was an automotive distributor head, which he had wrenched from the engine of the bus on the beach, so that the angry driver Hank, played by James Ward, could not speed away.

The crew watched Burton's mannered Stratford-on-Avon performance with fascination. Standing on the periphery of the set were still photographers Josh Weiner and Gabriel Torres, who were taking publicity shots that would later be sent to newspapers and magazines.

Bud Acord was on hand for the beginning of shooting. He recounted the filming of that memorable scene. "Burton walks up to the hotel and announces grandly: 'Hey Maxine, I'm back!' Ava comes out onto the terrace and says: 'Fuck you, Shannon!' Then she goes back to her dressing room, which was located behind the kitchen out of the camera's range. 'Cut!' yells Huston. 'We'll do it again.' They did another take and Burton calls out in his marvelous English voice: 'Maxine I'm back!'

"Gardner says to Huston: 'I can't come on this way with him!' and storms off to her dressing room," continued Acord. "They did the scene a third time and Gardner pleads with Huston: 'For god's sake, tell him to come down, he's way up there in Shakespeare land!' Finally Burton crawls up the hill and says meekly: 'Maxine, it's me Shannon, I'm back.' Gardner smiles and says: 'I've missed you Shannon!' Relieved, Huston called out: 'Cut! Print it!'"

The crew applauded. Gardner, as everyone knew from her frequent tirades, hated acting. She was a spontaneous performer. Burton, on the other hand, was a consummate actor, schooled in the classics. He relied on his formal training. They were communicating on two various levels. After that minor disagreement, the actors adjusted their performances and the movie found it's relaxed pace.

Standing on the sidelines was Elizabeth Taylor, modeling a provocative assortment of St. Tropez beachwear and applying pink lipstick from a makeup case in her Chanel handbag. Burton could never take his eyes off her; neither could anyone else.

One morning, Taylor was barely covered in a loose top and bikini bottom of sheer white batiste trimmed with red embroidery. "She had no bra on," recalled Thelda Victor, who played one of the schoolteachers, "and you literally could see the complete upper structure." Taylor was there, as everybody knew, to protect her Welsh investment.

Although it seemed improbable that Burton would stray, his sexual threat was apparent to everyone, especially Gardner, whom Victor commented was "livelier and lovelier around him."

In a weak moment, Gardner told Taylor: "Richard is the man I should have married. If you hadn't got him I certainly would have tried to get him."

Burton himself gave Taylor something to ponder after playing his first scene with Gardner. "She gave me that old tingle," he bragged to Taylor, arousing her jealousy.

Taylor wasn't worried if some of the female crew members such as costume designer Dorothy Jeakins or Huston's script supervisor Angela Allen flirted with Burton or he with them; that was all in wholesome fun. But she intended that Gardner, who was a three times married divorcée, keep a respectable distance. "The press was not just covering a congregation of some of the world's greatest talents and personalities in a remote Mexican village," said biographers Sam Kashner and Nancy Schoenberger, "they were waiting – hoping? – that Burton and Taylor's vaunted love affair might founder on Ava Gardner's dangerous shoulders."

Could Gardner steal Burton from Taylor? It was a ludicrous suggestion, most likely concocted by an overzealous newspaper man – or woman. But many city desk editors with a hankering for a delightful story gave the idea credence by running it on their front pages. To be fair, Burton may have done the dirty with Gardner if circumstances were different, even though he had pledged his love to Taylor. Just the same, she was not taking any chances.

Like Cleopatra, Taylor was a first-class seductress, who knew how to catch a man and keep him. She had already exerted her strong influence over Burton, forbidding him from being photographed with Sue Lyon, lest their appearance together be misconstrued as proof of a romantic involvement. Now she would do the same thing with Burton and Gardner, censoring his interviews and preventing any opportunity for incriminating photographs.

What to say and when to say it, was a lesson Taylor had learned at the beginning of her career. Ever since she was a smiling debutante, Taylor had fielded questions about her love life with the slickness of a politician. She needed to be that smart if she was going to keep her latest accusers at bay.

"Elizabeth was really a fallen woman," said Acord. "Maybe she was a little frightened and intimidated about her predicament which is why she wanted to be with Burton in Mexico."

Even though most of the newspapers treated Burton and Taylor's romance with frivolous indulgence, there were serious legal and moral implications arising from the couple's illicit union. "After all, they were infamously cohabiting, still technically married to other people," stated Kashner and Schoenberger. "In 1963, that was still shocking, but the public couldn't get enough of it."

Each day, the crowded flight from Mexico City to Puerto Vallarta was packed with reporters from the United States and Europe armed with Olivetti portable typewriters. There were journalists from important publications such as *Life*, *Time*, *The Saturday Evening Post*, *The New Yorker*, *Esquire*, *Look*, *McCall's* and *Cosmopolitan*, along with writers from some of the country's leading newspapers: *The New York Times*, *New York Daily News*, *Los Angeles Times*, *Los Angeles Herald-Examiner*, *San Francisco Chronicle*, and *Pittsburgh Press* – to name a few of the nationwide deputation.

For experienced wire service correspondents like John Alius of United Press International and Morris Rosenberg of Associated Press, who made the long trek to Puerto Vallarta, it was a return to the fighting trenches, but for new recruits like Stan Hochman of the *Philadelphia Daily News* it was their initiation into the big-league. "It was my first assignment in the field," Hochman recounted, "and I honestly didn't know what to expect. Ernie Anderson was of tremendous help, introducing me around, and furnishing background material."

Across the Atlantic pond came representatives from London's *Evening Standard, Daily Express, Daily Mail* and *Daily Sketch.* "Writers from the *Ladies' Home Journal, Show* magazine, a London *Times* reporter and the BBC," noted Victor. "Everyone is here but the *Police Gazette.*" There were feature writers from the movie fan magazines *Photoplay, Modern Screen, Screen Stars, Movie Life, Silver Screen* and *Screen Stories,* along with delegates from various French, German, Italian and Spanish film journals – all eager to spin tales of romance and intrigue among the palm trees.

The influx of journalists was a huge boon for charter boat owners. A new fleet of thirty-two-foot, twenty-knot-per-hour, fishing cruisers with ship-to-shore radios were pressed into service to transport reporters and photographers from Puerto Vallarta to Mismaloya. Gleeful sightseers rented sixteen-foot speedboats outfitted with thirty-five-horsepower motors to take them to the film location. The twice-a-day dash, sometimes resulting in minor collisions, resembled a drunken regatta.

Without a coast guard or harbor patrol, the town's miniscule police force was powerless to control the chaotic situation. Assistant director Tom Shaw took to using a bullhorn to warn intruders away from the beach. "This is private property," he bellowed. "No trespassing allowed!" Few people heeded his announcements. Photographers camped out in the jungle or hid behind rocks, training their 300-millimeter telephoto lenses on the actors.

"Puerto Vallarta had seen nothing like it since the conquistadors had traipsed through four hundred years before," described Lee Server. "Most locals seemed to enjoy the excitement and the spike in commerce, but there were those who complained about the hedonistic ways of the foreign invaders." Even at the annual Cannes Film Festival, which was accustomed to displays of outré behavior from visiting stars and starlets, there had never been such shameless exhibitionism as the kind that occurred in Puerto Vallarta.

Every morning, boatloads of rowdy visitors crisscrossed Banderas Bay, angering local fishermen, whose nets became tangled in the suction of whirring propellers. In the afternoon, vessels returning to port narrowly missed getting hit by yachts of intoxicated revelers.

After the sun went down, there were bonfire parties on the beach that lasted until dawn. This unwanted disturbance, which inconvenienced commuters from other villages, who relied on the waterways for their livelihood, took place every day for three months.

At first everyone indulged the press, hoping they would go away. But with each crashing wave came another battalion of reporters asking more questions. Residents locked their doors and bolted windows against the onslaught of paparazzi and goggle-eyed tourists, who gathered on the beach in ever-increasing numbers. "The atmosphere," witnessed Deborah Kerr, "of 'no holds barred, anything goes, get drunk, smoke marijuana, behave outlandishly, nothing matters, nobody will see' is rather overwhelming." Luckily, for Kerr, she was not needed on the set until the following week and remained sequestered in her villa, learning Hannah's lines.

After several days of this forced confinement, Kerr's husband Peter Viertel decided to take his chances outside. Viertel got up from his typewriter, where he was putting the finishing touches to his latest novel. He grabbed his surfboard and announced: "I'm going after barracuda!"

THE SUDDEN RISE IN PUERTO Vallarta's population, which resulted from the making of *The Night of the Iguana*, caught village economists by surprise. Hotel rooms sold out, restaurants were emptied of food, and grocery stores stripped of beer, soap and toilet paper. Even fuel pumps went dry at the town's two gas stations. "It got to be a joke," recalled Helen Lawrenson, "that whatever you wanted, you couldn't get because it had all gone to Mismaloya." Overnight, a black market sprang up for hard liquor, soft drinks and cigarettes. There was a high demand for everything from toothpaste and aspirin to contraceptives.

What was totally unexpected was the rapid emergence of hard drugs and prostitution. Men and women, some of them as young as teenagers, participated in this illicit trade, selling locally produced cocaine and opium, as well as hallucinogenic drugs such as mushroom and peyote. The suppliers derived more income from one night's work than could be earned in a week of manual labor. The first seeds of monetary greed were sewn that busy tourist season, watered by a deluge of quick cash.

Competition for goods and services became rife among Vallarta's businessmen, whose friendly smiles hid glimmers of contempt for their foreign customers. Profiteering sprouted like weeds, never to be eradicated from the landscape.

Huston never anticipated this problem. Neither did the Mexican press who became huffy, according to Lawrenson, because it was not invited to Puerto Vallarta.

In revenge, newspapers started writing derogatory stories about the stars. Their accusations were based on secondhand accounts of wild orgies and drug-filled parties where some women went topless and a few men went bottomless. How the writers knew such intimate details without being there was not revealed.

There was one journalist, however, who had been keeping tabs on everyone since shooting of the movie started. His name was Raúl Velasco. He was, as yet, unknown but would go on to a distinguished career in television. His reporting was among the most comprehensive coverage of the film's production – from the arrival of each of the Hollywood stars in Mexico City to their final decamping in Puerto Vallarta. For three months, Velasco was a conduit for the Spanish-speaking reporters, as well as a few English-speaking journalists, whom he befriended in the village.

It was Velasco who first wrote about "beatniks and crazy women looking for the isolation of Puerto Vallarta to live in complete freedom" because he personally witnessed it. Velasco observed firsthand that "a group of undesirable American people are living here, and their immorality has scandalized the local people of the port, because the American women are always drinking and are all the time smoking marijuana, and the townspeople don't think this is a good example for their sons and daughters."

While set designer Stephen Grimes was in Mismaloya, his German girlfriend Cornelia frequented the bar of the Hotel Oceano, where she was seen dancing nude on the tables. But her indiscretions were not confined to the hotel. Beachgoers also witnessed the strange behavior of the white Aryan woman, dubbed Lady Godiva. "She rode a horse down the street with a whip in her hand and swastikas painted all over her body," remembered Bud Acord. "She really flipped out at that point. The owner of La Palapa went out to try and restrain her, she was just whipping the horse and it galloped down the beach. They ended up sending her back to Germany."

The shame that Grimes felt over the incident led to his early departure from Puerto Vallarta. He packed his bags and bid farewell to Huston. “See you in Rome,” said Grimes, whose next collaboration with Huston was *The Bible*.

While the American press chose to ignore such disreputable activities, the state run Mexican media was duty bound to report the misconduct of foreigners. The ruling Institutional Revolutionary Party (PRI) held firm control in Jalisco by fostering public distrust of any opposition to the government, and thus diverting attention away from its own corrupt administration.

The left-wing political newspaper, *Siempre*, which had been snubbed by Seven Arts, gave the filmmakers a savage mauling. “Mexico can still save Puerto Vallarta, whose people are being criminally despoiled of their land, their beaches, their way of life,” thundered the paper’s editorial.

“Mexican children of 10 and 15 are being introduced to sex, drinks, drugs, vice and carnal bestiality by the garbage of the United States: gangsters, nymphomaniacs, heroin-taking blondes,” accused the paper, which was read by outraged politicians, religious leaders and unionists.

At one bacchanal, the hostess, a woman in her sixties, took off her dress and pranced around the living room of the house in her underclothes, while similar diversions were enjoyed by guests in each of the bedrooms. “I must say that none of the stars was present at those festivities,” said Lawrenson, “although other members of the company were,” she added cryptically. Who, then, were these other unnamed members?

Was Huston among them? When asked to comment, he adopted the conciliatory tone of a diplomat, and quickly distanced himself from the questionable goings-on. “I have long since ceased to be disturbed by attacks from the press,” he responded. “And I am far too busy to spread any carnal bestiality.”

Huston, however, was a movie magician, well practiced in the art of sleight of hand. A director who hid his volcanic temperament under a well of equanimity, he also harbored a sadomasochistic streak. He could build up an actor's ego through careful flattery and seduction, or, if he felt displeased, destroy the actor's self-confidence through a slow, painful process of deprecation. That condemnation extended to his frequent mistreatment of women, some of whom were his wives and lovers.

Huston's friend Emilio Fernández was similarly inclined. "My father said the first time they went to see him at his place in Mexico City he was in the living room practicing the bullwhip on a cowering young girl," remembered Philip Veiller, the son of screenwriter Anthony Veiller. In his heyday, Fernández was known to pistol-whip slow-witted actors and interfering producers. Huston tried to make light of Fernández's actions. "Emilio's only weakness is his tendency to shoot people he doesn't like," stated Huston, who may or may not have been joking.

Fernández was very much in his element on the set of *The Night of the Iguana.* He chatted with the cast and crew about his filmmaking adventures and kept visitors entertained with bawdy tales about the men he had shot and the women he bedded. But after his fifth or sixth whiskey, he reverted to his outlaw ways. He pulled out a Colt .45 semi-automatic pistol and people fled from him in terror. At night, after the boats returned to Puerto Vallarta, he was often spotted prowling the streets, looking for someone to challenge in a duel or hoping to find a woman he could take back to his room at the Hotel Oceano.

When a London newspaper wired Vallarta's Telegraph Office for details of a news report that Fernández had killed two gringos in a gun battle, he was forced to explain himself before the local chief of police. Fernández swore he had not shot a man in seven years, but had merely knocked two tourists unconscious in a nightclub after they rudely asked a senorita to dance.

Whatever the true nature of the crimes and misdemeanors that were committed by members of the *Iguana* film company, producer Ray Stark was quick to set up damage control. In Mexico it is common practice for lawbreakers to give a *mordida* or bribe to officials rather than being taken to court. To make amends for any inconvenience caused by the film company to the community, Stark authorized the payment of $1,000 to the city. The gift was ostensibly to benefit a new kindergarten school being built in the Emiliano Zapata colony. Production manager Clarence Eurist personally presented the check to Puerto Vallarta Mayor Carlos Arreola Lima, and the event was gleefully recorded in the local papers.

RICHARD BURTON ALWAYS HAD a flair for the dramatic. "It's like bloody D-Day!" roared the actor from his vantage point on the set of *The Night of the Iguana* high atop Playa Mismaloya. Burton, as was his habit, had been bending the elbow since breakfast, consuming beer, champagne and tequila. As a consequence, he was reliving scenes from the highly-acclaimed movie *The Longest Day* – a full-size reenactment of the Allied invasion of Normandy, when nine army divisions, including three airborne and six infantry from the United States, Great Britain and Canada crossed the English Channel on five thousand ships under heavy clouds, landing on the coast of France.

Instead of 1,000 airplanes dropping camouflaged paratroopers, and amphibious craft depositing 130,000 armed troops into waist-deep water on five beaches, there were only two small planes and a dozen boats zooming around the bay of Mismaloya. Stretching across the beach, attached to two large poles sticking out from the sand, was a large canvas sign painted in big red letters, proclaiming: NO VISITORS.

Patrolling the southern perimeter was a surly young Mexican sentry, who was prone to finger pointing and raising his voice in an aggressive manner. His name was Pablo Albarran, and like many people working on the film, he was intimately acquainted with John Huston. In 1947, Albarran was a small boy living in Jungapeo, a tiny village in Michoacán, when he was legally adopted by Huston during the making of *The Treasure of the Sierra Madre.*

Now, Albarran was a thirty-year-old married man with three children. He was given temporary employment in the publicity department, working for Ernie Anderson and his secretary Virginia Lord.

Carrying a ballpoint pen and clipboard, it was Albarran's job to interrogate visitors to the set and turn away unwanted tourists. Lines of journalists filed past the sullen guard like soldiers reporting for duty. "Richard Oulahan, *Life* magazine!" announced the forty-five-year-old writer. Behind him a thirty-three-year-old voice called out "Dudley Doust, *Time*!" The men showed their press credentials and Albarran nodded his approval.

"Next!"

"I'm Pete Turner," stated the twenty-nine-year-old New York photographer. "I'm shooting for *Esquire* and *Look* magazine. A pioneer of modern color photography, Turner used a Nikon camera with special filters to achieve distinctive results when the majority of photographs at that time were still being processed in black and white. Albarran eyed his camera equipment suspiciously. "You must be very famous," he said.

"Why is that?" asked Turner, squinting from behind his eyeglasses.

"Because I've never heard of you," Albarran sneered.

The bulk of shooting that first week in Mismaloya revolved around two important scenes. The first was Shannon's heated altercation with Judith Fellowes, who sent a telegram to her brother, whom she claimed was a judge in Corpus Christi, complaining about being shanghaied. The second was Shannon's good-natured sparring with Maxine Faulk, owner of the Costa Verde Hotel, where he took the ladies on the bus, although the hotel was closed for the summer. There, Shannon sought to mend his broken spirit, and restore some normality to his life.

In the cool of the morning, Burton and Ava Gardner rehearsed their lines. "Baby, you're going to pieces, aren't you?" she said. "They are tearing me to pieces," he replied. "Honey, just lie down in the hammock," she suggested, "and I'll fix you a nice rum-coco."

"No," he insisted. "If I start drinking rum-coco's now, I'll never stop." The simple but intoxicating beverage, a variation of the Coco Loco that Williams first tasted in Acapulco, was prepared using four ounces of fresh coconut water and 1½ ounces of rum, mixed and poured over ice.

To help stay in character, Burton amused himself by drinking what he called "Mexican boilermakers" – straight shots of tequila with beer chasers.

He hadn't shaved for several days, in keeping with his role in the film, and had gone without sleep. "The script says I'm supposed to be drunk and feverish," muttered Burton, scratching his chin, "and I'm a Method actor."

His appearance on the set looking like a hobo instead of a man of the cloth elicited stares from the cast and crew. "It used to amaze me," said assistant director Tom Shaw, "seeing Burton at seven in the morning drinking beer. And he'd drink beer all morning long. By the time we finished he would have had a case of beer. And then he'd shift into high gear! He started into that tequila, and man, you'd never have known he'd had a drink! He was a big-league drinker. There was nobody in that league."

Burton was not the only tippler on the set. Huston maintained an early morning glow from a Coca-Cola bottle that mysteriously kept refilling itself between shots, while Emilio Fernández always had a full glass of whiskey in his hand.

Gardner reportedly had liquor bottles stashed in her dressing room, and James Ward chugged down a few beers behind the generator shed when he thought no one was paying him any attention.

No prude herself, Deborah Kerr confessed: "I must cut down on the marvelous thirst-quenching Mexican beer. I shall not be a very Miss Thin-Standing-Up-Female-Buddha," as Shannon refers to her character in the movie. Even Cyril Delevanti was caught nipping at a silver hip flask that his doctor had approved for "medical purposes."

But if Burton was already showing signs of alcoholism, it was his fierce protector Taylor, who was his enabler. "Elizabeth went so far as to encourage Richard to drink," said Stephen Birmingham, a thirty-one-year-old writer, who was on assignment for *Cosmopolitan* magazine, "and nobody could figure out the reason. He'd perch on a bar stool and comment, 'I'm not going to have anything to drink tonight because I'm supposed to do close-ups in the morning.' 'Oh, Richard, have a little bourbon, have a little wine,' Liz would coax him. She'd implore him to drink something, and after an initial pause, he'd say, 'All right,' and twenty-seven drinks later they'd carry him home and put him to bed."

Following Maxine around the premises of the hotel were two copper-toned beach boys, Pedro and Pepe, in tight-fitting white cotton pants, each of them shaking a pair of maracas. In the Broadway stage version, the boys, originally named Pedro and Pancho, were played by two American actors: James Farentino and Christopher Jones, in dark makeup.

Naturally, Huston wanted Mexicans to portray these roles on film. Since the parts required very little dialogue, it didn't matter if the boys could act or not, just so long as they looked good and moved well.

Local auditions had been held over the summer. After a brief search, Huston selected two fine specimens of manhood as Pedro and Pancho – renamed Pepe because the Mexican censors objected to the derisive use of Pancho, which is the abbreviated name for one of their patron saints Francisco.

The lucky man that was chosen for the role of Pedro was Roberto Leyva – a former *clavadista* or cliff diver from Acapulco. Like many men, Leyva, twenty-six, had been lured to Puerto Vallarta by the promise of easy money and had gone to work on the beach. He had been spotted by Sandy Whitelaw giving waterskiing lessons to tourists on Playa Los Muertos. He was compact, lean and strong, with a sexy grin that attracted the ladies.

One of those smitten women was Carol – a young school teacher from Toronto, Canada. She had gone swimming, met Leyva on the beach and fallen in love with him. Two months before the start of filming in Puerto Vallarta she found herself pregnant and made the decision to have his baby. "Back in those days there was a lot of waterskiing, not so much now, you see lots of parachutes and fishing, but you don't see waterskiing," recalled the couple's daughter Lindsey Leyva, who was born in 1964. "It was a show. People still talk about when my parents got together and went waterskiing – someone so dark and someone so fair and the contrast – to watch them young and madly in love."

Huston's second choice, Fidelmar Duran, who played Pepe, proved to be less ideal. The brawny, curly-haired novice was foisted on the production by Churubusco Studios, which supplied the Mexican film crew. Shortly before the company relocated to Mismaloya, it was learned that Duran lacked one necessary skill. Anthony Veiller's script specified that Pepe "has the grace of a tiger. He never walks. He dances." Fortunately, Leyva was quick on his feet, and after Huston saw him make some nimble moves, their character's actions were reversed, making Pedro the tiger.

Gardner was very impressed with Leyva when she met him that first day on the set. She took one look at his gleaming pectorals and proclaimed he was the most handsome man she had seen in Mexico.

Because Leyva and Duran didn't speak English, any bits of direction had to be translated by the Spanish-speaking assistant director Jaime Contreras, who choreographed their movements. "They never walked in the movie," said Tom Shaw. "I used to watch John dancing to show them what he wanted them to do."

Filming started in Mismaloya most mornings at nine o'clock and lasted until four or five in the afternoon. As usual, John Huston watched the action from his director's chair with typical detachment. He rarely moved from the spot, just looked up from time to time to check the facial expressions of the actors then bowed his head and listened to the beat of their lines.

At the end of each scene, Huston asked Gabriel Figueroa if the shot was good and then ordered it to be printed. "He must have been imbued with some sort of divinity," observed Bud Acord, "because Huston seemed to know when to make a suggestion and when to leave things alone."

But when Grayson Hall persisted in nervously rolling her eyes and tapping her feet, he stopped the filming. "My dear Judith," he called out with withering disapproval, using the name of her character, "that little time-step you persist in doing is quite unnecessary for the dramatic development of this film." The actress then excused herself and went to the bathroom.

When she returned, Hall mentioned she didn't feel well and asked for some medication to relieve her nausea. "I still haven't got used to this heat," she told Angela Allen, the script supervisor.

It wasn't a bad of case of nerves that troubled Hall, but a mounting sense of fear. Prior to coming to Mexico, Hall had been advised by the actress Myrna Loy to be wary of Huston, who, she said, was a "known sadist." According to Hall's biographer Rebecca Jamison, "Loy said Huston always found one person on every set to hate and make miserable. Loy told her to never be sick, even if she was dying."

Actually, Huston was quite fond of Hall. Exactly how much he liked her would not be apparent until much later, when her sharp-edged performance received some of the film's best reviews.

Burton, of course, admired Hall's theatricality; in her he found a kindred spirit who shared his love for the theatre. He felt the only thing she needed was some quiet encouragement, and he put a reassuring arm around her shoulder. "You, love, are unique," said Burton. "When that camera is on you, the rest of us might as well not be there at all." After that reassuring comment Hall lost the jitters and her confidence soared.

The same could not be said for some of the less important actors, several of whom were not real performers but friends and neighbors – "the Gringo Gulch girls," as they were called on the set. Their presence was more like a cheering squad than a troupe of professional artists. Each morning Bernice Starr, Dorothy Vance, Billie Matticks, and Barbara Joyce met at Liz Rubey's house, where they piled into her brightly-painted Jeep, which took them down to Playa Los Muertos. The women were joined on a waiting ferryboat by Mary Boylan, Eloise Hardt, Gladys Hill, Thelda Victor, and Betty Proctor, for the regular commute to Mismaloya.

Rubey's daughter, Lowe Wilson was a twenty-two-year-old divorced mother with two children. "I was paid ten dollars a day," recalled Wilson, who was Deborah Kerr's stand-in, "and I think the schoolteachers were paid twelve dollars a day. The ones that spoke got paid a little bit more. It wasn't a lot of money. I don't think anyone did it for the money; they did it for the fun of being in the movie."

During the long hours of filming, the eleven schoolteachers were required to stand under the blazing sun in their long dresses, hats and shoes. It wasn't only the ultraviolet rays that caused potential harm to the women; they were assaulted by an onslaught of buzzing flies, biting mosquitoes and stinging wasps.

Changes in the weather were a daily occurrence. Afternoon squalls, the crackle of thunder and flash of lightning interrupted filming. One day, the makeup artist Jack Obringer remarked that the women's faces looked unusually pale, and when one of the teachers said she felt faint, Tom Shaw summoned the company doctor.

Dr. Pedro Pérez Rivera announced there had been an outbreak of dysentery and that Entero-Vioform pills – a standard prophylactic for traveler's diarrhea – would be issued to the cast and crew. Ironically, a key aspect of the story involved one of the teachers, Miss Peebles, suffering from Montezuma's Revenge. Her repeated insistence on needing to find a restroom was meant to inject some humor into the acerbic script, but nobody on the location found it amusing, merely an irritant as much as the medical condition itself. It was particularly galling for some of the actors, because they seemed to be living their parts – just as Huston had wanted from them.

For many of the *Iguana* film company, who had dreamt of a romantic holiday, life in the tropics was not all that it was cracked up to be. Sue Lyon, James Ward and Cyril Delevanti had to be given Sulfatracine pills and liquid Kaomycin after they ate contaminated food on the beach. Ward's girlfriend Julie Payne also came down with a bad case of dysentery that kept her in bed for several days. Dr. Pérez Rivera cautioned everyone against drinking the water and eating any meat, fish or vegetables unless it was thoroughly cooked.

That same week, costume designer Dorothy Jeakins fell on the rocks and broke her toe. The next day, publicity secretary Virginia Lord tripped while climbing out of a boat at the small dock and cut her shoulder on an iron spike.

"Everyone was on edge from the heat and sickness," commented Eloise Hardt. "Scorpions and iguanas hopping on your bed. You never knew if you were going to be bitten by something or stranded by a storm."

When there was a stretch of good weather, Shaw persuaded the cast to come to the set at 7:30 a.m. and finish around one o'clock in the afternoon, so they could have the remainder of the day to themselves and enjoy the beach. On Saturdays, the cast worked only a half day. Gardner practiced her waterskiing at Playa de Oro while Kerr went swimming. At Kerr's urging, Peter Viertel joined Gardner, his onetime romantic flame, in the water. "He paddled out to her boat and decided to have a turn with the skis. He went round and round in great style and I was very proud of him," said Kerr without a trace of jealousy. "Then at the last he had to let go and fall, because two kids were swimming out and he thought he was going to slice their heads off."

After the trio had exhausted themselves at the beach, they headed back to Kerr's villa. "Ava followed us home for a drink and we all sat in the kitchen and ate peanuts and sardines on crackers," said Kerr. After her third drink, Gardner confessed to Kerr that she adored Burton, "professionally speaking, of course." Kerr caught the gist of her remark. "And I adore you, personally speaking, of course," she said. When Viertel left the room to fix them another round of drinks, Gardner asked Kerr if she was truly happy. "Yes I am," she replied, "very much." Gardner was genuinely pleased. "I'm glad to hear that," she said, "because Peter's such a good man."

Later, Sydney Guilaroff stopped by Gardner's house. "I've come to say goodbye," he said. "Don't go," she begged him. Guilaroff was returning to Hollywood, where his services were required on other films. "I have to, darling," he said. Her eyes filled with tears and they embraced each other. Gardner was sad to see him leave, and when he walked away she blew him a long, slow kiss.

WHILE RICHARD BURTON, ELIZABETH TAYLOR, Ava Gardner and Deborah Kerr enjoyed their luxurious accommodations, the American and Mexican film crew had to make to do with less hospitable surroundings. For three months, they worked and lived side-by-side in Mismaloya, sharing the twenty-five cement bungalows with red-tiled roofs that were located across from the hotel set on the other side of the hill. Each hut was furnished with a small living room and kitchenette, twin beds with mosquito netting, a bathroom sink, shower and toilet.

At the end of every day, the crew sat on their porches, drinking beer and playing cards or listening to music on portable gramophones. One of the favorite pastimes was playing Conquián – the ancestor of gin rummy, which dated back to seventeenth century Central America. The game was introduced to Texas from Mexico in 1897. Players were dealt ten cards each from a Spanish deck, which they had to meld into pairs, discarding unwanted cards and choosing new ones to form a winning hand.

Before retiring for the evening, the men sprinkled the floors and steps of their bungalows with Boric acid – a white crystalline powder. This natural insecticide was used to repel a nocturnal hard-shelled predator with eight legs and two claws, known by its Mexican name *alacran*, but whose presence instilled fear among humans in any language.

Scorpions usually attack when disturbed from their hiding places under rocks and beneath trees, or if stepped on by an unsuspecting foot. The hills surrounding Puerto Vallarta are home to some of the more poisonous species of this voracious arthropod: *Centruroides*, which have light-brown stripes, and their darker cousin *Vaejovis*. A scorpion's venom can paralyze the limbs of its victims, inducing swelling, convulsions and vomiting.

In Mismaloya, the crew was extremely vulnerable. No one liked the prospect of finding a scorpion in their bed, so maids swept the huts daily to keep away these dreaded pests. The men were at greatest risk when they got up in the middle of the night to go to the bathroom. As an added precaution, a crewman wearing protective clothing and heavy boots regularly inspected each of the buildings. The man carried an ultraviolet lamp, which he shone under the railings and stairs. Scorpions glow in the dark; their exoskeletons contain a chemical that makes them fluorescent under black light.

On the back side of one hut the man spotted a small cluster of the glowing offenders – six adults, each measuring four inches in length, their heads, abdomens and tails pulsating under the UV light. He sprayed gasoline over the ugly creatures and set them alight, their bodies writhing and twisting in agony. After this horrid experience, some disgruntled crewmembers took to calling the place "Abismaloya," which is not to say that life there was truly abysmal, but it was bad enough.

While the cast and crew fretted over their safety, Grayson Hall received good news. Her husband Sam Hall, a fifty-two-year-old writer of television soap operas, flew to Puerto Vallarta with their five-year-old son, Matthew, on the third weekend of October. Warned ahead of time about the health risks, father and son came armed with a scorpion vaccination kit. The town was still cleaning up from heavy rain caused by Hurricane Mona, which struck the west coast of Mexico on October 19.

The Hall family reunion was tempered by concerns over his wife's frail appearance. Since coming to Mexico, she had been steadily losing weight – the result of increased smoking and poor diet. The actress denied it was from excessive drinking, saying the unsanitary living conditions were to blame. Hall's roommate Thelda Victor complained of having spiders in her hair, stomach cramps and dysentery. "All this for $100 a week," she griped. Everyone was taking anti-diarrheal medication to relieve the painful symptoms of what was jokingly called the Aztec two-step, though no one felt much like dancing.

"There was a while there," said Hall, "when if you hadn't had *la turista*, you were considered sort of a pariah. Everybody hated you." Fearful of getting sick, Kerr stayed at home. She refused to eat any food unless it was prepared by her husband. Every day, Peter Viertel went spear fishing and returned with armfuls of red snapper and yellow tail, which he grilled and served with fried rice and steamed vegetables.

Only John Huston seemed impervious to disease. He had made the happy discovery of *raicilla* – a 180-proof distillate of the maguey plant that was far more potent than tequila. "It will kill just about anything," Huston reassured a curious reporter. After tasting the kerosene-flavored hooch, Burton agreed. "If you drink it straight down," he said, "you can feel it going into each individual intestine." Huston added, "I think that's because they left in the needles." But most of the production company preferred to drink Scotch – a tried-and-true remedy against bacteria-carrying parasites.

One morning, Emilio Fernández was standing on the bluff when he spied a pretty maid with large brown eyes and thick black hair cleaning one of the bungalows. The girl was reminiscent of the Mexican actress Dacia González. She wore a white cotton dress, shell necklace and sandals.

"What is your name?" asked Fernández.

"Narcissa," she replied.

"You are very beautiful," he said. "Come back with me to Churubusco Studios and I will make you a movie star!"

The girl told him she lived in the village with twelve brothers, several of whom were given jobs on the movie set. One brother had recently committed suicide by hanging himself. The family was still grieving his loss. Fernández offered to buy a new dress for her *quinceanos* – the coming-of-age party for fifteen-year-old girls that is celebrated throughout Mexico.

Narcissa's boyfriend, who was wearing an embroidered vaquero shirt and brown pants, ran up to Fernández. "Leave her alone, senor," pleaded the boy, a scowl on his young face. "We are going to be married!"

"Get out of my way or I will shoot you!" warned Fernández, grinning maniacally.

The boy grabbed Narcissa and they ran away.

oooooooo

On the morning of Monday, October 28, Deborah Kerr was drinking a cup of coffee on the terrace of Casa del Cielo, when publicist Ernie Anderson rang the doorbell. "I'm sorry to bother you," said Anderson when Peter Viertel opened the front gate. "Deborah is needed on the set. There's going to be a special presentation." Kerr showered and dressed. Then she left with Viertel and Anderson for the lengthy pilgrimage to Mismaloya. But their trip took longer than expected.

Progress through the city streets to Playa Los Muertos, located a half mile away, was hampered by a more important pilgrimage. Hundreds of people were carrying religious effigies and painted cloth banners honoring Dia de San Judas or St. Jude's Day.

The yearly festival, held at the end of every October, commemorates the Patron Saint of Lost Causes – a symbol of hope for many poverty-stricken Mexicans. Mass services dedicated to the Last Apostle of Jesus are a common start to the day followed by communal banquets and evening fireworks. These festivities created almost the same excitement as Mardi Gras.

Wearing a headscarf, Kerr cowered with Viertel, Anderson and their driver Miguel in the rolling Jeep, as church bells tolled incessantly and a parade of men, women and children sang and chanted around them. It was one o'clock in the afternoon when Kerr, Viertel and Anderson arrived by boat at the small pier in Mismaloya. Their boat dropped anchor, and Kerr climbed up the rope ladder to the dock.

After lunch, the cast and crew gathered on the set of the hotel verandah. Looking like an aging intern in his white shirt and pants, Huston presented small pine boxes with gold hinged lids to the five leading members of the *Iguana* film company.

Richard Burton and Ava Gardner were dressed in their costumes, Deborah Kerr in casual attire, Sue Lyon, a striped cotton blouse, blue jeans and sandals, and producer Ray Stark, a pale-green sport shirt and chinos. There was also a sixth recipient: the company's million-dollar mascot, Elizabeth Taylor, who was swathed in purples and pinks, to whom Huston paid special attention.

Still photographers Josh Weiner and Gabriel Torres were on hand to record the event, which had been orchestrated by Huston and Anderson. Afterwards, captioned photographs would be sent by telephonic wire service to media outlets around the world.

"We all had to sit around a table and John made a dramatic speech which we started to take seriously and finally realized must be a joke!" recollected Kerr, who suspected that something was afoot.

Huston finished his preamble and the cast apprehensively opened their gifts. Inside the black velvet-lined boxes were gold-plated derringers with ivory handles and five .38 caliber bullets engraved with the names of the other people.

"Are these things real?" asked Stark, brandishing his pistol.

"Yes," replied Huston. "They're double-barreled handguns, guaranteed to hit their mark up to twenty feet."

The custom-made weapons that Huston handed out that day were called Texas Defenders. This sort of armory is no longer manufactured except for ceremonial occasions because of the high cost. Their modern-day equivalent, made from stainless steel with cherry wood handles, sell for between $400 and $500 each. "I sensed a certain nervousness in the laughter and the thanks of everyone concerned," said Kerr. "It was almost like the start of an Agatha Christie murder novel."

Huston's choice of weaponry was no accident. The Derringer Pistol was created by famed gunsmith Henry Deringer in 1852. So many companies copied the design that the double "r" spelling of the name, which was created to avoid the legal trademark, has stuck over time. The Derringer received worldwide attention when it was used by John Wilkes Booth to assassinate President Abraham Lincoln. A Confederate sympathizer, who opposed the abolition of slavery, Booth entered the president's box during a performance at Ford's Theatre in Washington DC, and fatally shot Lincoln in the back of the head. Ever since then the Derringer pistol has had the reputation as a "Hitman Special."

Stark toyed with the ornate weapon, curling his forefinger around the pistol's trigger. The cast-metal handgun, though small, felt heavy in his hand. "Go on Ray," teased Huston. "I'm sure you'll find a willing opponent. I hear Deborah is an excellent marksman."

"You mean a markswoman," interjected Kerr from across the table. Gardner, who was sitting next to Stark, smiled at Huston out of politeness rather than gratitude. "Naturally, the old fox hadn't put *his* name on any of the damn bullets," she recalled. After the ceremony, Gardner locked the box containing her pistol in a suitcase, and never looked at it again.

As Burton contemplated the deadly firearm that rested before him on the table, the perversity of Huston's gesture sent shivers up and down his spine. Burton's memory flashed back in time. The year was 1955, the film *Prince of Players*, written by Moss Hart and directed by Huston's friend Philip Dunne. Recreating a piece of theatrical history, Burton had portrayed Edwin Booth, a magnetic nineteenth century American stage actor famous for his Shakespearean roles, but whose place in history was reduced to an ignominious footnote as the grieving older brother of Lincoln's murderer.

Born a century apart and two continents away, Booth and Burton were both regarded as the greatest Hamlets of their generation – until fate intervened. Booth's accomplishments were smothered by political tragedy, while Burton's reputation had been sullied by his affair with Elizabeth Taylor. Would he ever regain his stature in the theatrical world? Now, sitting with a replica of the same pistol that had killed a president, Burton's mind reeled at the implications of Huston's joke. He fumbled with the box, then got up from the table and went to get a drink.

Viertel watched him go inside the hotel and trailed after him. In the kitchen, Burton's hand shook as he lit a Pall Mall cigarette. "I wonder," he stammered, "what makes Huston think that I would find it so amusing to revel in someone else's misfortune – my misfortune for that matter," he said, pointing at himself. Viertel smiled reassuringly. "You don't know him as well as I do, Richard. Everything he does is calculated for effect. In Africa, he almost killed Katharine Hepburn. The man is a sadist. He only gets pleasure from other people's misery. It's all a game to him."

Burton opened a bottle of Carta Blanca beer and took a swig. "Well, Pete, I am not playing his game, now or never."

Back at the table, Taylor was comparing her pistol to an antique gold ring that adorned her right hand. The valuable piece of jewelry, which she said was given to her by the king of Indonesia, was clustered with pearls, rubies and diamonds. The reflection from the gold was almost blinding. "What a perfect match!" she exclaimed. "Look at the way it shines in the light!" She aimed the pistol at Huston's heart, grinning wickedly like a femme fatale. "Why Elizabeth," demurred Huston, sounding like a Southern gentleman caught cheating at cards, "You wouldn't shoot an unarmed man!" At that moment, Burton returned, still drinking his beer. He took Taylor by the arm and led her away. "I think it best you leave now," he said. "We have to finish the next scene. I'll see you on the beach."

After the group disbanded, Huston filmed the sequence of Gardner shaving Burton while he lies in a hammock. It was a simple bit of business, with no physical exertion required. Yet both actors felt strangely lethargic as if the life had been sucked out of them. Gardner hardly had the strength to hold the razor, and Burton felt like his body was made of lead. An uneasy stillness hung over the set. Even the wind in the trees had disappeared. It was a tropical languor – the calm before a storm. Only Gardner's mixed up dialogue managed to lighten the somber mood.

Reprimanding Burton in the scene for wanting to tear the telephone out of the wall, she was supposed to say: "In a pig's eye you are!" But what came out of her mouth was: "In a pig's ass you are!" At least everyone laughed. "Cut!" said Huston. "It's the eye of the pig we wish to concentrate on. Can you remember that, dear?"

After filming wrapped for the day, the actors returned to Puerto Vallarta under darkening skies. That evening another tropical storm burst forth from the heavens.

Torrential rain transformed burbling streams into gushing rivers. Flash floods dragged broken tree branches and heavy silt deposits into the ocean, changing the color of the water from midnight blue to blood red.

JOHN HUSTON'S GIMMICK OF handing out real pistols with live ammunition on the set of *The Night of the Iguana* had its desired effect – perhaps more than even he expected. "The press was attracted in great numbers," he said. "There were more reporters than iguanas – I don't think any picture I've made has called forth as much interest. There were reporters and photographers from all over the world, and though they arrived and left in flocks, there always seemed to be at least a dozen hanging around, waiting for the great day when the derringers were pulled out and the shooting started."

The Derringers were a clever ruse, of course, calculated to grab the media's attention. The director stirred up quite a controversy by telling his actors: "If the competition gets too fierce you can always use the guns!" But if Richard Burton was a coward when it came to firearms, Elizabeth Taylor was not, while Ava Gardner and Deborah Kerr were more than able to defend themselves.

Broadsheets and periodicals were not the only news publications that dispatched writers to Puerto Vallarta that summer. Correspondents from Britain's top selling scandal sheet *News of the World*, along with the European tabloids *Paris Match*, *France Soir* and *Il Tempo* descended on the fishing port, where they attempted to barter for hotel rooms and meals with pounds sterling, liras and francs. They all had the same objective, which was to get exclusive interviews and take candid photographs.

Blending in among the legitimate journalists were several reporters of dubious provenance. In 1963, Hollywood's biggest scourge, whose bimonthly appearance on newsstands was dreaded by anyone with a reputation to uphold, was a twenty-five-cent magazine with the ominous name *Confidential.* Its publisher, a New York smut peddler named Robert Harrison, printed lurid exposés about celebrity fetishes and infidelities with scant regard for the truth. His magazine was the progenitor of modern-day imitators such as *National Enquirer*, *The Globe* and *Examiner* with their shocking revelations and tell-all confessions.

Harrison recruited his errant workers, as criminals are inclined to do, from the shadows. On his payroll were busted cops, disbarred lawyers, expelled journalists, and syphilitic starlets. They carried fake identification cards and masqueraded as V.I.P.s, friends and relatives of the rich and famous. A number of these informants were sent on special assignment to Puerto Vallarta. The slick connivers managed to penetrate the film's wall of secrecy by befriending some of the inebriated cast and crew at the Hotel Oceano.

Taylor was unwilling to let Burton out of her sight, so she stayed with him on the verandah of the bar. That evening they were joined by a chatty British newspaperman who made the mistake of trying to match drinks with Burton. If the reporter was hoping to ingratiate himself with the actor, his plan backfired. After the intoxicated newsman staggered out in the street twice in as many hours to throw up, he finally disappeared.

By the end of the day, Burton's drinking had caught up with him. He started reciting poetry to everybody at the bar, whether they were interested in his slurred recitations or not. Cyril Delevanti, who was enjoying an Old Fashioned, thought Burton was trying to mock him because he was playing the role of a geriatric poet. Burton humbly apologized and informed everyone: "The only thing in life is language – not love – not anything else."

Taylor started crying and went to sit with Josh Weiner, who massaged her feet. While she was away, Burton proclaimed: "It is ridiculous to get married or have a contract of any sort, because you feel tied and want to get away from it, whereas if you feel you can walk away from anything, it's better. I'm not going to marry Liz. Of course, I haven't told her that yet."

Production assistant Thelda Victor, who was keeping a secret diary that was later published to the dismay of Seven Arts, suspected someone was leaking information to reporters; it may have been Victor herself. But even she was not about to lose her job for ratting on her coworkers. On the other hand, there were some people, who had no qualms about selling information for the right price. Victor thought she knew the culprit's identity and even named him. "Skip Ward goes over and sits down like an avid movie fan to listen in on everyone else's interviews," she stated. "Someone here is also supplying Los Angeles columnists with all the dirt, some true and some not."

The person that tipped off the press to potential trouble on the set was not an angry member of the cast or crew bent on revenge – it wasn't even an outsider who might have held a grudge. The real perpetrator of this baffling charade was none other than Ray Stark. The smiling producer put the squeeze on influential friends; he demanded favors and insisted that publishers and editors give the film the attention that he felt it deserved. "I may have screwed John up a bit by exploiting the picture," said Stark with characteristic duplicity. "It was one of the most publicized pictures of its time."

Because Gardner openly despised the press, she became easy bait for the producer's hook. Now *Confidential* was ready to spill the beans on her rumored conquest of Burton. "Will Ava Gardner steal Burton from Liz?" inquired the magazine. Acutely aware of the monetary value of a racy headline, Stark made sure that the press always got an eyeful of Gardner, even though he knew it inflamed her strong hatred of them. "She was the most popular single lady in that part of Mexico at the time," he said. "Every eligible Mexican was after her."

But Gardner was no fool. She knew what Stark was up to and refused to work if there were any photographers around. So the set at Mismaloya was ordered closed to the press. Anyone without an invitation had to wait at the restaurant or sit in the bar until the cameras stopped rolling. "There was no getting away from them, day and night," complained Gardner. "Elizabeth Taylor was marvelous because she's very good with the press, she's fearless. So she did a lot of that which would have fallen on my shoulders. I've never been very good with the press because I'm frightened of them."

In all, some 150 members of the world's press overran the village in expectation of a lovers' quarrel or a crime of passion. They weren't all anonymous scribes and picture takers, some of them were celebrities in their own right, who were asked to adjudicate on the questionable morality of the moviemakers from front row seats in the press gallery.

These names represent a time when accomplishment was more valued than ambition: Bestselling author Robert Ruark had written extensively about Africa's independence in *Uhuru* and the Mau-Mau uprising in *Something of Value*; Barnaby Conrad was the former American vice consul to Seville, Malaga and Barcelona, and wrote the acclaimed novel *Matador*; while the fedora-wearing investigative reporter Erskine Johnson played himself in such movies as *A Night for Crime*, *The Corpse Came C.O.D.*, and *Al Capone*.

Also weighing in on the movie's state of affairs was Pulitzer prize-winning *San Francisco Chronicle* columnist Herb Caen, who pioneered three-dot journalism – the use of three ellipses that separated his column's short items; the glib Hollywood insider James Bacon, who spent six decades chronicling the lives of numerous movie stars and befriended eight US Presidents; and pseudonymous New York society writers Igor Cassini aka Cholly Knickerbocker, Aileen Mehle aka Suzy, Robert Sylvester, and Bill Kennedy – dubbed "Mr. L.A." They were an intimidating lot.

When the actors refused to give incriminating interviews, newspapers tried to stir up rumors of a vicious feud: "LIZ, RICHARD, AVA AND SUE – MIGHTY TENSE IN THE JUNGLE" and "LIZ KEEPS HER EYE ON BURTON AND AVA." But this half-baked soufflé of lies, concocted by a kitchen full of resentful cooks, refused to rise. A more appetizing dish was the truth.

"Elizabeth Taylor and Richard Burton have discovered paradise — and they freely admit it," wrote Hollywood journalist Marilyn Beck. "In this tiny tropical village they have found their heaven on earth, where they can openly display their love for each other, freer than they have ever been from notoriety and criticism."

Deborah Kerr joked that she was the only one who wasn't having an affair with anybody. But the same questions from nosy reporters, who accosted her every day, to and from work, quickly tried her patience. "I am a bit bored with being asked if I think Elizabeth and Richard will be married, and is Ava as difficult as 'they' say and is she on the make for Burton, or is Sue Lyon?" Kerr even took a well-aimed jab at the producers. "I think it would serve them all right if I suddenly developed temperament, had hysterics, became an unmanageable sexpot, threw temper tantrums, or something."

Somehow, Kerr always remained in control of her emotions. "She is without a doubt the loveliest creature among us," said Victor. "She is beautiful in the quiet, English way." Except that Kerr was Scottish and a star of the first rank. Eclipsed by the Burton-Taylor juggernaut that overwhelmed the film's production, Kerr's own hardships, which had been considerable, were forgotten. There was a painful divorce from her first husband and a bitter custody battle over their two children. Unlike Taylor, who was plagued by illnesses, real and imagined, Kerr never became a figure of pity, and she never caused embarrassment to anyone or lost her dignity as did Gardner.

After waiting almost three weeks, during which she did nothing except read scripts and attend rehearsals, Kerr filmed her first scenes as Hannah Jelkes on October 29. Stark and Huston inspected her costume prior to the scene. "Ray felt it looked too elegant," recalled Kerr. "And John felt it was not quite humorous enough." But Kerr liked the noble simplicity of her dress. "After much hemming and hawing," she said, "it was decided to use it as is."

When the cameras rolled midmorning, Kerr emerged from the jungle on the cobblestone pathway in front of the Costa Verde Hotel, "a fastidious Pilgrim," as costume designer Dorothy Jeakins described her, "clothed in raw silk" and carrying a blue parasol.

At Kerr's side, wearing a crumpled white linen suit, gentleman's hat and string tie was Delevanti as her ninety-seven-year-old grandfather. In the glaring heat both actors gave the realistic appearance of having walked several miles instead of just a few feet. "I think you may have heard of us. We've had a good many write-ups," Jelkes informs Maxine Faulk. "My grandfather is the oldest living and practicing poet. He gives recitations. I pass among the tables during lunch and dinner slowly. I wear an artists' smock picturesquely dabbed with paint."

Afterwards, Kerr said that she was relieved to finally "break the ice," but her impeccable diction hid any traces of nervousness. Later on, she sat with Jeakins, watching the costume designer do a sketch of Burton for an upcoming scene. Then Kerr ran lines with Burton for the next day's shooting.

On the return trip to Vallarta, Kerr's boat was caught in a thunderstorm. By the time the actress arrived back at her house, she was completely drenched. Peter Viertel opened the front door to find a wet cocker spaniel named Deborah standing on the mat, shaking the water from her hair. He wrapped a towel around his sweetheart, brought her inside and she dried off in the bedroom, removing her sodden clothing without any inhibition.

Viertel marveled at his wife's nakedness; he kissed her from behind and she turned and embraced him. The couple made love, slowly at first, then with increased passion. After taking a hot shower, the couple dined by candlelight, and then retired to bed.

oooooooo

Once or twice a week, a small delegation from Mismaloya, headed by Ray Stark, John Huston, Anthony Veiller, Gabriel Figueroa and Emilio Fernández, viewed unedited scenes of the film, called "rushes," at Puerto Vallarta's open-air movie theater, Cine Morelos, located on the south side of the plaza across from the malecón.

The English term "rushes," which refers to the speed at which prints of the film are developed, or "dailies" as they are usually called in Hollywood, are the raw, unedited footage shot during the making of a motion picture. They are called this because the footage from each day's filming is normally developed that same night, synced to sound and printed on film for viewing the next day by the director and some members of the crew.

Except in the case of *The Night of the Iguana*, the exposed film took one day to be flown from Mexico City to Los Angeles, another day to be developed at the laboratory, and a third day, to be sent back. As the need arose for a quicker turnaround, it was arranged to send the footage to Churubusco Studios for processing, which cut one day off the four-day schedule.

After the processed film arrived back in Puerto Vallarta, the news of a private screening was enthusiastically relayed through the village.

"The townspeople caught on quickly," remembered Huston. "When they saw Ralph Kemplen, our editor, and Eunice Mountjoy, his assistant, going into the theater with film cans, word would spread. By the time the rest of us arrived, the front of the house would be filled with locals of all ages. For the most part, they didn't understand a word of what they were hearing, but they were delighted to recognize the places, and thoroughly enjoyed themselves."

A highly experienced craftsman, Kemplen, age fifty-one, had trained in the editing rooms of Gaumont, Ealing, and Two Cities Films. He knew precisely when to cut a scene or, conversely, when not to cut it, which was much harder. In 1951, Kemplen began a long association with Romulus Films. He edited *Pandora and the Flying Dutchman*, *The African Queen* and *Moulin Rouge* for which he received the first of three Oscar nominations for Best Film Editing.

On a nod from Huston, the manager dimmed the house lights. The projectionist turned on the movie projector's carbon arc lamp by bringing two electrified rods together, filling the lamp with brilliant white light. At the same time, he started the motor and the long strip of perforated thirty-five millimeter film was pulled down from the top spool and into the machine by rotating metal sprocket wheels.

The descending black numbers on the film's leader flashed on the screen: 7, 6, 5, 4, 3, 2... It was followed by the projected image of the second camera assistant Salvador de Anda holding a wooden slate clapperboard and the sound of the "clapstick" being registered at the beginning of the designated scene and its corresponding take:

THE NIGHT OF THE IGUANA
Scene 18 Take 1
DAY
J.HUSTON
DIRECTOR

Watching the actors' facial expressions and gestures magnified in close-up was unnerving for some performers unaccustomed to the sight – and just as disquieting for others who had witnessed this process done in the past. "I saw the first film I was ever in and thought they had cut out all my best scenes," recollected Burton. "I started to dislike the director and the cutter and probably they were right, and so I decided that in order to make myself feel amiable towards everybody on the set I would never anymore go to see rushes."

For Huston, viewing this unadorned footage was like admiring a beautiful face with blemishes. He had the highest regard for Figueroa's photography but realized that some shots would have to be redone because of small imperfections: white flaring on the edge of the film, caused by overexposure to light, for example, or scratches to the negative that occurred in the laboratory. Occasionally, the outline of the boom microphone intruded into a shot, ruining an otherwise superior take. There would be plenty of time for retakes, of course, in the coming weeks.

Initially, the filming process had been slow, a mere twenty-one pages in the first two weeks. By the end of the second month, however, the production was five days ahead of schedule.

DIA DE LOS MUERTOS or Day of the Dead, is a traditional Mexican festival in memory of dear departed loved ones that combines both Catholic and pagan elements. This national holiday, which occurs each year on the first two days of November, honors children on All Saints Day and adults on All Souls Day, when it is said the spirits of the dead will return.

Unlike Halloween, which is rooted in fear and superstition, Day of the Dead is a time of joyful remembrance. Mexicans use this occasion to mock death, serving chocolate coffins and sugar skulls, which are eagerly devoured by children wearing spectral masks. This ghoulish carnival of dancing skeletons and grinning corpses is held every year in triumph of life over death – or is it death over life?

In Puerto Vallarta, the townspeople constructed private altars containing wedding photographs and items of clothing from the dead. Religious artifacts such as bronze and silver crosses and paintings of the Virgin Mary were displayed along with ornate wreaths of marigolds and dozens of ceremonial wax candles. Women baked *pan de muerto* – sweet egg bread made in the shape of skulls – and decorated with white frosting to resemble bones. They also served *atole* – a boiled drink made from maize.

As the sun rose over the town on Friday, November 1, 1963, there was collective mourning for the dead, lighting of candles and praying at churches.

Then the two days turned into a cheerful celebration, with revelry in cemeteries, eating and drinking on gravestones, and dancing in the streets.

Everybody on Playa Los Muertos was in a joyful mood when Ava Gardner and Deborah Kerr arrived there shortly after daybreak. Both women were wearing one-piece bathing suits, and tourists marveled at the two attractive stars as they joined hands and courageously dipped their toes in the ocean. They planned to water-ski to Mismaloya, but it was too late by the time the boats were organized.

The beachfront hotels were festooned with marigolds and painted *calaveras* – papier-mâché skulls with people's names written on them. Between the palm-woven umbrellas stood brightly-costumed *catrinas* – life-size wooden figures of upper-class women with skeleton faces. "Now I know why they call this the beach of the dead!" exclaimed Kerr.

Gardner was in unusually good spirits; she waved and laughed at the beach boys, inflaming their sexual desire with her shapely posterior which shone in the dawn like a mermaid's silvery tail. Then she dived into the water, and swam out to the boat with long strokes. "She has the strength of an ox, that girl!" marveled Kerr, who took a deep breath and followed her lead.

Gardner's chauffeur Ramón was waiting for them on the speedboat. He lifted each of the women into the stern, where they dried off with terrycloth towels. Then he started the motor and the boat roared to life. "We sped across the bay," recounted Kerr, "the sky quite marvelous, with the moon still vivid on the horizon to the west and the sun rising in the east, and the water like flat syrup."

In Mismaloya, the Mexican crewmembers erected personal shrines around the hotel set and bungalows. At the base of each monument were placed *ofrendas* – small offerings of food and beverages that had been brought from the village to entice the spirits of the dead.

The perimeters of the set glowed with so many candles that the hotel took on the appearance of an old Spanish church.

If any spirits were forthcoming from the shadows they certainly took their time. Kerr recalled that it was a long day's work. She and Burton did not finish their scenes until six o'clock, dispelling the myth that filmmaking is easy. "We had some difficult setups, and Ava and I filled in time rehearsing the long scene in the kitchen we have together."

They were about to pack it in for the day, when a familiar-looking figure in a short-sleeve cotton shirt and belted summer slacks strolled onto the set. He had a large head of thick graying brown hair and lively blue eyes that looked out from a chubby face. John Huston got up off his director's chair and the two men firmly shook hands.

"How's the fishing, Budd?" inquired the director.

"Well, I just arrived today," he replied. "On Sunday we are going to Punta de Mita and catch some marlin."

"That's swell," said Huston.

Seymour "Budd" Schulberg was a famous screenwriter and bestselling novelist who fought back against social injustice with a typewriter instead of using his fists. Although he was well respected in literary circles for exposing graft and corruption, not everyone liked him. His first novel *What Makes Sammy Run?* – a negative depiction of the movie business – incurred the wrath of the film industry for its crudeness and bigotry, even though, like the story's antihero, Sammy Glick, he was Jewish.

Schulberg's six-year membership of the Communist Party, which he voluntarily admitted before the House Un-American Activities Committee, made him some bitter enemies for his naming of seventeen people who had also been members. Widely ostracized by the film community, he had been living in Mexico City since 1959. But he never stopped working. He had written a new novel and was busy adapting a play for Broadway.

Now, standing in front of the film crew, Schulberg, age forty-nine, looked like one of the bruised prizefighters he had written about in *On the Waterfront* and *The Harder They Fall*; he had a bulbous nose, a chipped front tooth and the weary insolence of a man who had gone too many rounds. But he hadn't lost his sense of humor or his craving for a good stiff drink. He sat down at the bar with Huston, and ordered tequila with a wedge of lime and a pinch of salt.

Huston and Schulberg had more in common beside their past political affiliations. Both men were also lifelong fans of boxing. They feigned some punches; Huston aimed a left jab and Schulberg gave an uppercut. Burton's personal trainer Bobby La Salle, who had once been a professional boxer, joined them at the bar.

But if Schulberg was given a warm welcome by Huston, he was less well-received by others on the set. "It was slightly uncomfortable for him when he saw Peter Viertel," stated Lawrence Grobel, "because they had a troubled past: Schulberg's first wife divorced him and married Viertel." The woman, Virginia Ray, had one child by each husband.

Viertel divorced Ray and subsequently married Deborah Kerr. In 1960, Ray accidentally lit her nightgown with a cigarette, suffered horrible burns, and died a month later in hospital. She was fifty-six.

Schulberg also held a grudge against producer Ray Stark, who had bought the rights to his bleak novel *The Disenchanted* and wanted to turn it into a love story with a happy ending. Neither man would concede that the other was at fault and their friendship turned to hostility. When informed that Schulberg was in town, Stark refused to meet him.

Puerto Vallarta may have been beneficial for Huston but it proved unlucky for Schulberg. The same night he visited the movie set, Schulberg and his second wife Victoria Anderson had a loud brawl, which led to their divorce. The following year, Schulberg married the actress Geraldine Brooks.

"When we all went to the rushes," said Thelda Victor, "they wouldn't let Schulberg come. Ava, who likes him, took up the cudgels for him, but she was ineffective."

Taylor felt sorry for Schulberg and on Sunday she took him for a walk along the beach with her daughter Liza. "We're all star babies," Taylor told him, using a term that held deep significance for several generations of Hollywood children. "Whatever I do for Liza," she said, "I will never expose her to the kind of experiences my parents forced me to endure." At that moment, a speedboat approached the shore, its bow looming above the waves like the fin of a great white shark.

Out of the corner of her eye, Taylor spotted the lens of a press camera pointed in her direction, and she turned to face her attacker. While Schulberg looked on, Taylor screamed "Get away! Get away! You son of a bitch! Get out of here! Stop following us! I'll break your goddamn camera!"

What happened next took Schulberg by surprise. "She waded out into the ocean in the direction of the boat, throwing sand and pebbles and shouting at the photographer," he said. "She continued advancing until the crew turned the boat around and sped off."

Later that evening, Schulberg, who spoke Spanish, took Burton to a small cantina near the embarcadero. They ordered a round of drinks and joined drunken *charros* – cowboys – and *marineros* – sailors – singing the traditional Mexican song *Cielito Lindo*. Burton sang the chorus: "Ay, ay, ay, ay, canta y no llores," which Schulberg told him meant "sing and don't cry."

Taylor was woken up by the sound of their carousing as they staggered up the street, arm in arm, to Casa Kimberly at three o'clock in the morning. "Richard!" she yelled from the balcony. "Get your ass in here!" Taylor raced down the stairs and flung open the heavy gate. "You should be ashamed of yourself!" she reprimanded him. "And you too, Budd."

On an impulse, Schulberg grabbed Burton and gave him a big sloppy kiss. "If you don't watch out," he slurred, "I'll marry him!"

Taylor was livid. "How dare you!" she cried and slapped Schulberg across the face. Burton was crestfallen. "Your majesty," he said, going down on one bended knee, "I beseech thee; resist temptation to do harm to my learned friend." Taylor dragged Burton inside by his collar and locked the gate behind them, leaving Schulberg standing on the street.

The next day, Taylor had forgiven Burton but her suspicions lingered. Whenever the actor was drunk, his mood became noticeably gayer. He openly showed affection for other men and often called them "sweetheart." One day, when Burton was on the set, Herb Caen watched Taylor swallowing him with her violet eyes, while he entertained her with his effeminate act. "You, too?" she hooted.

Burton often speculated that many actors were latent homosexuals "and we cover it with drink." But he always denied being homosexual. "I tried it once," he said, referring to an incident from his past, "but it didn't take." On the nights when he came home late or not at all, Taylor was left wondering.

While the world's press was starving for a juicy headline, the actors sated their hearty appetites twice a day at the Iguana Café. The restaurant, which cost more than $2,000 a week to maintain, was managed by Rick Rubin – a tall, affable New Yorker. Fifteen years earlier, Rubin was managing a hotel in Cuernavaca when a visiting movie company asked him to provide food for their cast and crew. Within seven years he was the biggest caterer for foreign movies in the country.

It was Rubin's job to buy fresh produce and transport it by boat to Mismaloya. Unlike the simple preparation of tacos and tortillas, the process of cooking and serving à la carte meals to 130 people for two months in Mismaloya was a complicated task.

"First, we had to buy the food in Mexico City," explained Rubin, "and then put it in giant freezers there. Next, we packed the food in dry ice and shipped it to the airport, loading it on planes for the flight to Puerto Vallarta."

From there, the assorted items – sides of beef and pork, hams, sausages, chickens, turkeys, as well as Brazilian coffee, English tea, burlap sacks of rice, flour, salt and sugar – were transferred onto several boats for the twenty-five-minute journey to the film location. Rubin supplemented the daily food supply by fishing for mahi-mahi, tuna and mackerel in the bay. "But because we didn't have much freezing space in Mismaloya, we had to put all food not used up immediately back into freezers in Puerto Vallarta!"

Not only was Rubin an experienced chef, he also had to be a culinary wizard. The special requests he received on *The Night of the Iguana* ranged from kosher salami to a three-tiered birthday cake. "One day Sue Lyon asked me if I could bring in some gefilte fish and red horseradish. I found it." In the case of Ava Gardner, "she liked hot, spicy food, the spicier the better." One of her favorite meals was baked devilled fish, adapted from a North Carolina seafood recipe, which Gardner gave to Rubin. The tasty dish proved to be an unexpected hit.

AVA GARDNER'S DEVILLED FISH
1 ½ lbs. fish fillets or steaks
3 tablespoons chili sauce
2 tablespoons prepared horseradish
2 tablespoons prepared mustard
1 ½ teaspoons salt
Few dashes red pepper

Any firm, fine-textured fish will do. Sprinkle with salt and red pepper. Roll up fillet to form a coil, skin side out. Fasten with toothpick. Stand on ends side by side in buttered loaf pan. (For fish steak, lay in flat pan.) Mix chili sauce, mustard and horseradish and pour over fish. Cover and bake in 400-degree F. oven for 25 minutes. Uncover and bake 20 minutes more. Serve piping hot. Cucumber and onion salad makes pleasing side dish. Serves 5.

"In addition to feeding the 130 people in our cast and crew," Victor wrote in her diary, "we must also take care of a lot of freeloaders – visitors and ladies and gentlemen of the press."

Those freeloaders ranged from John Huston's friend Rose Covarrubias, who was the widow of Miguel Covarrubias – the noted Mexican artist and anthropologist, to Buckminster Fuller – the American architect celebrated for his invention of the Dymaxion House and the geodesic dome. Huston had invited the sixty-eight-year-old futurist to Mexico, hoping to interest him in the planned vacation resort Club Mismaloya.

Huston thought Fuller's igloo-shaped domes were the cleverest thing in construction. When he introduced the architect-engineer to the cast and crew, the director told them he was thinking of having Fuller put up one giant dome over all of Mismaloya.

"Lush tropical vines would cover the roof, creating a beautiful soft green light for the interior," explained Huston. "We could all live under this immense dome, sleeping as the Japanese sleep, on slabs of polished wood."

One afternoon, Michael Wilding showed up for lunch with a cleft-chinned, thirty-four-year-old New York actor named Joseph Sirola. Today, Sirola is best known as the voice of the Empire State Building Tour, which is heard by millions of visitors each year. But in 1963, his acting career was in low gear. Wilding thought he could help get Sirola noticed and offered to show him around the set, where he posed for a photograph with Wilding's biggest client, Richard Burton.

Could Wilding, once the darling of the British silver screen, truly have been happy in his new career as a glorified factotum? "To have been Taylor's husband and working as the personal assistant to his ex-wife's lover must have embarrassed him," said Bud Acord. For a short time, at least, Wilding seemed to enjoy the job of press agent.

Tipped off to all the Mexican partying, the magnesium-blonde sex goddess Kim Novak contacted Ray Stark's office to ask if she could come down to Vallarta for a brief spell. The thirty-year-old actress had zoomed to stardom in a succession of gossamer romances: *Picnic*, *The Eddy Duchin Story*, *Pal Joey*, and *Vertigo*. Novak's reputation had been scandalized by her reported dalliances with Prince Aly Khan and Frank Sinatra, as well as a highly-publicized interracial romance with the black singer Sammy Davis, Jr. She needed some good, clean exposure.

Novak's current beau was Roderick Mann – a dashing forty-year-old Fleet Street journalist, who wrote for London's *Sunday Express*. When Mann gave Novak an engagement ring he became fodder for his own newspaper. He relished the opportunity to slip away to Mexico with Novak, and renew his acquaintance with Burton, who was a drinking buddy. "That's all we need!" complained publicist Ernie Anderson.

On November 4, Herb Caen interviewed some of the actors during a lunch break in the Iguana Café. Sounding like a male version of Barbara Walters, he asked the probing question: "If you had one choice in your life as a way of life, what would you want?" Ray Stark answered: "Peace." Richard Burton intoned: "Adventure." Elizabeth Taylor called out: "Wealth." Ava Gardner exclaimed: "Health." Deborah Kerr admitted: "Happiness." Peter Viertel responded: "Success." Then Caen pointed the microphone at Huston. "And what about you, John?" The director grew pensive, as if trying to remember a long-forgotten word. "That's a tricky question," he replied. Then he took a deep breath and said: "I believe the answer would be interest." Caen repeated the word. "Interest," he said. "That's a very good answer."

TO THE CASUAL OBSERVER, life among the pampered movie stars in Mismaloya in 1963 must have resembled a summer vacation on Santa Catalina Island. "Everybody was drinking quite a bit. Richard Burton hit it very hard. And John Huston always did," said Budd Schulberg. "They were all having a good time. It was a happy company. You couldn't believe they were making a movie."

By now the local teenage boys had taken to hitching rides on the boats or following the actors in canoes hoping to get small jobs and take some money home to their families. Most of all, they wanted to reach out and touch the most enticing icon of feminine beauty they had ever seen in their lives: Elizabeth Taylor.

One morning a cocky youth with a ducktail hairstyle approached Taylor in front of El Dorado restaurant. The actress was smoking a Salem cigarette while waiting for the arrival of her launch *Taffy*. Taylor was wearing a tiny white mesh top and bikini that barely covered her crotch.

When the boy asked for a cigarette, she handed him one from her pack. "No," he said, pointing to the one in her mouth, "that one." With a shrug, she took the lipstick-smeared cigarette from between her lips and gave it to him. The boy, his eyes wild, took a deep drag and went into a spasm of orgiastic delight.

This incident was typical of the adolescent frenzy that followed Taylor wherever she went in the world.

"The beach boys around, who all appeared to be stoned, were beside themselves," wrote Burton in his diaries about one such encounter. "And as we left they shouted various invitations to her and offered to kiss her in various parts of her anatomy – the mini-dress was also very low cut – including sundry offers of fornication. They were careful that I was on the boat and moving rapidly away before these gracious offers were made."

It must have been exhausting for Burton and Taylor having to constantly look over their shoulders; they never knew who was following them. Fans and photographers were always hanging around, sometimes literally as it turned out. One time, Burton caught the infamous paparazzo Ron Galella hiding in a tree at Casa Kimberly and he was arrested. That is why an armed guard was posted outside the house and police regularly patrolled the street.

Following the shock of being kissed by Schulberg the other night, Burton didn't want to embarrass himself again, so he remained in a corner of the house reading. After an hour of excruciating silence, Taylor, who was on her fifth vodka tonic, blurted out "Richard, for Christ's sake have a drink! You're so dull when you don't have a glass in your hand!" Burton looked up from his book. "Elizabeth," he said peevishly, "is it too much to ask for me to have one day's sobriety?" Taylor got up and went to the bar. She filled a glass with ice and vodka, brought it back to the table and placed the mixture in front of him. "I dare you," she said viciously. "Take it."

Burton stared at the drink. Then he put the book down and gave in to temptation. "Good," smirked Taylor after the glass was empty. "Four more to go and we're even." But if Burton was weak willed at home he was letter-perfect on the set the next morning. Unfortunately, he was so hung-over after lunch that he fell out of a chair on the hotel verandah and slashed his thigh. The doctor patched him up, according to Thelda Victor, but he had to do a scene in which he carries Sue Lyon out of his bedroom. They shot it ten times, and each time she repeatedly kicked him in the sore leg with her foot.

Burton told her, "You're a real method actor. Stanislavsky would be proud of you for making me suffer."

Carrying Lyon in his arms was the closest Burton had been to her physically since they started the film, except for the day they went swimming at Playa Conchas Chinas. It was only natural for him to be attracted to her; she was beautifully proportioned, sexy as hell, and as Lyon herself was fond of saying: "I'm only seventeen!" In some American states, that was jail bait – like her character in the film.

Many of the crew noticed that she had matured a great deal since *Lolita.* Her breasts were larger, her hips fully rounded, and her voice soft and beckoning like a cat's purr. She was shaving her legs and inclined to be bitchy on the third day of every month when she had her period. Whenever that happened the air was fraught with sexual tension. "People kept saying that maybe Burton would fool everyone and run off with Sue," said Helen Lawrenson, "but that seemed the wildest of press agent dreams, although, admittedly, anything was possible in that atmosphere."

The trouble was that none of the cast was cooperating. Lyon had no romantic interest in Burton, which was fine with Taylor, but wreaked havoc with the film's publicity. After all, Burton's character was supposed to be lusting after this ripe young girl, who had a crush on him, but it wasn't working. Even Huston noticed the lack of onscreen chemistry between them.

Part of the problem, of course, was Taylor's insane jealousy. The other problem was Burton's rampant drinking, which had impaired his libido. "He drank so much at night the next morning the alcohol literally oozed out of his pores," said Lyon. "He gave off a terrible odor. Playing a scene with him could be most unpleasant."

It hardly mattered to Lyon, who already had a boyfriend – the actor Hampton Fancher. Very soon, she hoped, he would pop the big question.

At the end of every work day, after taking off her makeup, Lyon returned home for private schooling with her tutor Eva Martin. Two hours later, Fancher joined Lyon for dinner, and they talked and held hands until nine o'clock when he was banished from the premises with a severe case of blue balls.

That weekend, Lyon's widowed mother, a small woman in her middle fifties with graying blonde hair, arrived at the Hotel Playa de Oro and promptly moved in with Joann Fancher. The stress of having her fiancé's wife living with her own mother caused Lyon's face to break out with pimples.

Everybody settled into temporary domesticity in their designated homes throughout the city. Even Huston succumbed to the joys of fatherhood, spending the nights with Zoë Sallis and their infant son Danny. The press had been hoping for fireworks and when there was no explosion it was a big letdown.

Then, without warning, there was an unexpected bombshell. "Ava's New Mexican Flame is a Pistol-Packin' Firebrand," the *Los Angeles Herald-Examiner* announced the first week of November. Teletype machines in the world's newsrooms printed out the short item:

> Actress Ava Gardner will be married tomorrow. Mexican actor-director Emilio (Indio) Fernandez said he and Miss Gardner are making plans for the wedding. Fernandez said he was going to Los Angeles and that the wedding will take place there or at Puerto Vallarta, Guadalajara, or the fishing village of Mismaloya. Miss Gardner was not available for comment.

When the erroneous story broke that Gardner was going to marry the film's associate director Emilio Fernández, the rumor was traced back to James Ward, who was always seen hanging around Gardner. Maybe Fernández, who had taken a strong liking to the actress, planted the story himself.

Thelda Victor thought the whole thing was a sick joke. "To my knowledge," she said, "Ava couldn't stand him." But the damage had been done. Cables jammed the Puerto Vallarta Telegraph Office from newspaper editors in twenty countries demanding more details. The story made Gardner appear desperate to find a husband. What eligible bachelor would want to be involved with a drunken nymphomaniac? Once again, her chances for a serious romance had been ruined by the media. "She was very upset and rightly so," agreed Kerr. "Needless to say there wasn't a *word* of truth in it."

In protest, Gardner drank six martinis at the bar with her maid "Reenie" Jordan, and then vanished for several days. Huston had to film around Gardner until she sobered up. When she returned to Mismaloya, a hopeful journalist persisted in trying to have the actress confirm the trumped-up romance. "You *did* kiss Mr. Fernández, didn't you, Miss Gardner?" asked the writer. Gardner stared at him bleary-eyed then broke into an evil laugh. "Hell, yes!" she lied. "Everybody kisses everybody else in this crummy business all the time! It's the kissiest business in the world! If people making a movie didn't keep kissing, they'd be at each other's throats!" Then she dashed off to her dressing room, slammed the door and collapsed on the bed in a fury of tears.

During Gardner's absence, Kerr became the film's deputized female star, taking over the reigns as she had when riding a toboggan with Peter Viertel after he sprained his ankle skiing on the slopes of Klosters. To make up for lost time Huston took the unusual step of shooting several scenes out of continuity – a rare though necessary occurrence. Between camera setups Kerr wrote letters to her two daughters Melanie, age sixteen, and Francesca, twelve, as well as Viertel's eleven-year-old daughter Christine from his marriage to Virginia Ray. "The most boring part of making a movie is the hanging around," admitted Kerr, "and you must keep your energy going and your mind alert in case you are suddenly plunged into a scene!"

It took two days to film a lengthy sequence with Gardner and Kerr cutting and steaming fish in the kitchen. C. G. Kim, a Chinese-Mexican actor, played the role of Chang, the stoned cook, who looked like he had crawled out of an opium den. "I've warned you before," says Maxine Faulk when she sees him smoking a reefer. "I don't allow this stuff on the premises! Remember the time you got it in the enchiladas?"

Gardner was so nervous she kept forgetting her lines, referring to her character's husband as Frank instead of Fred, which caused the crew to break up with laughter at her unintentional reference to Sinatra.

When Maxine says "I still got my biological urges, but even I know the difference between loving somebody and just going to bed with them," it sounds as if Gardner is describing herself. Kerr had to endure the worst part of the scene, chopping off the smelly fish heads with a machete. It turned out to be more difficult than she expected because the spines of the fish were unusually tough. Property man Sam Gordon beheaded the actual fish in the final shot.

Afterwards, Huston filmed the scene of Kerr bandaging Burton's bleeding feet after he throws Sue Lyon out of his bedroom while walking on broken glass. "We live on two levels," Shannon informs Hannah, "the realistic level and the fantastic level." When her grandfather Nonno falls over in his room they run to help him and she laments her predicament. "So here we are," says Jelkes, "like a couple of scarecrows on this windy hilltop over the cradle of life."

The week concluded with Burton as he frantically tries to remove the gold cross from around his neck, saying "I've got to break the chain," followed by his mad dash into the jungle. In doing so he mimics the actions of the captured iguana that wants to be given his freedom.

It was also in this scene that Hannah asks the all-important question: "Why did they lock you out of the church?"

Shannon answers truthfully: "Fornication and conduct unbecoming a man of the cloth." His sexual dalliance with a young Sunday school teacher ended when she tragically cut her wrists with a straight blade razor. "Not fatally but it made a scandal," says Shannon, who had a nervous breakdown and was committed to a mental hospital. After Miss Fellowes accuses him of seducing a minor he becomes depressed and wants to end it all.

The two beach boys, Pedro and Pepe, chase after Shannon and try to catch him. Jelkes calls out: "Mrs. Faulk, stop him!" In shooting the action, Huston had Burton clamber across the sharp rocks, while the boys grasp and claw at him like they are trying to catch the iguana. Shannon says he is going to take "the long swim to China" because he wants to drown himself. This was a difficult shot because it required Burton to take a running leap off the rocks and dive headfirst into the sea. Incredibly, the scene was performed without a stuntman. Everyone marveled at the actor's retentive memory and unflagging energy – the result of his excellent stage training.

The segment where Kerr sketches Burton demonstrates the clever illusion of film. Although Kerr's hand was seen holding the artist's pad and pencil, another person's hand drew the actual caricature. Dorothy Jeakins had done some profiles of Burton's face during rehearsals.

When it came time to film the scene Burton sat directly facing the camera. Huston picked up the pad and proceeded to draw Burton's face as it appeared in the scene. "I'd had a certain gift for drawing from the time I could hold a pencil," said the director, who was not only a good sketch artist but an accomplished painter. Kerr got to show off her wit in the scene where Hannah passes among the schoolteachers at lunch and tries to sell them some of her paintings.

Kerr had been grumbling about her role being watered down from the original play. Anthony Veiller put back the missing dialogue which gave more depth to her characterization.

But when Huston kept telling her how to play the scene, she grew indignant. “How would you like me to balance a glass of water on my nose?” she asked. A comedic highpoint of the scene was Burton’s singing the chorus from *Three Little Fishies*, which was reprised from the first scene with the teachers on the bus.

The hot weather turned unusually humid that weekend, and both temperatures and tempers flared. The cast relieved their discomfort by submerging themselves in the tepid ocean but the sweltering heat refused to go away. On Saturday, as everybody tried to stay cool, a dark shadow passed between the palm trees and the electric generator. Moments later the motor coughed and spluttered and then fell silent. The lights in the huts went out and an eerie silence crept over the set. For three days there was no power; the only illumination came from kerosene lanterns and battery operated flashlights. All filming ceased while the generator operator Jorge Garcia attempted to fix the problem.

Whether it was an act of god or sabotage was never proven, but the crew had their own theories. Some thought that Emilio Fernández had broken the generator out of spite, while others suspected the Mismaloya natives of tampering with the engine. But the most common belief was that Richard Burton wanted to give everyone a couple of days off in celebration of his thirty-eighth birthday on Sunday, November 10. The previous morning, he had already polished off a bottle of Buchanan’s whiskey given to him by Ava Gardner. “We’ve worked six days a week since the beginning,” commented Thelda Victor, who welcomed the break in filming.

That weekend the company departed for Puerto Vallarta – taking part in the same activities that have since been enjoyed by millions of tourists. Burton and Taylor picked up Liza Todd from Casa Kimberly and took her to Playa de Oro, where they joined Grayson Hall and her family on the beach for a picnic. While the adults imbibed the kids built sandcastles and miniature dams.

James Ward played a game of burro polo with some of the American crew. Cheering spectators watched two teams of eight players with straw brooms hitting a soccer ball up and down the sand. It became a contest to see which players could hang on to their charging steeds without toppling to the ground.

Sue Lyon and Hampton Fancher hired a boat and went snorkeling. Their sixteen-year-old driver and his brother took the young lovers to a small reef. Wearing diving masks and snorkels the actors jumped overboard and swam amongst the eagle rays, puffer fish, and clown fish. Fancher tickled Lyon's feet and she giggled with excitement.

Back on the beach, Cyril Delevanti sat under a shady palm tree with a copy of the tenth James Bond novel *On Her Majesty's Secret Service.* After reading one chapter he put the book down and took a siesta. For the throngs of reporters, who hung around like vultures waiting for a tasty meal, the day was a bust. The press had to make do with tiny morsels to satisfy their hunger. The only romance, noted Stephen Birmingham, was the "flickering interest between Liza Todd and Grayson Hall's five-year-old son Matthew," who had been teaching her the alphabet.

"ILLUMINATION," GABRIEL FIGUEROA STATED, "is the privilege of the photographer because he is the owner of the light." On Monday, without any electricity, Figueroa demonstrated that remarkable talent by shooting two crucial scenes using a minimum of natural light. The first shot of the day took place on the hotel verandah when Maxine Faulk reveals Judith Fellowes' lesbianism and tells her: "Why don't you buzz off on your broomstick!"

When Miss Fellowes informs Shannon she is going to swear out a warrant for his arrest, Maxine comes to his defense. "You know what you're sore about? That little quail of yours has a natural preference for men!" The second shot was the departure of the schoolteachers on the bus, which was filmed on the beach at dusk. Maxine watches them leave and says: "Watch out for the fleas at the Ambos Mundos!"

Grayson Hall kept blowing her lines. In a corner of the set, Sue Lyon and Hampton Fancher were locked in a passionate embrace, kissing each other. Hall told John Huston: "I cannot act while those two lovers are necking in the corner. Here I am, trying to concentrate on my lines, with the two of them going at it hot and heavy on the sofa! It's just too damned distracting!" When Richard Burton added to her complaint, Huston had Fancher barred from the set, causing Lyon to throw a tantrum. The assistant director Tom Shaw had to restrain her. "If you want to neck, that's okay," said Huston, trying to pacify the actress. "But just don't neck on the set, honey. It bothers the people who are not necking."

A reporter from the *New York Journal-American* asked Lyon to comment on allegations that Fancher had been thrown off the set for attempting to tell Huston how to direct the movie. "Mr. Stark said he didn't have a role in the picture and he made everyone nervous," she pouted. "Well, Elizabeth Taylor doesn't have a role in the movie and she makes me nervous. How come she isn't barred?"

The generator, which had been out of action for three days, was repaired by lunchtime on Tuesday. Huston was impatient to resume work and they plowed into the next dramatic scene: a heated confrontation between Hannah Jelkes and Faulk, who resents the painter's intrusion. "The trouble is Shannon," she says. "I caught the vibrations between you two."

One bit of business that proved exhausting in the noonday torpor was a shoving match between Shannon and Maxine on the hotel verandah. Burton and Gardner pushed a heavy liquor cart laden with booze back and forth at increasing speeds until it nearly veered off into the jungle. Deborah Kerr rushed out to try and stop them. "This is childish! Stop it at once!" she yelled. "It's disgraceful!" There were repeated takes until Huston was satisfied that the scene had achieved the right level of sarcasm.

Shortly after filming resumed, several of the Mexican crew began complaining of severe headaches and muscle pain. When two of the men collapsed, Dr. Pérez Rivera discovered they had contracted dengue fever, which is transmitted by infected mosquitoes. The contagious illness was similar to malaria with victims complaining of sore eyes, bleeding gums and a painful skin rash. The men were confined to bed where they lay perspiring and convulsing for almost one week. Because there was no vaccine available, they had to take aspirin and sweat it out, tossing and turning in their delirium until the fever passed.

The tension on the set increased as more press arrived. The intrusion didn't seem to bother Elizabeth Taylor, who was in her element, but the other actors started getting jittery.

"Ava got mad at there being so many photographers and newsreel people clicking and whirring while she was working," said Kerr. "I agree with her – it *is* terribly distracting. But, unfortunately, it completely throws her, and the anger inside her gets on top of the situation and she just can't function."

Standing on the sidelines, out of camera range but within eyesight of the actors, was the Albanian pioneer of photoflash photography, Gjon Mili, who was on special assignment for *Life* magazine. Mili, age fifty-nine, wore a red beret, black silk shirt, grey pants and sandals. He kept running out of film and reloading his Leica camera. After fifteen minutes of him pointing and rapidly clicking the camera, Gardner called out: "That's enough!"

When Mili refused to stop taking photographs, she ran over, lifted her foot and kicked him solidly in the stomach. He fell over backwards, still holding on to the camera. "You want some more?" she asked, straddling Mili like a wrestler. The winded photographer got up, dusted off his beret and scurried over to Huston. "They sent for me!" he protested. "If I can't take pictures, I go home." Huston said nothing, just smiled broadly. The next day Mili was gone.

In her off hours, Gardner tried to numb the pain of loneliness by reaching out to any willing young man. The lights burned late at Casa de la Luna. "She threw parties many nights," said Lee Server, "and the beach boys would fill the villa – drinking, smoking marijuana, and dancing the twist." They probably didn't even know her name; just that she was a single white woman looking for some hot action. One of those boys became infatuated with her – and she with him.

Antonio Sanchez was a twenty-three-year-old water-ski instructor with broad shoulders and narrow hips. One day he met Gardner on the beach and offered to give her waterskiing lessons. She invited him home and they had sex twice that night.

"He was not so handsome. I don't think so," said Nelly Barquet. "Very skinny. Maybe she liked this kind of person. Cheap looking. She wanted to be with him, and he moved into the house."

Burton thought the beach boy was a hustler and advised Gardner to get rid of him. "He bleaches his hair," said Burton, "and any man who does that is trouble." Ignoring his advice, Gardner embarked on another disastrous love affair. Several weeks into their courtship, she threw a birthday party for Sanchez. Gardner decorated the house, cooked Southern fried chicken and baked him a cake. For some reason, he didn't show up until very late and by that time nearly everyone had left. "She was drunk by then," recalled the script supervisor Angela Allen, "and I thought this is going to end up in a very messy thing, and I don't want to be here mopping up the blood! So I decided I was not going to hang around, and I got out."

Burton's premonition proved to be correct: Sanchez was trouble. Beach boys are opportunistic by nature and will take advantage of any circumstances that will benefit them. It was the only way they could improve their lives, because most of them had never had anything. But Gardner couldn't tear herself free of him. Could it be she confused sex with love? All her lovers had been Casanovas. What she lacked from men in a long-term commitment, she made up for in short-term excitement. "Tony's great in bed," Gardner told one of the film crew. Every day she craved sex with him, but her obsessive nature and hysterical temperament eventually drove him away.

All too soon, their affair ended as it had begun: on the beach. Hollywood columnist James Bacon witnessed Gardner and Sanchez having a loud argument down by the speedboats. "They were going at each other, and the kid started hitting her. It was right in front of the tourists, and he was slapping her around pretty good. And she was taking it." Gardner cried for two days after they broke up.

The following year Sanchez married a bright woman named Marsha and they had two children. But Gardner never settled down and started a family; she flitted from one lover to another, her life a spinning carousel of one-night stands.

On November 16, six days after Burton's birthday, Peter Viertel turned forty-three. He celebrated by surfing and fishing for lobsters in Bucerias. His speedboat was driven by a thin, bearded teenager named Carlos and his twelve-year-old assistant Virginio, who took turns riding Viertel's surfboard.

That night, Kerr hosted a spaghetti party at their house in El Cerro. Music was provided by a flamenco guitarist that she met on the beach, and everyone sat around drinking beer and tequila. Huston arrived with a pre-Columbian mask and Sue Lyon brought a small gift. "Elizabeth and Richard were supposed to come, but at the last minute a very charming present arrived, but not them," said Kerr. The culprit, as usual, was Burton's fondness for alcohol, which rendered him unresponsive by midevening.

The Night of the Iguana, despite its many interruptions and delays, was now five days ahead of schedule. By some miraculous feat, the company had reached page 114 of the shooting script, which meant they were more than two-thirds finished. John Huston felt pleased with himself for reshaping the play to fit the location. But his good luck was about to run out.

"Untie me!" shouted Richard Burton, a look of fear in his eyes. "A man can die of panic!"

"Not when he enjoys it as much as you do," said Deborah Kerr facetiously.

The actors were performing their roles on the verandah of the Costa Verde Hotel in front of the camera crew on Monday, November 18.

It was the first night of shooting, which would last until three or four o'clock the next morning. The set was ringed with lights, and the boom microphone operator, sound recording men, electricians and grips carried out their tasks in the semidarkness.

Huston was filming the climactic duel of words between the three main characters, Reverend Shannon, Maxine Faulk and Hannah Jelkes, which would be shot over five consecutive nights. The mammoth scene stretched for more than twenty-two pages – almost one half-hour of screen time. In the script, Shannon has been brought back to the hotel by Maxine's two beach boys and tied up in the hammock to prevent him from killing himself. "You think I enjoy being tied up in this hammock like a hog in a slaughterhouse?" he cries out.

"No, who wouldn't like to atone for the sins of themselves and the world if it could be done in a hammock with ropes instead of on a cross with nails, on a green hilltop instead of on Golgotha, the place of the skulls," sneers Hannah. At that moment, high in the sky above the hotel, there was a flicker of lightning from some place far away. The mood was prime Tennessee Williams, the dialogue heavy with symbolism.

"Why have you turned against me?" pleads Shannon. "I haven't turned against you," says Hannah.

"All women, whether they want to face it or not," he complains loudly, "want to see a man in a tied-up situation!"

Maxine brings Shannon a tray of hot poppy-seed tea, which, she explains, is a mild sedative. But he doesn't want to drink it. He screams and thrashes about in the hammock like a wild animal. "I'm gonna call Doctor López and have you carted off to the Casa de Locos!" Maxine tells him. Shannon, his lips scalded from the hot beverage, becomes indignant. "May I make a suggestion, Maxine? Why don't you go moonlight bathing with your beach boys?"

"You bastard," hisses Maxine tearfully. "You no-good bastard!"

Huston yelled "Cut!"

There was a fifteen-minute break from the torrent of angry words. Elizabeth Taylor walked over to where Burton lay tied up in the hammock, and gave him a cigarette. Kerr, wearing her artist's smock, maintained her composure, while Gardner in her poncho top and black leggings showed increasing signs of nervousness. They had already been at it for several hours.

"Okay," said Huston. "Let's try it one more time." Taylor patted Burton's head and went to wait on the other side of the set. Shortly before Huston called out "Action!" to the actors, Gardner wearily shook her head. "I'm sorry," she apologized. "I can't do this." She abruptly left the set and went to the bar to get a drink. "For Christ sakes!" fumed Tom Shaw, the assistant director.

Filming of the scene continued with Burton and Kerr. After a short time, Gardner returned to the set, but it was useless, she was drunk. "The more we'd go on, the more Ava would drink," said Shaw. The hours ticked by. Gardner kept fluffing her lines. Huston was slowly losing his patience.

At 2:15 a.m., Shaw checked his wristwatch and said, "John, we're wasting our time. I don't think she's going to get it. We better call it a day." Huston nodded in agreement and the company was dismissed. The bright lights were doused. Shaw's assistant Terry Morse untied the ropes from around Burton's hands and feet and he got up from the hammock. Taylor put her arms around Burton and kissed him. The lightning continued to flicker in the sky. The crew packed up their equipment and everyone strolled back down the hill to their bungalows.

The pervading symbolism of the scene was not limited to Williams' prose. That night held special significance on the Aztec calendar.

It was three days before the end of the fourteenth Aztec ceremony honoring Quecholli, Precious Feather, which commemorates dead warriors, and celebrates the rituals of hunting and war. Prisoners were traditionally bound like deer and sacrificed to the gods. Huston had most likely not known the importance of that day, nor would anyone else unless they were Aztec. But that night, reenacting this ancient rite on the hillside, the film company was tempting fate.

The jungle was eerily quiet; the mountain could be seen only in silhouette, the palm trees outlined like black paper cutouts against the pale night sky. There was the intermittent exchange of male voices coming from inside the huts and then gradual silence as doors were closed and lights turned off.

Shaw uncapped a bottle of beer in the kitchen of his two-story bungalow. On the table were call sheets for the next day and a copy of the shooting script. Shaw went outside, leaned over the railing and saw Terry Morse walking along the pathway below. "Come on, sit down for a minute," he said. "We'll talk about tomorrow's work."

Morse nodded and walked up the stairs to the patio where Shaw handed him a cold bottle. They sat down on the railing and were about to take a sip of beer when they heard a terrible groan. Seconds later, the terrace beneath them gave way like a giant trapdoor and Shaw and Morse were tossed headlong down the hillside.

At first the Mexican crew suspected there had been an earthquake. They ran from their rooms, some of them carrying flashlights, and hurried over to Shaw's cottage. Huston put on his moccasins and sprinted after them.

Peter Viertel was the first to reach the injured men, who were lying twenty feet below in a ditch. "I landed right on my head," Morse recollected, "and it was just luck that I wasn't killed. I came to and Deborah Kerr was looking at me, holding my head up. They thought Tom Shaw might have been dead."

Huston was horrified at the sight of his two assistant directors lying semiconscious in a pile of rubble. “They had sat down on the balcony, which was supposed to be reinforced concrete and it had collapsed,” he remembered. “Terry was soon able to stand up, but Tommy just lay there, and we realized that he was seriously hurt.” Several of the crew ran for the doctor who was at the top of the hill and brought him down in a Jeep. The men carefully placed Shaw’s body on a mattress and lifted him into a room on the ground floor of the bungalow. By now he was awake and moaning in pain.

Twelve burly crewmembers improvised a stretcher out of a wooden bed frame. They put Shaw on a fishing boat with Huston in command and headed for Vallarta. By the time the boat reached Playa Los Muertos it was almost sunrise. Huston, who was the tallest of the group, jumped into the water fully clothed but realized it was too deep. “Help me!” he yelled, sinking up to his neck. The other men leapt overboard and they lowered Shaw, who was lashed to the stretcher, into the sea. They had to lift him high in the air in water that was almost over their heads. Each of the men held their breath as their faces disappeared beneath the waves. “I’ll never forget the sight of those hands holding the stretcher above the surface,” said Huston, “while the men walking on the bottom brought Tommy to shore.”

Clinging to life, Shaw was transported by truck to the Red Cross hospital where a doctor took X-rays showing his back was broken in two places. Seven Arts chartered a special plane and that same morning he was flown from Puerto Vallarta to Los Angeles for emergency treatment. At the time of Shaw’s accident, however, it was uncertain if he would survive the ordeal. Only because he had been a college star athlete and was in superb physical condition did he make a full recovery.

JOHN HUSTON WAS SO ENRAGED over what had occurred in Mismaloya in the early hours of the morning that he returned to the bungalows the following afternoon. Standing on one of the balconies, he raised his foot and with a swift kick demolished the balustrade. A few days later, the roof of Cyril Delevanti's room caved in, almost hitting the old man on the head. Then it was learned that the cabins were infested with termites and spiders, and the people that were living there had to be evacuated. Everyone was appalled.

"I think the accident serves to show up the basic quality of this location: that the whole place seems to have been put together with chewing gum is all too obvious and dangerous," recounted Deborah Kerr. "Apparently the cement was mixed with beach sand, which because of the high saline content doesn't cement."

The catastrophe delayed Huston's plans of turning the hotel and accommodations into a tourist resort. "We had a sixty-day schedule and half the bungalows started to fall apart after sixty days," said Ray Stark. Ironically, the only structure that was not damaged was the main set, which Stephen Grimes had insisted be made from different sand. Inconceivably, Guillermo Wulff, who had built all the cottages, absolved himself of any responsibility for the accident by saying that printed signs reading: CEMENTO FRESCO – WET CEMENT had been placed on the terraces of the bungalows as a warning to the men. It was an indefensible excuse, hardly justifiable considering the buildings were two months old.

But there was still a film to be made and three or four key scenes that needed to be completed. Twenty-four hours later, Ava Gardner had sufficiently regained her confidence to face the cameras again.

Although everyone was emotionally and physically drained from the near tragedy that had occurred, they wanted to put the experience behind them. No one felt guiltier than Gardner, who kept telling people it was her fault because she thought her drunkenness had contributed to the accident. Determined to make it up to everyone, she girded herself for the most controversial scene in the film: Maxine's erotic swim with her two male concubines.

The provocative moment, when Pedro and Pepe make love to her in the water, takes place at the shallow end of Playa Mismaloya, where future generations of tourists would go swimming.

But Gardner was embarrassed about her weight and told Huston that "I can't do it in the daytime. If it was night it wouldn't be so difficult." So he changed it to night but she was still frightened about being photographed in a bathing suit so he told Gardner not to worry, that she could go in the water wearing her poncho top and stockings.

The shot was planned for the evening of November 20 – coincidentally the fifty-third anniversary of the Mexican Revolution. Emilio Fernández engrossed the crew with tales of his own derring-do as a rebel soldier, and demonstrated his marksmanship by shooting at pineapples that had been lined up along the parapets of the hotel.

That afternoon, as Gardner sat drinking at the bar, Huston and cinematographer Gabriel Figueroa made advance preparations to ensure that everything would go off without a hitch. They planned to record the scene in one continuous take using multiple cameras with the rocks for backlighting.

The cameras were set up at five o'clock and covered with palm fronds to make them look as inconspicuous as possible. If all went well, Huston would roll the cameras three hours later when it was getting dark. The master shot would be photographed by Figueroa, while his camera operator Manuel González and their assistants Pablo Rios and Salvador de Anda handled the secondary shots of Gardner embracing the beach boys.

It was almost eight o'clock when Terry Morse, his head wrapped in bandages, came down to the beach and spoke to Huston. "I've got bad news," Morse informed him. "Ava is in the bar. She says she's not ready." Huston walked over to the bar and quietly sat down next to Gardner. "What are you drinking?" he asked. "Tequila," she replied. "Do you want some?" He answered "Yes."

The bartender brought them two shots of tequila, which they drank in one gulp. "It's been a hell of a week," said Huston. "Boy, you can say that again," agreed Gardner. "Too bad we have to cancel tonight," he said casually. "What do you mean?" she asked. "Weather forecast says rain," mentioned Huston. "In one hour there'll be too many clouds." Gardner looked him straight in the eye. "Are you putting me on?"

Huston shook his head. "No. It looks like we're going to lose the shot. I feel embarrassed for Gaby." Gardner gave him a quizzical look. "What's Gaby got to do with this?" The bartender refilled their glasses. "It's that you don't know all that he did," explained Huston. "He chose the beach, he got an extraordinary effect of moonlight and he was working with passion. I'm embarrassed to tell him that we have to do the scene on another day." Gardner quickly sobered up. "Wait a second," she said. "For Gaby I'll go to work." They finished their drinks and walked down to the beach where Figueroa stood facing the ocean. He was admiring the view. "It's a beautiful night," he said. "Sure is," Gardner smiled. They stood together watching the moon. "Hey, show me that dance again, will you?" she asked.

“You mean this one?” said Figueroa. He took off his shoes and demonstrated the various steps. “It’s called a *bailar huaracha*, a barefoot Cuban dance. Here, it’s easy.” He put his arms around Gardner’s waist and began to lead her back and forth. Roberto Leyva and Fidelmar Duran walked over and started shaking their maracas. For a few precious moments, everybody’s attention was focused on Figueroa and his partner dancing barefoot on the sand. When it came time to do the actual scene, however, Gardner was overwhelmed with fear. She wouldn’t budge from her spot on the beach. Huston must have thought, “Here we go again!” But he never complained, just smiled beatifically and took her by the hand. She started objecting and pulled away. He held on and slowly drew her closer to him.

Huston and Gardner waded into the ocean. Figueroa stood watching them holding hands, his eyes alert to the moment when he would roll the cameras. After getting accustomed to the temperature of the sea, Huston said to Gardner: “You all right, kid?” She nodded. “Yes. I’m fine.” Then he slowly let go of her hand, which was the signal for Figueroa to start the cameras. Huston motioned to the beach boys and they took up their positions in the water. Then they performed the scene exactly as it had been written in the final script:

> CAMERA is close on Maxine in Pepe’s arms. Pedro, his eyes gleaming, stands a foot or two away, playing his maracas. Pepe and Maxine are dancing to the rhythm but only their bodies move, their feet merely shifting in the sand. Maxine’s eyes are closed as she surrenders to the full sensations of her body. Suddenly, Pedro shifts both maracas to his left hand, making the rhythm more frenetic. Simultaneously, his body is pressed against Maxine’s back, his right arm encircling her as Pepe’s mouth closes down on hers. Now all three bodies are swaying in unison. Then suddenly Maxine starts struggling and breaks away from them. The two beach boys look after her in bewilderment as she runs down the beach.

When Huston called out "Cut!" he knew he had created something magical. Gardner turned around and strolled down the beach, a big smile on her face. "She had wanted the special attention," said Lee Server, "and Huston gave it to her, and in return she gave him all that she could. The scene was done, beautifully, in a single take." There was enthusiastic applause from the crew. "That was great," said Huston. Figueroa was overjoyed and started singing *O Sole Mio* at the top of his lungs. "I didn't know you could sing Italian opera," commented Huston. "Neither did I," said Figueroa, pulling out a half-empty bottle of Sauza tequila from behind the camera. They all headed up to the restaurant in high spirits.

Huston's favoritism towards Gardner during the making of *The Night of the Iguana* elicited mixed feelings from the cast and crew, who suspected that the director and actress may have been more than just friends. "You could tell by the way Huston indulged Gardner that there was something special between them," commented Bud Acord. But if that was the truth, their relationship had been a fleeting one, or perhaps nothing more than a strong case of mutual admiration. Regarding the scene, Gardner later confessed: "I was nervous about doing it, and John, bless him, understood. He stripped down to his shorts and got into the water with me for a rehearsal, showing me exactly how he wanted it to go, then directed the scene soaking wet. That is my kind of director."

That same night, Huston shot Hannah's confession with Shannon, who is still tied to the hammock on the hotel's verandah. The lengthy scene, which was the third act of Tennessee Williams' play, is the dramatic highpoint of the film. Huston filmed it simply with a minimum of movement and kept the camera on Kerr's face for most of her performance. The effect was like watching an actor on the stage delivering a passionate speech. "Have you never in your life had any kind of love life?" asks Burton, his hands and legs bound. "There are worse things than chastity," admits Kerr. "Yes," snorts Burton, "lunacy and death."

Hannah reveals to Shannon that she has had only two sexual encounters: once when she was molested in a Nantucket cinema at the age of sixteen, and more recently in Hong Kong when an Australian traveling salesman propositioned her in a sampan and masturbated while holding a pair of her stockings. "It was ten and a half pages," said Kerr, "and at the end of shooting I felt I had been talking for a week." She didn't get to bed until 4 a.m.

On Thursday, Huston filmed the emotional scene where Hannah's grandfather Nonno finishes writing his poem. With the jungle as his mute witness, Cyril Delevanti reads the composition from memory while Kerr writes it down:

How calmly does the olive branch?
observe the sky begin to blanch,
without a cry, without a prayer,
with no betrayal of despair...

Gardner and Burton look on in wonderment as he continues his recital:

A chronicle no longer gold
of bargaining with mist and mold,
and finally the broken stem,
the plummeting to earth, and then

An intercourse not well designed
for beings of a golden kind
whose native green must arch above
the Earth's obscene, corrupting love...

By the poem's end his energy is almost spent:

Oh, courage! Could you not as well
select a second place to dwell?
Not only in that golden tree
but in the frightened heart of me?

The experience proves so liberating for Nonno that he dies, prompting Shannon's moving observation that "God has set him free." After the scene was finished, everyone rushed over to Delevanti and congratulated him on his performance. "Thank you," he beamed. "Let's hope it's a step up the ladder for me." During filming, Huston had taken a special interest in the dandified actor, who reminded him a little of his own father, Walter Huston, who probably could have played the role if he were still alive. "Cyril was from that time on in demand," said Huston. "He was never again without an offer, and the last years of his life were happy ones."

Before night's end, Burton, after being untied by Kerr from the hammock, cut the iguana loose – metaphorically freeing his demons. But it took more than one slice of the rope to banish the cunning devils. Early on, Herb Caen had noticed a wooden crate filled with captured iguanas at the back of the set. Some of the lizards' mouths had to be sewn shut after one of them bit an electrician on the leg and it was feared the man might catch rabies so he was given a tetanus shot. Now the morose reptiles, accustomed to their captivity, looked as bored as everybody else. "For that final shot we need an iguana straining at the leash," said Huston expectantly. Tom Shaw's original plan had been to use a little turpentine and apply an electric prod to the animal's tail, so it would scamper back to the jungle. But since he was hospitalized nobody else seemed to know what to do.

When the time came to release the iguana, it refused to move. Twice Burton untied the sluggish creature, but it just sat there. One of the grips sprayed it with water and somebody else tried hitting the lizard with a broom. Finally, one of the electricians rigged up two wires and zapped it with 110 volts of electricity from the generator. The gimmick worked, if somewhat dangerously. Burton, whose hands were touching the iguana, felt the electric current pass through his body. He shot straight up in the air and crashed to the ground. Huston tried to make light of the incident. "Boy, I hope there isn't a Society for the Prevention of Cruelty to Iguanas," he joked.

Between shots, the cast met with hosts from radio and television, who had arrived to cover the last days of filming. "I have never seen so many cameras and recording machines on one picture," commented Kerr of the mass of Bell & Howell news cameras, portable quartz lights, electric sunguns, reel-to-reel tape recorders and microphones.

Richard Strout, the national correspondent for *The Christian Science Monitor* and *The New Republic*, flew in from Washington. The actors recorded on-the-spot interviews comprised of two parts: "closed-end" featuring a complete interview with Strout and "open-end" which provided a script so that local radio station announcers could ask live questions and get prerecorded answers.

Much of the manufactured hype was destined for M-G-M's publicity department, who distributed it to various outlets. An authorized 13½-minute promotional short, *On the Trail of the Iguana*, was photographed and directed by Ross Lowell. "There was a lot of drinking going on, and Huston had to work around many problems, but he was holding it all together," Lowell reminisced. "Burton was very friendly and insisted I have some beers with him. Ava Gardner was very sweet when sober. But I was advised to be awfully careful with her after noontime. One afternoon I was filming her, trying to frame a shot of her through some flowers, and she must have thought I was trying to sneak some shots of her, and she had a fit."

Lowell's lush footage of Mexico's beaches and jungles, which was shot with Kodak Ektachrome color film, provides a striking contrast to Figueroa's black-and-white cinematography. Moreover, it gives a sense of what might have been possible between Ray Stark and John Huston if they had been in greater accord over their artistic vision.

ON FRIDAY, NOVEMBER 22, 1963, Deborah Kerr came down to Playa Los Muertos at 4:30 p.m. to take the boat to Mismaloya for the last night of filming. That is when she learned about the murder of President John F. Kennedy, who had been fatally shot by two sniper bullets as his motorcade sped through Dallas, Texas, at 12:30 p.m. (Central Standard Time). The president was pronounced dead at 1 p.m. and the public announcement was made one half-hour later.

Radio news of Kennedy's death was just reaching Puerto Vallarta by the time Kerr arrived on the beach. At first it was difficult for her to comprehend what had happened. But as she sat in the speedboat, her eyes gazing out to sea, the full force of the tragedy hit home. "The complete flood of disbelief, horror and shock left me with a thumping heart and a knotted stomach," Kerr said. After the boat docked in Mismaloya, she climbed up the stairs to the bar and slumped into a chair next to Ava Gardner and the other actors, who were drowning their sorrows. The bartender brought Kerr a drink.

"Everyone was in a state of shock, of course," remembered Ross Lowell. "And there was a lot of disbelief and waiting to get confirmation because communication down there was so terrible. The radio was full of static."

Then, after what seemed like an eternity, John Huston called everyone together and asked them to follow him to the hotel set.

When everybody was assembled on the verandah, their backs to the sun, Huston addressed the group in a somber voice. “I am not a religious man,” he began, “but if there is a God, or whatever we call a god, I hope that at this tragic moment in time, he is giving comfort to the family of President Kennedy, who served his country in a time of war, and continued to serve her in a time of peace. Until today when he was so brutally taken from us, this dedicated young man, husband and father, who devoted his life to the leadership of the USA, was our greatest hope for the future.”

Some people wept openly, while others held each other. Assistant director Jaime Contreras, who had taken over from the incapacitated Tom Shaw, read aloud the Lord’s Prayer at the conclusion of which was heard a murmuring chorus of “Amen.” Contreras then made a special request to the cast and crew. “I respectfully ask everybody, whether they are American or Mexican, to observe one minute’s silence in memory of the president.”

The congregation stood motionless and bowed their heads. There was no noise, only the sound of breaking waves on the rocks below. Then, after sixty seconds had elapsed, Huston, Figueroa, Fernández and the rest of the company opened their eyes and looked up. Standing before them was a male trio, not heavenly angels, as one might have expected, though they certainly appeared wise and humble.

Propitiously, a three-man television crew from David Wolper Productions had arrived in Puerto Vallarta that afternoon to record interviews for a proposed documentary about the making of *The Night of the Iguana*. The twenty-five-minute program, which offered a tantalizing glimpse into the art of moviemaking, was scheduled as the nineteenth episode of the TV series *Hollywood and the Stars*. Greg Morrison, chief of publicity for Seven Arts, had sent a telegram to Huston, informing him of the importance of the upcoming special. “The footage that this crew takes will be screened for its principals and no shots taken will be used until cleared.”

Heading the film unit that visited Mismaloya on that gloomy day was writer-director-producer Bill Kronick, age twenty-nine, from Amsterdam, New York, his thirty-five-year-old cameraman-editor David Blewitt, a native of Los Angeles, and the assistant cameraman John Orland, twenty-four, from New Jersey. It was Orland's first major assignment, and he was understandably nervous being so far from home. "There was the additional emotional burden of knowing that President Kennedy had just been assassinated and wondering if the United States would come under attack by unnamed Communist forces during our absence," he said.

For three days, Orland had to transport all the camera gear to and from the movie location, first by dugout canoe to a waiting yacht and then to a raft and finally onto the dock at Mismaloya, where it was carried up to the set and back twice a day. Another concern was the battalions of mosquitoes that invaded Orland's room at the Hotel Rio, which didn't have window screens. "Sometimes in the middle of the night when the mosquitoes were on the attack I would spray DDT onto the nude body of our producer, Bill Kronick, and he would return the favor."

Orland's biggest worry, however, was making sure that the Arriflex 16-millimeter camera, which he had never handled before, as well as the rolls of undeveloped film that he sometimes inadvertently loaded backwards, were kept dry. "I sweated bullets until we returned to Hollywood and the film dailies were processed without a hitch."

On Saturday night, while the USA was still coming to terms with their first presidential assassination of the twentieth century, Burton and Taylor welcomed Deborah Kerr and Peter Viertel to Casa Kimberly, where they grilled four Texas steaks for dinner. They sat up until 3:30 a.m., "debating the details of the whole incredible happening," said Kerr, and swapping conspiracy theories about JFK's murder. They ate, drank and smoked, trying to forget the recent horrific events that had plagued the film.

Then, on Sunday afternoon, came the news that Kennedy's alleged assassin Lee Harvey Oswald had been shot and killed at 1:07 p.m. central time. "I began to feel like we were all living in a lunatic asylum," confessed Kerr.

"By late November, Iguana's jungle location had lost its charm for nearly everybody," said Lee Server. On Tuesday, Huston directed the first part of the film's final scene when Shannon and Hannah part company on the hotel verandah following the death of Nonno. Anthony Veiller had rewritten some of the dialogue, which added to the scene's poignancy. "I'm going to try my luck in the plaza," Hannah tells Shannon, echoing what many struggling artists coming to Mexico have done over the years. To brighten their mood between scenes, Burton and Kerr donned bowler hats, which they found in a costume box, and sang an old English music hall ditty:

There was I waiting at the church,
Waiting at the church,
Waiting at the church,
Then I found he'd left me in the lurch,
Lor' how it did upset me,

All at once he sent around a note,
Here's the very note,
This is what he wrote:
"Can't get away to marry you today,
"My wife won't let me."

Laughing, Burton said to Kerr; "I think we're singing my song." They removed their hats and bowed for the appreciate crew who responded with shouts of "Bravo!"

As the hours counted down to the last two days of filming, almost everyone became anxious to get their business over with and go home. On November 28, Ray Stark did his best to boost morale by having a traditional Jewish Thanksgiving dinner of turkey, pastrami, corned beef, sauerkraut, potato salad, pickles and cheesecake, flown in from New York.

At six o'clock, Elizabeth Taylor's two sons, Christopher and Michael Wilding Jr, aged eight and ten, visited the restaurant and sat in the bar watching their mother and Burton swilling tequila with beer chasers. Taylor was wearing a frilly white cotton top, with a bracelet of gold coins and a pair of hoop earrings. Next to her was a copy of Mexico City's English-language newspaper *The News*. The main headline was "Nation Mourns President Kennedy" with a photograph of New Orleans nightclub owner Jack Ruby shooting Lee Harvey Oswald in the basement of the Dallas Police Station.

The final scene between Shannon and Maxine was concluded the following day. For the first time since filming began, Burton and Gardner were completely sober, which showed their relief at nearly being finished. The scene was difficult for them to play; their characters had become emasculated because Huston feared audience rejection of a spider devouring her mate, as he put it, even though that was what had made Bette Davis so riveting in the Broadway play. But then Huston never cared much for the play, only the opportunity to make another film in Mexico. Kerr openly voiced her objections: "The end should be more savage, and it isn't, it's soft. One should feel that Shannon is left to his purgatory, and not that everything is going to be sweet and lovely with a really nice girl from El Paso."

Huston had no comment. He already had made up his mind, as he had when advocating that the film be photographed in black-and-white. But were his decisions made out of artistic respect for Williams' prose or monetary expediency? His philosophy of "win the battle, lose the war," which applied equally to moviemaking, was similar to the reasoning that governed much of his own life. That same logic also applied to Huston's code of moral behavior, covering up his frequent indiscretions, so it made sense for him to let Shannon escape his punishment.

Thus, Maxine's invitation to join her in hell became a thinly-veiled proposal of marriage: "Why don't we go down to the beach?" she asks kindly.

"Well, I can get down the hill," replies Shannon, "but I'm not too sure about getting back up."

"I'll get you back up, baby," Maxine smiles. "I'll always get you back up." These words were not written by Tennessee Williams; rather they were the invention of Tony Veiller, who also had a hand in the subsequent scene.

Charlotte Goodall's wild dance with Pedro and Pepe, which Sue Lyon had been rehearsing for two days, was scheduled for Saturday, November 30 – officially the last day of filming. The shot was made in a specially constructed ramada on the beach at the mouth of the Rio Mismaloya.

The area where Lyon performs the routine is located in front of Las Gaviotas – the oldest restaurant in the village. Eight customers sat at wooden tables drinking bottles of Bohemia beer and shots of tequila, while a mariachi song plays on an old windup Victor gramophone.

The *patrón* or boss, a tall, mustached, saturnine man, who looks like Paladin, was played by Emilio Fernández. This was not the first time that Fernández stepped before the cameras; he had previously acted in a number of important films, both in Hollywood and Mexico. He would go on to play villainous roles in three films directed by Sam Peckinpah, most famously *The Wild Bunch*.

Fernández relished the opportunity to appear in Huston's movie. "Charlotte has been drinking," described the script. "Her hair has become disarrayed from the violence of the dance which becomes more hectic as Pedro suddenly tosses the maracas into the air. Without missing a beat, Pepe catches them expertly and continues playing them as Pedro seizes Charlotte and continues the dance."

Originally, Huston wanted to use the popular tune *La Viuda Abandonada,* which had been recorded in 1961 by Amalia Mendoza. When RCA was unable to trace the music's copyright owner, he was forced to choose another song. Fernández suggested *La Negra,* a standard in the mariachi repertoire, made famous by the musical group Mariachi Vargas.

The cantina dance was representative of the culture clash between the Americans and Mexicans in Mismaloya. Fernández rants at Lyon's character: "No more! Stop it I say! Senorita, go home! Take your dollars with you. I am a rich man. I do not want your dollars. I do not want you dancing to my music. No more music! We do not want our sons to know that young girls can be like you! Muchachos, take her away!"

The scene continued with Hank rescuing her from the two boys. "If Judith's performance on the beach was a dance macabre, the fight that ensues is a ballet mechanique," indicates the script. Fernández changed the record on the gramophone and played a livelier tune called *La Raspa.* "Still dancing to the beat of the maracas, Pepe's jabbing fists cut Hank to ribbons." Makeup artist Jack Obringer painted a big shiner under James Ward's left eye, to make him look like he had gone several rounds. "Dancing like a pair of fighting cocks, Pedro and Pepe prance off. Charlotte falls to her knees beside Hank. Cradles his head to her breast."

Filming of the dance was completed shortly after lunch and when it was finished principal photography of *The Night of the Iguana* came to an end. It should have been a moment of joy for the cast and crew. Yet again, the occasion was marred by another tragedy that was broadcast that day on the ship-to-shore radio. Just twenty-four hours earlier, the worst air disaster in Canadian history occurred when a Trans Canada flight crashed in Montreal, killing 118 people. The grim news was of serious concern to Richard Burton and Elizabeth Taylor because Montreal was where they planned to get married when their respective divorces were finalized. Burton, in particular, viewed it as a bad omen.

All doubts were put on hold as preparations were made for that evening's festivities. Caterer Rick Rubin and his staff decorated the Iguana Café with colorful balloons, piñatas and paper streamers. After the sun disappeared behind the horizon, Rubin flipped a switch on the generator and the outline of the beach was illuminated in multicolored lights. A fifteen-piece mariachi band played traditional Mexican songs.

Ava Gardner was the first to arrive by boat from Puerto Vallarta, looking radiant in a brightly-patterned Pucci harem outfit which Ray Stark had given her. At eight o'clock Richard Burton and Elizabeth Taylor walked from the dock along the pathway to the beach. He was wearing his favorite green cardigan sweater which showed off the color of his eyes. She wore a white jersey blouse and matching slacks with a large diamond-encrusted rose-shaped pin at her bosom. The sweet smell of citronella and Jungle Gardenia perfume mixed with the spicy aroma of fried tacos and enchiladas.

Chefs cooked strips of *carne asada* – thinly sliced sirloin steak – and pork tenderloin on the grill. A local specialty, *pollo a las brasas* – grilled chicken roasted over hot coals – was served with finely chopped cabbage and sliced radishes, accompanied with homemade *gorditas* – thick tortillas – and hot Tomatlan salsa. There were buckets of cold beer on the restaurant tables, plus bottles of wine, vodka, gin, and whiskey. "We drank up everything in sight," said Thelda Victor, "and then we began to draw on the supplies of tequila brought by the more than 200 Mexican townspeople from Puerto Vallarta who had been invited."

When they ran out of tequila, the bartenders started pouring *raicilla* from jugs with cork stoppers. Even in small quantities the potent brew had a powerful effect. As the music from the party became louder and people got progressively drunker, the numbers of dancing couples increased until the beach was covered in gyrating bodies. Marijuana cigarettes were liberally passed around. People ate wild mushrooms and chewed peyote leaves that had been cooked in boiling water.

These hallucinogenic drugs altered the user's perception of time and space. Inanimate objects were transformed into ungodly figures and normal images distorted into bizarre shapes.

The beach was no longer a tropical oasis but a posh Hollywood nightclub, the trees and rocks an enclave of cozy booths and tables; the silver sands a mirrored dance floor. Men were outfitted in formfitting jackets and stovepipe trousers, blow-dried hair covering their foreheads and ears; women in smart dresses and miniskirts, their long curls teased upwards in flips or beehives. Flashy pendants adorned plunging necklines. Dancers shook their arms and legs to the hyperactive electric guitar rhythms and pounding drums of that summer's hit song *Wipeout*, played by the Surfaris.

The sound of the rolling surf was a strong aphrodisiac. Inhibitions were lost as people took off layers of clothing like snakes shedding old skin. Eager hands grabbed willing torsos; partygoers paired off and stumbled into the jungle. John Huston and Zoë Sallis caressed each other under the palms. Ava Gardner wrapped her arms around a sinewy young man. Sue Lyon and Hampton Fancher kissed in a dark alcove. Emilio Fernández grabbed an Indian girl and took her to one of the unused bungalows. Other couples, their passions aroused, dropped to the ground in a mating frenzy, moaning and groaning with pleasure.

Twelve hours after it started, the party broke up at 4 a.m. on Sunday, "and even John's pet iguana looked stoned," commented Axel Madsen. In the drug-induced euphoria few people missed Deborah Kerr and Peter Viertel, who had intended to go to Mismaloya and then changed their minds. "Had it been just us and all our boys, whom I have become so fond of, it would have been a different matter," stated Kerr. "I just felt I couldn't cope with Puerto Vallartan society. So I didn't go." Maybe Kerr was tired or perhaps she felt guilty, having already dismissed these people as "gross, overdressed or excessively underdressed, loud and very drunken." Clearly, she felt out of place.

The next day, after viewing the rushes, Huston felt that Kerr's performance could be improved. He arranged for a skeleton crew to stay behind and reshoot Hannah's confession even though Kerr was reluctant to go through the whole thing again. "The prospect of three more nights is hideous," she admitted, "but at least we are fortunate in that we *can* do it and, consequently, improve the whole." The night scene was filmed from Wednesday through Friday. Huston was a good sport about it, offering fresh ideas and making helpful suggestions.

On Sunday, December 8, Kerr left Playa Los Muertos at nine-thirty in the morning for one last retake of the end scene with Burton. The tenderness between Burton and Kerr was real, and they had to take care not to overplay their emotions. As they bid each other farewell, Shannon gives Hannah a present of his gold cross. "That's a real amethyst," Burton tells Kerr, "so don't let the loan shark give you less than 1,800 pesos for it." At the scene's conclusion, Huston called "It's a wrap everybody!" and the crew broke into applause.

AFTER SEVENTY-SIX DAYS OF MAKING a movie "in a Godforsaken, miserable, uncomfortable corner of the world," wrote Thelda Victor, the agony of living and working in Puerto Vallarta was finally over. "If this were *Cleopatra*," said John Huston melodramatically, "it would have been a massacre." Compared to the fiscal hemorrhaging, two fatalities and numerous injuries that plagued the making of that colossal film, the producers of *The Night of the Iguana* were let off lightly – or so everyone thought. There wasn't as much as a nick to the cast members or their producer from one of the thirty engraved bullets that accompanied Huston's gift to them of six gold Derringers.

The press reacted with profound disappointment that no blood had been spilt, especially from the veins of the film's director, who many observers hoped and prayed would get his comeuppance. "The publicity tom-toms boomed warnings. This looked like throwing a match into a powder keg," wrote Associated Press correspondent Morris Rosenberg, who was waiting for a loud detonation. But all too soon the fuse sputtered out. "The whispered fancies of the village gossips proved only to be part of the warm air waving the coconut palms," he lamented.

The only casualty, reported in *The New York Times*, occurred when Sue Lyon was bitten by an angry scorpion. But if such a thing did happen, it only temporarily dampened the actress's high spirits. Grayson Hall kept her scorpion vaccination kit close at all times, and Dr. Pérez Rivera was never far away.

After a final round of drinks at the Hotel Oceano, followed by a farewell dinner with Gabriel Figueroa and Emilio Fernández at Las Margaritas restaurant, Huston flew to Los Angeles, where waiting reporters buttonholed the arriving director at the Beverly Hills Hotel about his latest film. "Easiest picture I ever made," Huston boasted to Hedda Hopper, refusing to give her an ounce of grist for her gossip mill. "Everybody adored themselves and one another. A most serene experience." What about all those drunken orgies? Huston had no comment. But Hopper's eagle eye spotted something far more incriminating during their sixty-minute-long interview. And it wasn't a naked woman, though one was there in the form of Zoë Sallis, sleeping with her son Danny in the next room.

Sitting on the coffee table of Huston's plush $300-a-night hotel suite was a 200-year-old carved mastodon tusk and a pre-Columbian vase and sculpture that he had brought back from Mexico. There were no customs forms attached to the three items nor had they been declared. These archaeological finds were a good indication that he had been smuggling valuable relics out of the country. Huston first acquired his taste for purloined antiquities during the filming of *The Treasure of the Sierra Madre* in Michoacán, when he hid several pre-Columbian tomb figures in a Warner Brothers movie sound truck and had the priceless statues driven across the Mexican border. After losing his art collection to ex-wife Evelyn Keyes in a coin toss, he attempted to rebuild the collection by any means possible, wherever it was legal or not.

During the making of *The Bible*, Huston's secretary Gladys Hill smuggled various art treasures out of Cairo to Rome – a risky but profitable enterprise. Among the items that eluded Egyptian customs officials was an eighteenth dynasty wooden scribe worth around $75,000 and jewelry valued at $500,000. Their intended destination was a rich exiled family in Switzerland. "Many of the art objects with which I filled St. Clerans," Huston confessed, "arrived there as the direct result of Miss Hill's prowess as a smuggler."

Right then, however, Huston was unconcerned by latent allegations of piracy. Weighed down with Christmas gifts, including a $1,500 Florentine crossbow for his son Tony, who had turned thirteen, the director returned to St. Clerans to spend the holidays with his wife Ricki and their family. It was not a happy homecoming.

While Huston had been working in Mexico, his absent wife, whether motivated by loneliness or out of revenge, consummated an affair with a thirty-five-year-old British diplomat named John Julius Cooper. The man she took to bed was not merely a public servant; he was the second Viscount of Norwich.

When Ricki Huston became pregnant with Cooper's child, she decided to forgo an abortion. Her husband never suspected the affair until she informed him one afternoon while the maid was serving tea.

Incensed, Huston beat his wife with a metal poker and broke her wrist. On August 26, 1964, she gave birth to a daughter in London. The baby was named Allegra. The birth certificate stated: "Father unknown."

In Puerto Vallarta, life went on for Richard Burton, Elizabeth Taylor, Liza Todd and the two Wilding boys, Chris and Mike, who had settled into a daily routine at Casa Kimberly. It was a special time of year.

The festival of Guadalupe, which marks the anniversary of the day the Virgin Guadalupe made her miraculous appearance to a peasant in Mexico, was already underway. For more than 500 years, this annual celebration, which lasts twelve days, has been held in cities and towns around the country. Every afternoon at four o'clock, hundreds of people marched in a two-mile procession along Calle Juarez to the cathedral, where they attended a candlelit mass, followed by folkloric dancing, singing and fireworks.

But there were other practical reasons for Burton and Taylor staying in Mexico, one of which was a legal matter known as "proof of residency."

At the time, married American couples seeking a divorce had to comply with different state laws requiring between six weeks and one year's separate domicile to legally end a marriage. Alternatively, they could skirt the law by getting a Mexican "quickie" divorce. That involved one or both parties crossing the border, usually from El Paso, Texas, to Juárez in the state of Chihuahua. Once there, the husband or wife hired a Mexican lawyer, paid one dollar to the clerk of the Municipal Court and received a slip of paper certifying that they were in Juárez. A short time later, the local judge, exercising his authority, granted them a legal divorce.

By remaining in Puerto Vallarta, Burton and Taylor circumvented the long, drawn-out process of American law, which could have taken as long as two years. On December 16, 1963, Burton's divorce was finalized when his wife of fourteen years Sybil Williams was awarded a decree *in absentia* by Judge Arcadio Estrada Quiñónez in the Puerto Vallarta Supreme Court of Jalisco.

The Burtons retained the counsel of Aaron Frosch of the prestigious New York law firm Weissberger & Frosch. The lawsuit charged her husband with "abandonment and cruel and inhuman treatment," noting that he was "in the constant company of another woman." *Newsweek* called that "the throwaway line of the decade." Frosch, who spent the month in Puerto Vallarta drawing up divorce papers, became an indispensible part of the two actors' lives.

In celebration of the decree, Burton presented Taylor with an emerald and diamond ring, pendant earrings and matching bracelet, which completed the Grand Duchess Vladimir Suite that he purchased from Bulgari.

The date was important for another reason: it was the first day of the Mexican religious celebrations called *posadas* that were held every night, reenacting the journey of Mary and Joseph to Bethlehem and their search for an inn where Mary could give birth to the baby Jesus.

At twilight, Burton and Taylor returned home, walking up Calle Guerrero to Casa Kimberly. Photographers kept a respectable distance from the lovesick stars, who strolled hand in hand along the street, trailed by their bodyguard Bobby La Salle. On the sidewalks were *nacimientos* – small mangers made of wood and straw with painted ceramic models of the nativity scene. These displays of fertility made Burton feel glum. Taylor, as he knew, could no longer conceive a child. Eventually, she would undergo a hysterectomy.

Two days later, Burton and Taylor held a press conference at the Hotel Playa de Oro, which was attended by a blitz of international media. The jazzy Samba rhythm of the hit song *Blame It On the Bossa Nova*, recorded by Eydie Gorme, could be heard coming from the beach pavilion. With its exuberant refrain about the dance of love, the bubbly tune perfectly captured the hopeful mood of Burton and Taylor. The suntanned couple sat in two wicker fan back chairs behind a long bamboo table. As photographers and reporters crowded around them, Burton announced through a haze of flashbulbs: "We're very happy now but we'll be happier when we're married." Several journalists yelled out "When will that be?" Burton smiled "Just as soon as possible and the sooner the better."

In response to one reporter's comment about Eddie Fisher wanting to get a quickie divorce in Juárez, Taylor was adamant: "I want this marriage to be thoroughly legal." This was the first direct word from the pair that they intended to climax their lengthy romance with wedding bells. The resultant headlines made front page news around the world:

"BURTON AND LIZ TO WED SOON"

> PUERTO VALLARTA, Mexico, Dec. 18 (AP) – Richard Burton said today that he and Elizabeth Taylor will be married somewhere in Mexico "just as soon as possible – and the sooner the better." He said, "the date depends on Mr. Fisher," referring to Eddie Fisher, Miss Taylor's estranged husband, with whom divorce proceedings have been an on again, off again matter for months. Miss Taylor said the question of whether she or Fisher would get the divorce had not been decided. The pair made the statement in an interview at the bar at the Playa de Oro Hotel in this tropical West Coast resort...

Coincidentally, on that same day, Sue Lyon and Hampton Fancher obtained a marriage license at the courthouse in Santa Monica, California. The wedding date on the invitations, which Lyon's mom hastily mailed out, was Sunday, December 22, 1963. Oddly enough, the first invitation was given to Fancher's ex-wife, Joann, who happily accepted. But if Lyon and Fancher hoped to steal the limelight from Taylor and Burton, they only snatched a couple of beams.

The young couple was married in a civil ceremony at Dorothy Jeakins' two-bedroom apartment in Los Angeles. The seventeen-year-old bride wore a sleeveless white satin dress and veil, while the twenty-five-year-old groom had on a black suit and tie. Family and friends threw rice as the harmonious voices of the Beatles could be heard singing their newest record *She Loves You* on the radio.

A champagne reception was held outside on the small patio of the apartment, where, it was noted, there were more newsmen than guests. If the location that was chosen for the nuptials seemed odd that's because Jeakins had formed a special bond with Lyon on the movie set.

Although the actress was sometimes accused of being moody, Jeakins knew differently. They were both loners who dreamt of finding true love with a special man. Wasn't that every woman's dream? After returning to Los Angeles, Jeakins threw herself into work. Spread out on the kitchen table was pencil sketches and fabric swatches of lederhosen costumes for the nine Trapp Family Singers that would take the talented designer to Salzburg, Austria, for her next film assignment *The Sound of Music.*

Back in Puerto Vallarta, Burton played host to ten newspaper reporters, who had been invited by Taylor to Casa Kimberly, where the butler poured Veuve Clicquot champagne and eighteen-year-old Dewar's Scotch, and the maid served trays of canapés. It was a yuletide gesture of goodwill to the press, many of whom were known to the couple on a first name basis. Seated in the living room was their friend and neighbor the CBS news correspondent Charles Collingwood, along with visiting showbiz correspondents James Bacon and Roderick Mann. Doing his best to spread good cheer, Burton reportedly downed a dozen glasses of whisky and Taylor tried to keep pace with four gins and tonic.

On Christmas Eve, Taylor's parents, the wealthy Beverly Hills art and antiques dealer, Francis Taylor, and his graceful wife Sara Southern, who was devoted to her daughter's career, arrived in Puerto Vallarta – "she is beaming and prattling on as usual in her little girl's voice, he with his cool, uncertain expression," commented Donald Spoto.

On the same flight were the actress's brother Howard Taylor and his wife Mara Regan, along with Taylor's recently adopted German daughter Maria, holding a yapping Sealyham, which kept licking everyone's faces. The delicate two-year old girl, who had undergone several operations to correct a crippling hip deformity, and her slobbering pet were both escorted off the plane by a smiling English nanny.

Burton and his secretary Jim Benton met them at the airport. "Maria walked down the ramp without a trace of a limp," said Spoto. "After which, the child fell ill with a temperature of 104 degrees, and Elizabeth became frantic trying to find a local doctor to treat her." But the girl made a full recovery and celebrated her third birthday at the house two weeks later.

That night, the Burton-Taylor family attended a midnight mass at the Church of Our Lady of Guadalupe. Afterward, they enjoyed a traditional Mexican Christmas dinner of roast suckling pig, turkey, *romeritos* – sprigs of a wild plant – served with patties of dried shrimp and potatoes in a mole sauce.

Taylor's friend Ava Gardner may have wished she was there. Instead, at the same moment Burton was passing the gravy dish across the dining table, the actress was running a gauntlet of paparazzi at the Basin Street West nightclub in Hollywood, where she had gone to celebrate her forty-first birthday on December 24.

While Gardner was necking with her male escort at a corner table, a photographer honed in on them. What happened next made the morning papers: "The camera went off, and the escort grabbed for it, shouting, 'You can get your head broken for that!' The two men scuffled, Ava running out, the escort catching up, a Cadillac sedan screaming out of sight," said Lee Server.

But the biggest mishap of the year was yet to come. Ray Stark was skiing in Sun Valley, Idaho, over the Christmas holiday season, when he tumbled off his skis on the downward slope. A first aid patrol skied out to where Stark lay in the snow, crying out in pain. They placed the injured producer on a stretcher and carried him back to the resort.

A local doctor found Stark had suffered a compound fracture to his right leg. His broken limb was put in a splint until he could be taken to the hospital for medical treatment.

Huston was at St. Clerans when he heard the bad news. "Dear Ray," he wired back, "Hope this little accident doesn't get you down or keep you off your feet too long. Love, John."

Determined to put the past behind him, Huston rang in the New Year with as much fanfare as possible. He knew big things were in store for him, and he eagerly welcomed the arrival of 1964. On Friday, January 3, the American director became an Irish citizen. After a decade of living in Ireland, he had no problem relinquishing his American ties. "The step I'm taking represents a sincere desire to get to the roots of my ancestors. I've had this on my mind for a couple of years," he said, visiting the Dublin office of Justice Charles Haughey.

Ultimately, Huston's decision to leave the United States was not so much a desertion; it was more of a defection. "After Kennedy was murdered, what little glimmer of political optimism he had abruptly faded," stated Lawrence Grobel. "If he was ashamed of his country of birth, he was definitely proud to be considered an Irishman."

Three days after being granted permanent Irish residency, the director boarded a plane for Italy, where he started preproduction on *The Bible*. Holding the stamped travel document in his hand, Huston characteristically spoke his mind. "An Irish passport is one of the most valuable. It has no restrictions. With it I can go anywhere, even to Red China if I want to," he told the assemblage of reporters at Dublin Airport.

ON JANUARY 14, 1964, the Los Angeles attorney Milton "Mickey" Rudin, representing Elizabeth Taylor, filed an abandonment petition with the State of Jalisco Court and the same judge that awarded a divorce to Sybil Burton gave Taylor's husband Eddie Fisher twenty-two days to reply. A heavyset man with a raspy voice, Rudin had spent the holiday season in Puerto Vallarta as Taylor's houseguest, swimming and taking trips on Burton's boat.

The same day that Rudin filed the petition for Taylor's divorce, James Real, who represented the American investors in Club Mismaloya, sent an urgent telegram to John Huston in Ireland, apprising him of a developing crisis: "EL INDIO AND OTHER VULTURES TRYING TO STEAL MISMALOYA." In Huston's absence, Emilio Fernández had spoken with the Indians, who planned to usurp the investors by enforcing their land rights.

In the Los Angeles office of A. Morgan Maree Jr. & Associates, which assisted in the preparation of income tax returns and business investments, Huston's manager Jess Morgan smelled a rat. He held in his hand a deed that he had received from Guillermo Wulff. The letter, typed on pale blue Club Mismaloya stationery and signed by Wulff, granted Huston exclusive rights and title to his house on three lots at the centre ridge of the Mismaloya peninsula. The agreement was for twenty years inclusive from the execution of the contract between Wulff and Huston on December 1, 1963 until its expiration on April 1, 1982, when the terms of the lease could be renegotiated.

As Morgan read the letter, alarm bells sounded in his head. Where was the official Mexican government seal? Why hadn't the document been notarized? Morgan informed Huston that he doubted the legality of the document, which had not been legally drafted and contained numerous spelling errors.

Huston cabled Mexican President Adolfo Lopéz Mateos at Chapultepec Palace, as well as former President Miguel Alemán Valdéz, who was now the chief of the Mexican tourist bureau, requesting their help. Huston's secretary Gladys Hill also wired the Mexican attorney Victor Luna Gonzáles, who was a friend of the director, in Guadalajara. A separate telegram was sent to Gabriel Figueroa "because the president of Mexico is related to Figueroa and they play cards a couple of times a week," said Hill.

It became imperative to authenticate the deed and find out whether or not Wulff was defrauding investors. Norval Lavene, vice president of the advertising agency Fuller, Smith & Ross, which was promoting Club Mismaloya, flew to Puerto Vallarta to resolve the matter.

After meeting with the Mismaloya Indians, Lavene received written guarantees from village representatives that the club association could legally transfer the lease and protect their property.

By the end of January, Lavene had raised nearly $20,000 from club members to pay for legal costs and secure their ownership in the resort. But fate had different plans.

President Lopéz Mateos was bound to uphold the Mexican constitution which favored the rights of its citizens over foreigners. After being elected president in 1958, he distinguished himself by providing low-income housing for 100,000 people and increased the land distribution by allotting thirty million acres to individuals and *ejidos* or communal groups – more than had been done by previous administrations in eighteen years. He could not lose face by reversing his popular stand on land rights, even for the sake of diplomacy.

Likewise, Miguel Alemán remained loyal to similar causes, notably his promotion of Acapulco as the country's premier tourist resort, which took precedence over Puerto Vallarta. In this respect, Huston had erred by underestimating the Mexican legislature.

Faced with the reality that Wulff's assurances were nothing more than empty promises, Huston canceled his investment in Club Mismaloya and withdrew from the venture. The first rule of buying real estate is *caveat emptor* – buyer beware. In other words, if the land does not have title it is not a safe investment.

Fifty years later, the issue of land rights still has not been resolved. The continuing anger of Mismaloya residents, who have been dispossessed of their property by fraudulent real estate deals, was demonstrated by graffiti spray painted on a concrete wall: GRINGOS U ARE ILLEGALLY BUYING INDIGENOUS LAND.

On January 22, Burton and Taylor flew to Los Angeles en route to Toronto for the first tryout of John Gielgud's 1964 revival of William Shakespeare's *Hamlet*, in which Burton played the treacherous prince of Denmark. The classic tragedy, which was performed in five acts, replaced traditional costumes with modern street clothes in the hopes of attracting a more diverse audience.

Burton and Taylor had barely passed through customs at Los Angeles International Airport, when the rumblings of a press stampede spread through the concourse. Although it was nighttime, the airport was jampacked. Security guards escorted the actors through the labyrinth of corridors beneath the Pan American World Airlines satellite, but 200 photographers, reporters and gate crashers blocked their escape.

There was a chaotic twenty-minute fight to get to a waiting limousine that transported the world's most notorious lovers to the Presidential suite of the Beverly Wilshire Hotel.

"Photographers banged into garbage cans, one fell into a dog cage, others stumbled over luggage as they fought for good shots of the celebrated pair," described Jack Smith of the *Los Angeles Times*. "Teenagers squealed. One father held up a small boy to see the famous couple. The boy was crying. Police whistles split the air. The scene was turned to daylight by floodlights. The queen was home."

A press conference was held for eighty photographers and newsmen in the Beverly Wilshire's rococo meeting room, where the atmosphere was filled with tension. "I'm always afraid somebody's going to throw acid," grumbled Burton. "I hope as many people come to see *Hamlet*." Burton announced they would be taking the Super Chief to Chicago and travel from there to Toronto. Instead he and Taylor flew direct from Los Angeles and avoided the press by having Jim Benton leave two hours later with their luggage. Arriving in Toronto on January 28, Burton and Taylor took over the three-bedroom Royal Suite on the eighth floor of the King Edward Hotel. Armed guards stood outside the door while downstairs in the lobby the media swirled like a mini tornado.

In the meantime, Ray Stark had begun the elaborate task of getting *The Night of the Iguana* ready for worldwide release. Even though the producer was incapacitated with a broken leg, it didn't stop him from overseeing the movie's postproduction – the laborious process of cutting, editing and synchronizing music and sound effects that are necessary before a completed film can be shown to an audience.

On February 17, after screening a two-hour rough cut of the movie at the offices of Seven Arts in New York City, Stark dictated a two-page letter to Huston, accompanied by seven pages of editing notes with almost 100 comments and suggestions for improving every scene in the picture. He was assisted in this endeavor by a small taciturn lady wearing eyeglasses. Her name was Margaret Booth, and she was the supervising film editor at M-G-M – a post she had held since 1937.

A dedicated theoretician, Booth started her career in the dawn of cinema, before the silent movies learned to talk. She pioneered an editing technique known as "invisible cutting," which made the change from one image to another within the same scene almost imperceptible, so that most viewers were unaware of the transition.

For two days, Booth, age sixty-six, sat through several viewings of Huston's film. She informed Stark that many scenes needed adjustment; some of the shots chosen by Huston were, in her opinion, repetitive or redundant. (Huston had no personal involvement in the editing process. The right of final cut typically belonged to the producer. In any case, the finished picture, as Huston shot it, was incapable of being altered to any substantial degree.)

To make the movie conform to her rigid standards, Booth wanted to eliminate a panning shot of young boys standing on the road holding iguanas, which is one of the most striking moments in the film. Clearly, she disliked the scaly lizards and tried to reduce the savagery of the landscape by trimming anything that she considered to be inappropriate. Booth also wanted to cut out several of the teacher's reactions, which she thought were repulsive, and delete several close-ups that were unflattering to Ava Gardner.

When Tennessee Williams came up from Florida for an advance screening of the movie, he had his own criticisms. He commented about Huston's overemphasis on the beach boys, which he thought distracted from the main characters. He also harbored concerns about the end of the film, which, like Booth, he judged to be too abrupt. These were pertinent observations, though unlikely to affect the movie's overall quality. As much as Stark valued Booth's opinion, he ultimately refrained from changing anything of significance, believing that what he had was magic in a bottle – or, more appropriately, a film can.

After three weeks of rehearsals, *Hamlet* opened on February 26 at the O'Keefe Theatre in Toronto for a three-city Canadian run, which was completely sold out.

The joyful occasion called for a double celebration. The next day, February 27, was Elizabeth Taylor's thirty-second birthday. When she awoke in the king size bed of their hotel suite, Burton surprised her with a stunning emerald and diamond necklace from Bulgari. She squealed with delight and threw her arms around him.

On March 5, in Puerto Vallarta, Judge Estrada, who, by now, had grown accustomed to the whims of celebrities, ruled that Taylor was divorced, and judged that Eddie Fisher, by failing to present himself in court, had confessed to her charge of abandonment. Ten days later, Burton chartered a Viscount Turboprop aircraft for $3,000 to take him, Taylor and ten friends from Toronto to Montreal for a private wedding ceremony. Among the invited guests was Burton's agent Hugh French, his lawyer Aaron Frosch, and the couple's publicist John Springer. "The wedding," wrote showbiz columnist Earl Wilson of the *New York Post*, "was remarkable for its simplicity, haste, secrecy and general lack of circus flavor."

Burton and Taylor were married in the bridal suite of the Montreal Ritz-Carlton Hotel by a Unitarian minister, Reverend Leonard Mason, on Sunday, March 15, 1964.

Burton wore a blue suit, maroon necktie and matching pocket square handkerchief. Taylor was dressed in yellow chiffon with a headdress of white hyacinths, designed by Irene Sharaff, who also created the costumes for *Cleopatra*. Pinned to the right breast of Taylor's wedding dress was a gleaming emerald-and-diamond brooch, part of the Grand Duchess Vladimir Suite that Burton had purchased in Rome. Burton would later add two emerald-diamond bracelets to the set.

Even though this was Taylor's fifth wedding, she still managed to delay her entrance in true movie star fashion. "Isn't that fat little tart here yet? She'll be late for the Last bloody Judgment!" roared Burton, which prompted Taylor's annoyed response: "I don't know why he's so nervous. We've been sleeping together for two years!" As the amused guests looked on, Reverend Mason quietly performed the marriage ceremony.

Burton placed a sparkling diamond-studded wedding band around Taylor's finger, and they were pronounced husband and wife. The groom kissed the bride in customary fashion and the corks were popped from two dozen chilled bottles of Moët & Chandon champagne in celebration.

Photographer William Lovelace was among the selected group of press who were allowed to take wedding photographs. "It was a surprise for me to be invited because I had been hounding them for so long," he recalled. "But they knew who I was because they had seen me in so many countries. It was almost like I was a part of their family."

The following day the smiling newlyweds returned to Toronto, where Burton was given a standing ovation at the end of that evening's performance of *Hamlet*. After the curtain came down he brought Taylor out on stage, the two of them basking in the footlights. Holding Taylor's hand, Burton repeated Hamlet's promise to Ophelia: "I say, we will have no more marriages!" and the theater erupted in cheers.

That same night, actor Hume Cronyn, who played two memorable roles with Taylor and Burton: Sosigenes, the Egyptian prime minister, in *Cleopatra* and Polonius, the Danish lord chamberlain, in *Hamlet*, hosted a cocktail party for the married couple. Present at the reception was Cronyn's wife, actress Jessica Tandy and the play's director John Gielgud, along with cast members Alfred Drake, William Redfield, John Cullum, and Burton's friend, comedian Peter Cook. The clinking of champagne glasses lasted until 2 a.m. It seemed the pomp and ceremony would never end for Burton and Taylor.

IN MARCH, AT THE SIXTEENTH Annual Awards Dinner of the Writers' Guild of America, held at the Beverly Hilton Hotel in Los Angeles, John Huston arose to accept an award from his peers for advancing "the literature of the motion picture through the years." Waving an open bottle of champagne, he declared that he was drinking to them all "from an overflowing cup, with an overflowing heart." American comedy writer and song parodist Allan Sherman, who was dressed as a gaucho, paid tribute to Huston with a lampoon of the recent doings at Puerto Vallarta, which he sung to the tune of *The Streets of Laredo*:

> They were down there to film *The Night of the Iguana*
> With a star-studded cast and a technical crew.
> They did things at night midst the flora and fauna
> That no self-respecting iguana would do.

The festivities over, postproduction for *The Night of the Iguana* moved closer to its completion. Because the film was being assembled in London, it gave Stark access to a selection of technicians and artists that might otherwise have been unavailable to him in Hollywood. One of these fortuitous choices was the graphic designer Maurice Binder, who created the title sequence for *Dr. No* – the first installment of the profitable James Bond franchise. When asked to create the main titles for *The Night of the Iguana*, Binder was poised to make the jump into Sixties pop art with his psychedelic main titles for a succession of satirical films that were directed by Stanley Donen: *Charade*, *Arabesque*, *Two for the Road* and *Bedazzled*.

On *The Night of the Iguana*, Binder functioned as a visual consultant. Stark made his request explicit: "I would love to see us start the titles with the longest shot of the iguanas and end the titles with the tightest shot," he told Huston. Originally it was planned to intercut the lizards with other images of Puerto Vallarta but after seeing some test footage, Stark changed his mind. "I think the iguanas are so beautiful and so startling that it is a shame to intersperse the atmosphere shots with them during the titles." As a result, Binder's contribution to the movie was negligible, and he did not receive any official credit.

One of Stark's major concerns about the film was the lack of music. Huston preferred using the natural sounds of the jungle to highlight the dramatic scenes, while Stark thought the addition of "about fifteen or twenty minutes of music will enhance the picture tremendously." Williams echoed these sentiments, and it became imperative to hire a composer so the movie could be finished in time for entry in the Cannes Film Festival.

Stark favored the American composer Alex North, who had written the richly evocative score for *Cleopatra*. Unfortunately, North was in such high demand that it precluded him from taking Stark's assignment. "He screened the picture for me," North recalled, "and I told him I didn't think it was something I wanted to do." Consequently, another talented musician was brought to the producer's attention. When told the name of the composer, Huston gave his approval. His choice was not made for reasons of admiration or quality, rather for more obscure ones that resonated within him.

Benjamin Frankel had never written an original score for a Hollywood motion picture, though he had composed a variety of music for smaller British-made films. His original scores for *The Seventh Veil*, *Mine Own Executioner*, *The Man in the White Suit* and *The Importance of Being Earnest* helped put the scholarly composer in the vanguard of postwar European film composers. But his joy was tinged with sorrow.

Frankel had once been a darling of London society. His talents as a composer and arranger were eagerly sought for the musical revues and comedies of highbrow playwrights like Noël Coward and Terence Rattigan. Then whispers about Frankel's political affiliations scuttled his chances for greater success. At the center of this tempest was his candid admission, subsequently printed in newspapers, that Frankel had once been a member of the Communist Party. His theatrical reputation in disfavor, Frankel turned to the cinema, which musical purists regarded as a lesser form of artistic expression.

On March 26, 1964, Frankel recorded the original music for *The Night of the Iguana* with a chamber orchestra. Frankel's score consisted of ten separate compositions totaling twenty-five minutes of background music – nearly one-fifth of the movie's running time. "Prelude," played over the opening main titles, underlines the plot action when Shannon is banished from his small Virginia church and takes refuge from his accusers in Mexico. The "Hannah and Shannon Theme" highlights the solace and comfort of deep understanding Hannah gives to Shannon, whose suicide attempt is dramatized in "Shannon's Long Swim, while the "Maxine and Shannon Theme" emphasizes the sensuousness and profound love of the beautiful hotelkeeper.

Coincidentally, that same day, Barbara Streisand played her first public performance as Fanny Brice in *Funny Girl* at the Winter Garden Theatre on Broadway and West 50th Street in New York City. Ray Stark had spent thousands of dollars of his own money and several years turning it into a stage musical. The combined stress of producing the expensive show and overseeing the making of *The Night of the Iguana*, coupled with his recent skiing accident, had caused Stark's weight to drop fifteen pounds. His broken leg was still in a plaster cast when the curtain went up shortly after 8:00 p.m. At the end of the finale, Streisand received a standing ovation and twenty-three curtain calls. Before the year was over, *Funny Girl* rivaled *Hello, Dolly!* as the most popular Broadway musical of 1964.

Stark was unable to rest on his laurels – at least not yet. Ahead lay the finishing touches necessary to propel *The Night of the Iguana* from its launching pad and into the stratosphere.

Dubbing of the film was completed by March 31, and a finished print screened for Huston at Cinecittà Studios in Rome on April 25. After viewing the movie, he cabled Stark in Beverly Hills: "Dubbing on *Iguana* altogether brilliant. Music excellent and sound effects best I've ever heard. Know you will be delighted. Love, John."

Although the Motion Picture Association of America (MPAA) issued its certificate of approval for the film, several minor problems still nagged Stark. Five days later, following another screening, he wired Huston back: "Believe first part of film still slow but perhaps because end is so good. Church wants minor deletions but I have refused and am certain will win. I miss you. Ray." The American Legion of Decency gave the film an "A" rating but noted in its remarks: "Some dialogue coarse and crude."

In England, the film was given a compulsory X rating, allowing it to be shown only to people age sixteen and older. A small controversy arose in Australia when the Commonwealth Film Censorship Board reported its dissatisfaction with the film to the MPAA. As a result, the Production Code Administration issued a confidential report requesting the deletion of a kissing scene between Burton and Gardner at the end, which, paradoxically, hastened the fadeout.

As the publicity machine revved into top gear, Edward Feldman, the vice president of advertising and publicity for Seven Arts, organized two press screenings for *Life* magazine and the *New York Times*. "Each group was unanimous in their praise for the picture," Feldman wrote to Huston, who was staying at the Grand Hotel in Rome. "The people felt that *Iguana* is one of the most poetic films they have seen and we have been assured of a rave review in the magazine."

A deal was reached with the London *Daily Express* syndicate for them to serialize the making of the movie in seventy-five global newspapers, each running the story and pictures for one week. The total circulation was estimated at 4.4 million readers.

In Hollywood, Stark hosted a special screening of the film for 300 exhibitors at M-G-M studios in Culver City. "My opinion is that this motion picture has all the ingredients necessary to make it one of the outstanding films of recent years," Morris Lefko, the company's vice president and general sales manager, told the capacity crowd. Seated in the audience were producers Otto Preminger, Mike Frankovich, Harold Mirisch, and Charles Feldman. All were enthusiastic in their praise for the richly textured drama.

Among the well-wishers was Frank Sinatra, who had a keen interest in seeing the movie because one of the stars happened to be his former wife. "*Iguana* is a smasher! The cast is marvelous!" Sinatra wrote to Huston. "I loved every moment of it, and everything about it."

On July 2, Edward Feldman airmailed to Huston a copy of the film's promotional trailer, stating "I think we have finally achieved a combination prestige-action trailer." Feldman had good reason to smile.

Up until then, the majority of trailers – three-minute-long previews of coming attractions that were shown weekly in cinemas – had been routinely assembled by the studios, who were more concerned about their corporate image than engaging viewers in a visceral experience.

Feldman broke with tradition by asking Andreas "Andrew" Kuehn, Jr., a twenty-six year-old Chicagoan, who headed M-G-M's advertising and promotions department, to design him a provocative trailer for *The Night of the Iguana* that communicated the film's message on a strong emotional level.

But what Kuehn came up with far exceeded Feldman's expectations. "I saw an actor in an off-Broadway show that had a really hairy voice that I liked and I brought him in and taught him how to do a voiceover," recalled Kuehn. "It was James Earl Jones."

A strapping native of Mississippi with a resonating baritone, Jones supplied the trailer's powerful commentary: "One man... three women... one night! *The Night of the Iguana*! Since man has known woman, there has never been such a night!" His lines were recorded over a soundtrack of bongos, xylophones, flutes and maracas played by jazz musicians, creating a heavy atmosphere of sexual tension. The campaign was a huge success, drawing attention from the ticket-buying public as well as the media. *Q Magazine* called Kuehn's work "the first modern advertising campaign for a movie."

IN 1964, THE FACE OF American pop culture was redefined by a quintet of British rock ‘n’ roll musicians with shoulder-length hair, whose presence brought rapid changes to the entertainment industry.

On June 1, the Rolling Stones arrived in New York City for a three-week tour of the USA and Canada. Nobody anticipated the effect the group’s music would have on the plays of Tennessee Williams. His impassioned speeches, which galvanized theater audiences, became muffled by the shrill melodies and dissenting lyrics of songs that unified a newer generation, who were too young to have known about the playwright’s lost loves or care about his faded glories. Williams was unprepared for these changes, even powerless to stop them. Resigned to his fate, he drank from the cup of fame one last time.

On Tuesday, June 30, *The Night of the Iguana* was given its world premiere at the Philharmonic Hall of the Lincoln Center for the Performing Arts, in New York City. When it opened two years earlier, this state-of-the-art concert hall was intended as the permanent venue for the New York Philharmonic Orchestra.

The screening of films at the Lincoln Center was reserved for special occasions. “It is going to be a hell of a night and I only regret that you will be unable to attend,” Edward Feldman wired John Huston in Italy.

Ray Stark also cabled the director, saying "You really should be here tonight to take all the bows for *Iguana.*" But Huston had already moved on, believing that once the die had been cast, it was bad luck for him to go back and gaze into the furnace.

That evening, one thousand people each paid $100 to attend the gala, which benefited the American Heart Association. Twenty mounted policemen patrolled Broadway and 65th Street where wooden barricades held back hundreds of photographers and thousands of excited fans, who cheered the arriving guests in black tie and evening dress.

Outside the Lincoln Center, Steve Allen and Jayne Meadows held a "live" television interview with Ava Gardner for *The Steve Allen Show*. Their short conversation was frequently interrupted by people yelling and waving their hands. Gardner, who had fortified herself with several martinis, looked glamorous in a strapless blue satin gown and white lace greatcoat designed by Cristobal Balenciaga.

Grayson Hall wore a long-fitted dress and cape that her son Matthew, who attended with his mother and father Sam Hall, called her "Indian dress." Sue Lyon arrived with her husband Hampton Fancher, and James Ward was accompanied by his fiancée Julie Payne, whom he married six months later.

A loud roar went up from the crowd when they saw Elizabeth Taylor entering the concert hall amid a rapid detonation of flashbulbs. Wearing a long-sleeved blue evening gown with silver stars, Taylor was escorted by her frequent costar Montgomery Clift, whose once-handsome features had been ravaged by alcohol and drugs.

Joining Taylor and Clift was her husband's adopted father, Philip Burton, in a classic tuxedo. (Burton, a former teacher at Port Talbot Secondary School in South Wales, England, had ensured the academic future of a promising young student when he became his legal guardian and the boy changed his name from Richard Jenkins to Richard Burton.)

There were cheers when Roddy McDowall, who had appeared with Taylor in *Cleopatra*, walked inside the auditorium with his friend Lauren Bacall. Also in attendance were actor Red Buttons, singer Eydie Gorme, and actress Susan Kohner – the daughter of Huston's longtime agent Paul Kohner and his wife Lupita Tovar. Representing Seven Arts was Eliot Hyman, Ray Stark, his right leg supported by a metal crutch, and Clarence Eurist. Noticeably absent was Abe Steinberg, who died from a heart attack thirty days earlier. He was fifty-four.

Everyone took their seats inside the Philharmonic Hall with its retractable acoustic clouds and Aeolian-Skinner concert pipe organ. Gardner sat behind a clean-shaven Williams, whose guest that night was his mother Edwina, wearing a vintage stole made of muskrat fur. The playwright's face was calm from having taken the tranquilizer Miltown. After the lights went down, Williams or maybe it was Gardner produced a bottle of Wild Turkey, which they shared, passing the bottle back and forth in the darkness, taking turns sipping the sweet Kentucky bourbon. "As we watched the film," recalled Philip Burton, who had never been to Puerto Vallarta, "Elizabeth kept whispering to me about the place, pointing out what was off-screen in relation to what we could see."

When the lights came up after two hours, there was spontaneous, prolonged applause, which reached a crescendo when Stark gamely stood up on his crutch to take a well-deserved bow. The rejoicing continued long after the last reel of the film had been unspooled. According to Charles Higham, "the screening was followed by a champagne party and a banquet held on the second-floor balcony. It was a squealing, shouting confusion of TV crews, reporters, and fans. When Richard Burton arrived at the Lincoln Center after playing in *Hamlet* the shouts and screams became overpowering." He reached into his tuxedo pocket and presented Taylor with a fabulous gift: a black velvet case containing a gold-and-diamond encrusted Tiffany brooch in the shape of a dragon. She kissed him, and they embraced with the same fervor that characterized their romantic courtship and subsequent ten-year marriage.

The movie's sumptuous buffet featured Beef Puerto Vallarta – an incongruous dish since the Mexican port was better known for its excellent seafood than its mediocre beef. A more appropriate meal might have been the offer of Roberto San Roman, owner of the Hotel Spa Ixtapan, who wanted to serve a feast of baked iguana. But the opening night audience probably would have recoiled at the sight of cooked reptiles laid out on silver trays like small roasted pigs.

Halfway through the dinner, Gardner "got so mad at the press she chucked the party," according to Rex Reed. After throwing champagne glasses at photographers, Gardner fled out the backdoor, where she hailed a yellow cab, which took her to the Birdland nightclub to watch a jazz performance by Miles Davis.

In the approaching months, as *The Night of the Iguana* opened in cities around the world, the press, which had so keenly followed the exploits of the film since its transference from stage to screen, now gave their final verdict on its long-awaited cinematic presentation.

The critical reaction, especially in England, was ecstatic. Barry Norman of London's *Daily Mail* proclaimed it "the best film Richard Burton has ever made." Alexander Walker in the *Evening Standard* wrote "Miss Gardner's performance is brilliant," while Derek Prouse of the *Sunday Times* hailed Huston's direction as "his best work since *The African Queen*."

It seemed strange that closer to home, the film was mocked for the very thing it set out to create: an adult love story. "Mr. Huston has got some scenic beauty of the Mexican coast here and there in black-and-white," commented Bosley Crowther in *The New York Times*. "But the setting, at the last, becomes monotonous – just like the all-talk, no-play film." Some of the harshest criticism came from Hollywood itself. "The language is tirelessly profane or, in other spots, intramurally special to the world of the homosexual," criticized John O'Hara in the *Los Angeles Times*.

Such carping seemed irrelevant, however. The enormous success of the film, which grossed $10 million at the box office, restored Huston's reputation in the volatile film industry. After ten years of lukewarm successes he was now in demand again. Victory must have tasted sweet to him.

As a consequence of *The Night of the Iguana*, tourism to Puerto Vallarta more than tripled from 24,000 visitors in 1960 to 78,000 in 1964. "It's a place where most people forget worries and cares," wrote Charles Collins, travel editor of the *Milwaukee Sentinel*. But it was still a difficult place to get to; either a six-hour Jeep ride from Tepic, a day's boat ride from Mazatlan or a one-and-a-half-hour plane flight from Mexico City via Guadalajara.

Despite the huge increase in airline reservations, the bungalows at Club Mismaloya, which had undergone extensive repairs since filming ended, were unoccupied that season. Guillermo Wulff's money woes continued to plague the project and by the end of July 1964, investors were growing nervous at the prospect of a prolonged legal battle. When informed that additional money was required to pay lawyer's fees, transfer of leases and property assessments, many investors backed out of the deal because the safety of their investment could not be guaranteed.

That summer, as the rains came, a human hurricane of disgruntled villagers wielding hammers, chisels and screwdrivers blew through Club Mismaloya, its fury sweeping away everything in its path. Bedroom closets and doors were unscrewed from their frames, kitchen sinks and cabinets pulled from the walls. Bed frames, mattresses, headboards, nightstands, coffee tables, table lamps, six-draw dressers, and writing desks were taken from the bungalows, to be sold for cash or traded. Pieces of furniture were dragged down the hill and loaded onto boats for the journey to Puerto Vallarta, where the items were destined for private homes. Ten years later, the bungalows were still standing, though their condition had badly deteriorated, a combination of weathering and vandalism.

After renting Casa Kimberly, Richard Burton arranged to buy the house from owner Bill Wilson for $60,000. But even with six bedrooms, the existing premises were too small for the combined Burton-Taylor families, so they purchased the vacant lot across the street. It was there, where Burton had spent the previous summer watching pigs rolling in the mud, that he constructed a second house with four bedrooms, four bathrooms, a sundeck and swimming pool. London interior designer Jill Medford was hired to decorate both residences. "One house was Elizabeth's, the other Richard's," explained biographer Penny Junor, "and they built a bridge which connected the two, from Elizabeth's swimming pool area to Richard's first floor, where he went with his typewriter to work in the mornings."

American actor Philip Ober owned the adjoining three-story house Casa Juanita, which was dedicated to his third wife, Jane Westover, an NBC publicist, whom he married in 1961. Because the Obers were Burton and Taylor's closest neighbors, they became friendly accomplices against the constant threat of paparazzi. "There happened to be an underground passage from our house to theirs," confided Jane Ober about a small tunnel, which had been left there by the workmen. "If they wanted to go out and didn't want to bump into the tourists who occasionally congregated in front of Casa Kimberly, they would use the passage and exit from our place."

On November 25, 1964, Greg Morrison wrote to John Huston in Cairo, Egypt, where filming was underway on *The Bible*: "We on the home front have just started putting our Academy Award campaign for *The Night of the Iguana* into full swing. If things go according to plan," Morrison told Huston, "we will get at least eight nominations, including Best Picture, Best Director, Actor, Actress, Screenplay, etc."

Filled with confidence, Seven Arts paid $3,000 for the front cover of the thirty-fourth anniversary issue of *The Hollywood Reporter*, advertising *The Night of the Iguana* as "The Most Acclaimed Film of 1964!"

Morrison's announcement turned out to be premature, however. Many people in the industry thought the movie had been overhyped, and their reaction was one of cool detachment rather than warm embrace. Furthermore, there was some confusion as to the film's country of origin to qualify it for nomination under the guidelines of the Academy of Motion Picture Arts and Sciences.

The movie had, after all, been made entirely in Mexico, starring a Welsh actor, and two actresses, one Scottish, who resided in Switzerland, the other an American living in Spain. Furthermore, it was directed by an expatriate American with Irish citizenship, photographed by a Mexican cinematographer, and edited in England.

To Seven Arts and M-G-M, the film may have sounded American by virtue of its connection to Tennessee Williams, but not to Hollywood's embittered trade unions. "By forfeiting certain pension clauses," stated Axel Madsen, "the picture had lost its Americanness." But did it, in fact, ever have any such claim? The film's production offices were incorporated in the Bahamas and most of the salaries that had been paid out were deposited into foreign bank accounts. When asked to comment on the film's nationality, Huston reacted with puzzlement. "Hmmmm," he shrugged, "maybe it's Liberian, or Panamanian."

It was a cold overcast day in Los Angeles. Ray Stark sat in his office at Seven Arts. He was reading the list of nominations for the thirty-seventh Academy Awards, which were announced on February 23, 1965. Among the films nominated for Best Picture of 1964 were *My Fair Lady*, *Mary Poppins*, *Becket*, *Zorba the Greek*, and *Dr. Strangelove*. The Best Actor and Actress nominees included Rex Harrison, Peter O'Toole, Anthony Quinn, Peter Sellers, Julie Andrews, Anne Bancroft, Sophia Loren, and Debbie Reynolds.

To Stark's amazement *The Night of the Iguana* received only four nominations:

Grayson Hall for Best Actress in a Supporting Role
Dorothy Jeakins for Best Costume Design, Black and White
Stephen Grimes for Best Art Direction-Set Decoration, Black and White
Gabriel Figueroa for Best Cinematography, Black and White

Stark couldn't understand why the film was overlooked in the all-important categories of Best Actor, Best Actress, Best Screenplay, Best Director, and Best Picture. Later, he was told that the unsavory publicity generated by the film had adversely influenced many conservative voters, who threw their support behind that year's sentimental favorites: *My Fair Lady* and *Mary Poppins*, which won eight and five Oscars apiece. It was particularly galling for Stark since Seven Arts had such high expectations for *The Night of the Iguana*.

Overseas, the film gained several prestigious honors. At the San Sebastian International Film Festival, held each year in Spain, Ava Gardner was voted the prize for Best Actress, though she did not attend the awards presentation. Gardner was also nominated by the British Academy of Film and Television Arts for Best Actress, but she didn't show up in London either. In Los Angeles, the Directors Guild of America nominated John Huston for Outstanding Directorial Achievement in Motion Pictures.

The same year that *The Night of the Iguana* failed to get any major Oscar nominations, the film gathered five nominations at the 1965 Golden Globe Awards, which were sponsored by the Hollywood Foreign Press Association. Perhaps in gratitude for the huge amount of publicity generated by the film, members of the press nominated it for Best Motion Picture Drama, Best Motion Picture Actress – Ava Gardner, Best Motion Picture Director, Best Supporting Actor – Cyril Delevanti, and Best Supporting Actress – Grayson Hall.

At the Laurel Awards, hosted by *Motion Picture Exhibitor* magazine, Deborah Kerr was nominated for a Golden Laurel in the category of Best Dramatic Female Performance.

The Academy Awards telecast, emceed by comedian Bob Hope, was held on April 5, 1965, at the Santa Monica Civic Auditorium. The star-filled gala featured a live appearance by Judy Garland, who sang a touching medley of Cole Porter songs in tribute to the late composer, who died in 1964.

The only nominee from *The Night of the Iguana* to win an Oscar that evening was costume designer Dorothy Jeakins. It was the last time the award was given specifically for black-and-white films. To Stark, who had hoped for much bigger things, these tributes were of small consolation. He swallowed a mouthful of Pepto-Bismol and grimaced at the chalky taste. Then he buzzed his secretary on the office intercom and dictated a telegram to Huston.

All the frustration, anger and resentment that had built up inside Stark was about to be released in a fuselage of vulgar expletives. But all he could find in him were several words that expressed his bitter disappointment. When Huston opened Stark's telegram on the other side of the world, he smiled at its brevity. He threw back his head and howled with laughter. Stark's three-word telegram read: WE WERE ROBBED.

EPILOGUE

WHILE JOHN HUSTON BASKED IN the triumph of *The Night of the Iguana*, the victories of other people connected to the movie turned sour, their lives plagued by misfortune. Shortly after returning to California from a promotional tour of Australia, Sue Lyon received heartbreaking news. On October 18, 1964, her diabetic brother James Lyon was found dead in a station wagon near Tijuana, Mexico. He was twenty. An investigation of the vehicle by Mexican authorities discovered hypodermic needles and a white substance that was later identified as heroin.

Two days earlier, the distressed actress, age eighteen, had filed for divorce from Hampton Fancher on the grounds of mental cruelty, after ten months of marriage. Lyon was legally divorced from Fancher in Santa Monica Superior Court on December 8 and moved to a rented house in the Los Angeles suburb of Westwood.

The following year, Lyon and her fifty-nine-year-old mother were seriously injured in a automobile accident when their car collided with an oncoming vehicle, which was attempting to make a U-turn on the Pacific Coast Highway in Malibu. Lyon filed a lawsuit against the driver of the other vehicle and was awarded $225,000 for injuries sustained in the collision. Her mother received $42,000. She died in 1968, age sixty-two.

In 1964, Elizabeth Taylor's ex-husband Michael Wilding married Margaret Leighton, who costarred with Bette Davis in *The Night of the Iguana* on Broadway. In 1971, Leighton contracted multiple sclerosis. She continued making sporadic appearances in movies and television until her death, at fifty-three, in 1976.

Three years later, Wilding died after falling down a flight of stairs during an epileptic seizure at his country home near Chichester in Sussex, England. He was sixty-six.

Production manager Clarence Eurist proved indispensable on the Seven Arts Film, *This Property Is Condemned* – the twelfth screen adaptation of a Tennessee Williams play. Eurist returned to Mexico a fifth time to oversee the making of *The Undefeated* starring John Wayne. In 1976, Eurist was stricken with a fatal heart attack – seven months after the death of his wife, Elizabeth. He was seventy.

Inevitably, the specter of death reached out its ghostly hand and touched each of the film's participants on the shoulder. Anthony Veiller never wrote another screenplay after returning to Los Angeles from Puerto Vallarta. Veiller was diagnosed with cancer and died in 1965. He was sixty-two. His body was flown to England, the country he most loved, and buried in the family plot at St. Mary's Churchyard in Bepton, West Sussex.

In 1969, Huston's fourth wife, Ricki Soma, who had been separated from her husband for ten years, was driving with a friend through Strasbourg, France, on the way to visit her parents in Italy, when she was killed in a head-on collision. She was thirty-nine. Huston adopted his wife's four-year old daughter, Allegra, who became a sister to her half-brother Danny.

Emilio “El Indio” Fernández solidified his reputation as a wild man when he shot and killed a farmer in Coahuila, Mexico, in 1976. To avoid capture, Fernández drove across the border to Guatemala. After several days on the run, he surrendered to authorities. Fernández was extradited to Torreon, where he was convicted of manslaughter and sentenced to four and a half years in prison. He appealed the verdict and was paroled after six months. In 1986, Fernández died from a heart attack at his home in Mexico City. He was eighty-two.

Tennessee Williams wrote seven more plays, none of which were critically or commercially successful. In 1969, Williams was admitted to the psychiatric ward of a St. Louis hospital, where he was treated for drug and alcohol abuse. He was released six months later. His final days were spent in a delirium of self-induced paranoia. In 1983, Williams choked to death on the plastic cap of a medicine bottle in his two-room suite at the Hotel Elysee in New York City. He was seventy-one.

Richard Burton was nominated seven times for the Academy Award, but went unrewarded, while Elizabeth Taylor won two Oscars. Their lifestyle was the most lavish of any celebrity couple in the twentieth century. At the height of their fame, they earned $4 million each year and spent half of it. But fame and money could not insulate them from the harsh realities of life. After being hospitalized separately for various alcohol-related illnesses, Burton and Taylor were divorced in 1974; they remarried in 1975 but divorced again ten months later.

Burton returned to Puerto Vallarta and in 1978 bought a second vacation home, Casa Ciruelos, which he renamed Casa Bursus, as a Valentine’s Day gift for his third wife, Susan Hunt. When they divorced after four years, she kept the house and $1 million in cash. In 1984, Burton suffered a cerebral hemorrhage at his villa in the Swiss village of Céligny. The unconscious actor was taken to a Geneva hospital, where he died on the operating table. He was fifty-eight. Curiously, Burton’s death occurred on August 5 – the same day that John Huston celebrated his seventy-eighth birthday.

Grayson Hall was never offered another substantial film role after *The Night of the Iguana*. Hall found better success in theater and television, where she portrayed the recurring character of Dr. Julia Hoffman in the gothic TV serial *Dark Shadows* and its two movie spinoffs, which were written by her husband. A heavy smoker, Hall succumbed to lung cancer in 1985. She was sixty-two.

Cyril Delevanti, who was a lifelong smoker, died from cancer in 1975. He was eighty-six. His death occurred five months after the passing of his wife, Eva, to whom he was married for more than sixty years. Mary Boylan continued playing kooky roles in a variety of offbeat films in-between holding play readings and acting workshops. She died in 1984 at age seventy.

John Huston continued to make movies for another two decades, though financial wealth still eluded him. In 1972, Huston married his fifth wife, Celeste Shane, and the couple divided their time between Ireland and Puerto Vallarta, where they rented various houses: Casa Tres M's, Quinta Laura, and Casa Los Arcos – just up the street from Casa Kimberly.

After divorcing Shane and selling St. Clerans in 1977, Huston fulfilled his longstanding dream of building a beachfront home on the shores of Banderas Bay. The land, which he leased for twenty years from the Chacala Indians, was located five miles south of Boca de Tomatlan, between Quimixto and Majahuitas, on a long stretch of sand called Las Caletas with two crescent beaches separated by rock outcroppings and huge shade trees.

Designed by Freddy Romero, the sprawling compound, which generated its own electricity, consisted of six white stucco huts with red tile roofs, connected by a small network of stone bridges and pathways. Huston lived on the premises with his female companion Maricela Hernandez, three boa constrictors and a Rottweiler named Don Diego. The only contact with Puerto Vallarta was by shortwave radio and a forty-five foot cabin cruiser named *Tranquilizer*, which lay anchored offshore.

Huston's longtime secretary Gladys Hill, whose devotion to him bordered on unrequited love, died from a heart attack in New York during filming of the musical *Annie* in 1981. She was sixty-four.

Two years later, Huston became the eleventh recipient of the American Film Institute's Life Achievement Award – the highest honor for a career in film. The ailing director, who had undergone two heart operations, traveled from Puerto Vallarta to Los Angeles to receive the award.

In 1987, Huston was directing a movie in Newport, Rhode Island, when he died in his sleep of complications from emphysema, which destroyed his lungs. He was eighty-one. Huston's last completed film, which had been written by his son Tony and starred his daughter Anjelica, was ominously titled *The Dead.*

Production designer Stephen Grimes collaborated with the director Sydney Pollack on seven films. Their meticulous recreation of colonial Kenya in the epic love story *Out of Africa*, starring Robert Redford and Meryl Streep, helped it to win seven Academy Awards, including Best Picture, Best Director and Best Art Direction. In 1988, Grimes was stricken with a fatal heart attack in Positano, Italy, while working on the movie *Haunted Summer*. He was sixty-one.

Death was a busy caller on the violators of Mismaloya. In her sunset years, Ava Gardner experienced severe respiratory problems, the result of heavy smoking, which caused the actress to have a debilitating stroke. In 1990, Gardner succumbed to pneumonia at her home in London, England. She was sixty-seven. Sydney Guilaroff, who loved the actress in spite of her shortcomings, died in a Los Angeles nursing home in 1997. He was ninety.

Dorothy Jeakins received her final Oscar nomination for the traditional satin and lace evening costumes she created for the Irish wake in *The Dead*. Jeakins passed away in a Santa Barbara nursing home in 1995. She was eighty-one. Two years later, Gabriel Figueroa, who was repeatedly denied an entry visa to the USA because he was classified as an Undesirable Alien, died of a stroke following heart surgery in Mexico City. He was ninety.

Guillermo Wulff rebounded from the failure of Club Mismaloya to become a successful builder of luxury hotels and condominiums in Puerto Vallarta. But his family was not spared from misery. Wulff's eldest son Luis, who took over the management of El Dorado restaurant, suffered a double tragedy when one of his sons drowned and his depressed wife killed herself. Optimistic to the end, Wulff died in 2002. He was eighty-two.

Frustrated with acting in inferior roles, James "Skip" Ward eventually moved behind the camera, where he became associate producer of the TV series *The Dukes of Hazzard*, which gave him a lot more satisfaction than he ever achieved in front of the camera. Ward died in 2003 after a lengthy illness. He was sixty-nine.

Ray Stark left Seven Arts in 1967 and formed his own company Rastar Productions. He produced more than fifty films: five starring Barbra Streisand, eight directed by Herbert Ross, and eleven written by Neil Simon. In 1970, Stark's son, who intended to follow his father into show business, took a drug overdose and jumped to his death from a fourteen-story apartment building in Manhattan. He was twenty-five. As a memorial, Stark donated $1 million to the University of Southern California for the establishment of the Peter Stark Motion Picture Producing Program. In 1984, *Forbes* magazine calculated Stark's personal worth at $175 million, making him one of the richest men in Hollywood. The following decade, Stark was incapacitated by a stroke. He died in 2004 at age eighty-eight.

Citing a shortage of good roles for middle-aged women, Deborah Kerr retired from the screen in 1970, though she continued acting in the theater and on television. In 1994, Kerr was awarded a special Oscar. Ten years later, the actress' younger brother was killed in a road rage attack while driving in Birmingham, England. Inconsolable, Kerr died from Parkinson's disease in 2007. She was eighty-six.

The next month, Kerr's husband Peter Viertel died from lymphoma in Marbella, Spain, twelve days before his eighty-seventh birthday.

Raúl Velasco became a star reporter for the daily newspaper *El Heraldo de México*. Following a stint with Mexican Independent Television, Velasco joined the country's largest broadcaster Televisa, where he hosted the weekly TV variety show *Siempre en Domingo* from 1969 to 1998. Velasco was forced to retire when he contracted hepatitis and underwent a liver transplant. He died in 2006, at age seventy-three.

In 2008, Danny Huston, who followed in his father's footsteps to become a successful director and actor, endured unspeakable torment when his wife of six years, Katie Jane Evans, jumped to her death from the rooftop of a luxury apartment in Manhattan Beach, California. She was thirty-five. It was an inglorious end for the young couple, who had been married in Puerto Vallarta.

And what of Ava Gardner's two beach boys from the movie, Pepe and Pedro? Actor Fidelmar Duran later played minor roles as *charros* in several Mexican Westerns, and then vanished. Roberto Leyva, meanwhile, moved to Cabo San Lucas, where he sold fishing tours. He died in 2015 at age seventy-eight.

The most famous survivor from *The Night of the Iguana* was, not surprisingly, also the strongest. In 1990, Elizabeth Taylor sold Casa Kimberly and its original furnishings, art and other personal possessions to San Diego investors Maurice Mintzer and Toy Holstein, who managed the famous home as a bed-and-breakfast hotel and museum. Ten years later, the property was listed for sale at $1.75 million.

In 2006, the house was seized for unpaid liens and taxes and its owners evicted. Shortly after, the home was purchased by Janice Chatterton, a wealthy San Francisco madam, who once ran the largest escort service in the bay area.

(In 1983, Chatterton and her daughter Paula Carvajal were arrested by police and charged with pandering and pimping, two separate felony counts that each carry prison sentences of three to six years.)

This unexpected turn of events, in which a convicted prostitute took ownership of Taylor's house, put a wry smile on the aging star's face – if not for the buyer's audacity then for the irony of her actions. Chatterton had already bought Richard Burton's former home Casa Bursus and converted it to a boutique hotel named Hacienda San Angel, which opened in 2003. Her acquisition of Casa Kimberly was viewed by preservationists as an attempt to reunite Hollywood's most famous couple, the memory of which still looms large in the Mexican port and elsewhere. In 2011, Taylor died from congestive heart failure in Los Angeles. She was seventy-nine.

On the twentieth anniversary of the making of *The Night of the Iguana*, more than 526,000 Americans visited Puerto Vallarta. "They came to ride horseback in the jungle, take boat trips to otherwise inaccessible coastal villages with stunning, quiet beaches, or watch sunsets on an uninterrupted horizon, the water glistening red and gold for hundreds of miles," reported *The New York Times*.

In 1989, eager to capitalize on the explosion of tourism, La Jolla de Mismaloya, a 300-room hotel, was built on the beach, displacing families that had lived there for generations. A Mexican restaurant, "The Sets of the Night of the Iguana," opened for business where the movie was filmed. The director's house Casa Huston which was never occupied became John Huston's Seafood Restaurant. Both eateries were operated by the hotel until it was acquired by Barcelo Resorts in 2005.

According to the Mexico 2010 census, the official population of Puerto Vallarta is 255,681. Almost half the municipality's workforce is employed in tourist related industries such as hotels, restaurants, personal services and transportation, which were given impetus by the filming of *The Night of the Iguana*.

Despite outward signs of prosperity, there is aggrieving poverty. In some neighborhoods the roads are unpaved; there is no potable water and no sewerage system. Six or more members of one family live together in a two-bedroom house. Many people rely on public transportation because they cannot afford to buy a car.

In 2015, Puerto Vallarta welcomed nearly four million international and national visitors, generating more than $30 million revenue. While the bountiful rewards from tourism are shared by real estate developers and resort owners, their employees survive with minimum wages. Hotel workers are hired, fired and rehired to circumvent paying them benefits legislated by the Mexican Government.

But it is Puerto Vallarta's natural beauty that draws the eye, not its social inequality. Still visible on the hillside above the beach in Mismaloya are the remains of the Hotel Costa Verde, its empty archways beckoning absent guests through the overlapping palm leaves. For years, a Mexican caretaker occupied the premises. Now, the building is patrolled by armed guards. On the next hilltop are the foundations of the hotel bungalows, which rotted decades ago.

At sea level, a long concrete boardwalk, broken and cracked, leads to a rusting boat jetty, which is encrusted with barnacles. Pelicans swoop into the water hoping to catch fish in their long bills. On the surrounding rocks are numerous iguanas soaking up the sun – just as they have done for thousands of years. Behind a ten-foot high stone wall with a chain link metal fence and padlocked gates are two large painted signs, their words as dooming as a witch's curse:

PRIVATE PROPERTY
DANGER DO NOT ENTER
BEWARE OF THE DOGS

ABOUT THE AUTHOR

Howard Johns is a film historian, author and television personality. In 2004, he wrote the bestselling nonfiction book *Palm Springs Confidential: Playground of the Stars* (Barricade Books), which sold out through three printings. Two years later, he published the scandalous follow-up *Hollywood Celebrity Playground* with similar success.

From 1996 to 2002, Johns was editor-at-large for the monthly California prestige magazine *Palm Springs Life*. In 2008, he was a contributing editor for the magazine's 50th anniversary issue, providing a multilayered commentary about the history and development of this unique desert oasis.

Johns currently resides in Puerto Vallarta, Mexico, where he recently completed his third nonfiction book, *A Stolen Paradise*.

BIBLIOGRAPHY

Barzman, Norma. *The Red and the Blacklist: The Intimate Memoir of a Hollywood Expatriate*. New York: Thunder's Mouth Press/Nation Books, 2003.

Baxter, John. *Fellini*. New York: St. Martin's Press, 1993.

Bragg, Melvyn. *Richard Burton: A Life*. Boston, MA: Little, Brown and Company, 1988.

Braun, Eric. *Deborah Kerr*. New York: St. Martin's Press, 1978.

Burton, Philip. *Richard and Philip: The Burtons*. London, England: Peter Owen Publishers, 1992.

Cole, Lester. *Hollywood Red*. Palo Alto, CA: Ramparts Press, 1981.

Cordingly, David. *Under the Black Flag: The Romance and the Reality of Life Among the Pirates*. New York: Random House, 1995.

Cottrell, John and Fergus Cashin. *Richard Burton, Very Close Up*. Englewood Cliffs, NJ: Prentice-Hall, Inc., 1971.

Cummins, John. *Francis Drake: The Lives of a Hero*. New York: St. Martin's Press, 1995.

Félix, María. *Todas mis guerras*. Mexico: Editorial Clio, S.A. de C.V., 1993.

Fernández, Adela. *Traditional Mexican Cooking and Its Best Recipes*. Mexico: Panorama Editorial S.A. de C.V., 1985.

Ferris, Paul. *Richard Burton*. New York: Coward, McCann & Geoghegan, 1981.

Figueroa, Gabriel. *Memorias*. Mexico: Universidad Nacional Autónoma de México, Pértiga, 2005.

Fraser-Cavassoni, Natasha. *Sam Spiegel*. New York: Simon & Schuster, 2003.

Gardner, Ava. *Ava: My Story*. New York: Bantam Books, 1990.

Goldman, Herbert G. *Fanny Brice: The Original Funny Girl*. New York: Oxford University Press, 1992.

Green, Michelle. *The Dream at the End of the World: Paul Bowles and the Literary Renegades in Tangier*. New York: HarperCollins Publishers, 1991.

Grobel, Lawrence. *Conversations with Capote*. New York: New American Library, 1985.

__________. *The Hustons*. New York: Charles Scribner's Sons, 1989.

Grossman, Barbara W. *Funny Woman: The Life and Times of Fanny Brice*. Bloomington and Indianapolis, IN: Indiana University Press, 1991.

Guilaroff, Sydney, as told to Cathy Griffin. *Crowning Glory: Reflections of Hollywood's Favorite Confidant*. Santa Monica, CA: General Publishing Group, Inc., 1996.

Hadley-Garcia, George. *Hispanic Hollywood: The Latins in Motion Pictures*. Secaucus, NJ: Citadel Press/ Carol Publishing Group, 1990.

Hammen, Scott. *John Huston*. Boston, MA: G.K. Hall & Co.; Twayne Publishers, 1985.

Hayman, Ronald. *Tennessee Williams: Everyone Else is an Audience*. New Haven, CT: Yale University Press, 1993.

Hemingway, Ernest. *Death in the Afternoon*. New York: Charles Scribner's Sons, 1932.

Heymann, C. David. *Liz*. New York: Birch Lane Press, 1995.

Higham, Charles. *Ava*. New York: Delacorte Press, 1974.

Hodel, Steve. *Black Dahlia Avenger*. New York: Arcade Publishing, 2003.

Huston, John. *An Open Book*. New York: Alfred A. Knopf, 1980.

Jamison, R.J. *Grayson Hall: A Hard Act to Follow*. Lincoln, NE: iUniverse, 2006.

Junor, Penny. *Burton: The Man Behind the Myth*. New York: St. Martin's Press, 1985.

Kaminsky, Stuart. *John Huston, Maker of Magic*. Boston, MA: Houghton Mifflin Company, 1978.

Kashner, Sam, and Nancy Schoenberger. *Furious Love: Elizabeth Taylor, Richard Burton and the Marriage of the Century*. New York: Harper, 2010.

Kelsey, Harry. *Sir Francis Drake: The Queen's Pirate*. New Haven, CT: Yale University Press, 1998.

Keyes, Evelyn. *Scarlett O'Hara's Younger Sister*. Secaucus, NJ: Lyle Stuart, Inc., 1977.

Kohner, Pancho and Lupita Tovar. *Lupita Tovar: The Sweetheart of Mexico*. Bloomington, IN: Xlibris Corporation, 2011.

Leaming, Barbara. *Bette Davis – A Biography*. New York: Simon & Schuster, 1992.

Leverich, Lyle. *Tom: The Unknown Tennessee Williams*. New York: Crown Publishers, Inc., 1995.

Long, Robert Emmet, editor. *John Huston Interviews*. Jackson, MI: University Press of Mississippi, 2001.

Madsen, Axel. *John Huston: A Biography*. Garden City, NY: Doubleday & Company, 1978.

Marks, Richard Lee. *Cortés: The Great Adventurer and the Fate of Aztec Mexico*. New York: Alfred A. Knopf, 1993.

Marnham, Patrick. *Dreaming With His Eyes Open: A Life of Diego Rivera*. London, England: Bloomsbury, 1998.

McGilligan, Patrick and Paul Buhle. *Tender Comrades: A Backstory of the Hollywood Blacklist*. New York: St. Martin's Press, 1997.

Moldea, Dan E. *Interference: How Organized Crime Influences Professional Football*. New York: William Morrow & Co., 1989.

Montes de Oca de Contreras, Catalina and Yolanda G. de Garduno. *Puerto Vallarta: My Memories*. Guadalajara, Mexico: University of Guadalajara, 2002.

Moseley, Roy. *Bette Davis: An Intimate Memoir*. New York: Donald I. Fine, Inc., 1989.

Munguia Fregoso, Carlos. *Puerto Vallarta: The Hidden Paradise*. Puerto Vallarta, Mexico: Pro Biblioteca de Vallarta, A.C, 1996.

Navasky, Victor S. *Naming Names*. New York: Viking Press, 1980.

O'Reilly, James and Larry Habegger, editors. *Travelers' Tales Mexico*. San Francisco, CA: Travelers Tales, Inc., 1994.

Ordóñez, Marcos. *Beberse la Vida: Ava Gardner en España*. Spain: Aguilar, S.A. De Ediciones-Grupo Santillana, 2004.

Rader, Dotson. *Tennessee, Cry of the Heart*. Garden City, NY: Doubleday, 1985.

Reed, Rex. *Do You Sleep in The Nude?* New York: New American Library, Inc., 1968.

Reed, William with Sylvia Rosa Garcés Marroqui de Reed. *Escape to Paradise: A Mexican Odyssey*. Puerto Vallarta, Mexico: Garces Press, 2004.

Server, Lee. *Ava Gardner: "Love is Nothing..."* New York: St. Martin's Press, 2006.

Sheppard, Dick. *Elizabeth: The Life and Career of Elizabeth Taylor*. Garden City, NY: Doubleday & Company, Inc., 1974.

Spoto, Donald. *A Passion for Life: The Biography of Elizabeth Taylor*. New York: HarperCollins Publishers, 1995.

__________. *The Kindness of Strangers: The Life of Tennessee Williams*. Boston, MA: Little, Brown & Company, 1985.

St. Just, Lady and John L. Eastman. *Five O'Clock Angel: Letters of Tennessee Williams to Maria St. Just 1948-1982*. New York: Alfred A. Knopf, 1990.

Stevens, George, Jr., editor. *Conversations with the Great Moviemakers of Hollywood's Golden Age*. New York: Alfred A. Knopf, 2006.

Stine, Whitney. *Mother Goddam*. New York: Hawthorn Books, Inc., 1974.

Townsend, Richard F. *The Aztecs*. London: Thames and Hudson, 1992.

Viertel, Peter. *Dangerous Friends: At Large with Hemingway and Huston in the Fifties*. New York: Doubleday, 1992.

Williams, Dakin and Shepherd Mead. *Tennessee Williams: An Intimate Biography*. New York: Arbor House, 1983.

Williams, Tennessee. *Memoirs*. Garden City, NY: Doubleday & Company, 1972, 1975.

___________. *The Night of the Iguana*. New York: University of the South New Directions Publishing Corporation, 1961, 1989.

Winters, Shelley. *Shelley II: The Middle of My Century*. New York: Simon & Schuster, 1989.

MAGAZINES

"Away from the Resort Mob," Richard Oulahan, *Sports Illustrated*, January 21, 1963.

"The Cast Menagerie," *Time*, November 8, 1963.

"Stars Fell on Mismaloya," Richard Oulahan, *Life*, December 20, 1963.

"The Nightmare of the Iguana," Helen Lawrenson, *Show*, January 1964.

"The Days and Night of the Iguana," Deborah Kerr, *Esquire*, May 1964.

"Tropical Blooms," *Newsweek*, July 7, 1964.

"The Drama the Cameras Missed," Thelda Victor and Muriel Davidson, *The Saturday Evening Post*, July 11, 1964.

"Let My Iguana Go," Edith Oliver, *The New Yorker*, August 15, 1964.

"Whatever Happened to Puerto Vallarta?" John H. Davis, *Town & Country*, January 1980.

"A First-Class Affair," Sam Kashner, *Vanity Fair*, July 2003.

NEWSPAPERS

"Liz Taylor, Burton Find Solitude in Villa of Remote Mexican Town," *Los Angeles Times*, October 13, 1963.

"John Huston's 'Iguana,'" Paul P. Kennedy, *The New York Times*, December 1, 1963.

"Huston Calls Job a Serene Experience," Hedda Hopper, *Los Angeles Times*, December 24, 1963.

"Liz, Burton Fly Here to Riotous Welcome," Jack Smith, *Los Angeles Times*, January 23, 1964.

"Richard Burton: Belated Baccalaureate for a Brooding Welshman," Eugene Archer, *The New York Times*, June 28, 1964.

"Burton's Best," Barry Norman, *Daily Mail*, September 8, 1964.

"Explosive Burton," Clive Barnes, *Daily Express*, September 8, 1964.

"The Iguana's Night – But It's Ava's Picture," Alexander Walker, *Evening Standard*, September 10, 1964.

"It's a Night of 4-Star Passion," Dick Richards, *Daily Mirror*, September 11, 1964.

"The Iguana Survives," Derek Prouse, *The Sunday Times*, September 13, 1964.

"Shocked Flock," Penelope Gilliatt, *The Observer*, September 13, 1964.

"Picturing Painting and Passion," Peter Bart, *The New York Times*, September 27, 1964.

"Whatever Became of Richard Burton?" Vincent Canby, *The New York Times*, June 13, 1971.

"Pacific Mexico: Puerto Vallarta," Nick Madigan, *The New York Times*, February 26, 1984.

Made in the USA
San Bernardino, CA
27 May 2020